*The Myth of Educational Reform*

# The Myth of Educational Reform

## A Study of School Responses to a Program of Change

Thomas S. Popkewitz
B. Robert Tabachnick
Gary Wehlage

THE UNIVERSITY OF WISCONSIN PRESS

Published 1982

The University of Wisconsin Press
114 North Murray Street
Madison, Wisconsin 53715

The University of Wisconsin Press, Ltd.
1 Gower Street
London   WC1E 6HA, England

First printing

Printed in the United States of America

For LC CIP information see the colophon

ISBN 0-299-08840-5

This book is based on work supported by the National Institute of Education under grant
number OB–NIE–G–78–0217. Any opinions, findings, and conclusions, or recommendations
expressed in this publication are those of the authors and do not necessarily reflect the view
of the Institute or the Department of Education.

For Our Parents

Jacob and Anna Popkewitz
Harry and Sarah Tabachnick
and
Laura Schalekamp

# Contents

# Foreword

What happens to ideas and practices aimed at reforming curricula and administrative patterns when these ideas and practices are introduced into the "real world" of the schools? The conventional approach to this question has been either to determine the extent to which reform ideas and practices have been "implemented," or to measure the consequences of new programs in terms of anticipated outcomes such as student achievement. In their important study of the introduction of Individually Guided Education (IGE) into the schools, Professors Popkewitz, Tabachnick, and Wehlage have chosen to follow neither of these standard approaches. Rather, they present case studies of six elementary schools the IGE programs of which had already been judged to be "exemplary." Their attention is focused on the relationship of IGE as a reform technology to on-going patterns of schooling and the ways in which IGE was incorporated, revised, and even transformed in the institutional settings of the schools under investigation.

Specifically, the authors identify three institutionalized forms of schooling, each of which is characterized by distinctive styles of work by staff and students, conceptions of knowledge, and professional ideologies. Persuasive evidence is presented that in the schools representing these forms of schooling—labeled technical, constructive, and illusory—the reform ideas and practices were not merely adapted, but substantially altered. In the words of the authors: "Schools did not merely adapt the [I.G.E] program, making modifications to reach the same goal; rather they revised both the technology and its espoused goals. Such revisions helped to conserve quite different institutional conditions—in each of the schools a different style of work, conception of knowledge, and professional ideology was maintained."

In this connection, one is reminded of a central theme in E. Durkheim's distinguished history of secondary education in France—namely, that doctrines and schemes for educational reconstruction are, in all instances, transformed once they enter the domain of practice. "I do not know of a single historical case," writes Durkheim, "where the ideal proposed by an educational theorist has passed in its entirety and without essential modifications into practice." The significance of the present study lies in the empirical evidence it presents regarding the conditions within and outside the schools that influence the modifications that reform efforts such as IGE make when they enter the real world of schooling.

But the significance of this research lies also, and more generally, in its concepts, guiding questions, and methods that together serve as a promising model for the study of both schooling and the reform of schooling. For example, the authors contend that "the institutional patterns characteristic of the schools in this study may be generalized to other school settings as well." This is to be interpreted, I take it, as an invitation to other researchers to test the concepts and methods developed in this research in investigations of other schools in other community settings. Thus this study may be viewed as initiating a fruitful line of inquiry that gives promise of enlarging our understanding of the conditions of schooling and the possibilities for reform.

Arno A. Bellack

*Teachers College*
*Columbia University*

# Acknowledgments

This project began four years ago with a seemingly simple inquiry: what values and meanings are transmitted by reform programs in schools? Many reform programs have had unanticipated consequences and have concealed values that worked against the ethical and political intentions of the planners. Our study has proceeded as an intellectual odyssey, the first part of which was to discover the complex and interrelated implications of the question. As data were collected, our search involved relating our initial thoughts and conceptual perspective to the different conditions of schooling in which we found the technologies of a particular reform program, Individually Guided Education. During this time certain colleagues have been unfailingly helpful. Out of the many, we would particularly like to thank Thomas A. Romberg, who organized a general evaluation from which this study emerged and provided thoughtful comments on the manuscript. Different work groups within the Evaluation Project in the Wisconsin Research and Development Center offered comments and we profited greatly from our interaction with these individuals. Their deliberations about the data and analysis broadened our own understanding of the methods, findings, and limitations of educational science. These colleagues include Anne Buchanan, Gary Price, Deborah Stewart, and Norman Webb. David Hamilton and Arno Bellack gave us criticism which stimulated our thinking about the curriculum and schooling issues described in this book. Important and helpful reactions during the preparation of the manuscript were also provided by Dave Berliner, Michael Apple, Herb Kliebard, Pinchas Tamir, Thomas Fox, and Paul Willis. Finally, a debt is owed to the staff of the project, who helped collect some of the data, chased elusive references, edited, and generally met deadlines; these include Paula Bozoian, Barbara Esdale, Ruthanne Landsness, Mary Pulliam, and Sara Ann Selje. For any inaccuracies, conceptual lapses, or misplaced metaphors we are responsible and culpable.

T.S.P.
B.R.T.
G.W.

*Madison, Wisconsin*
*July 1980*

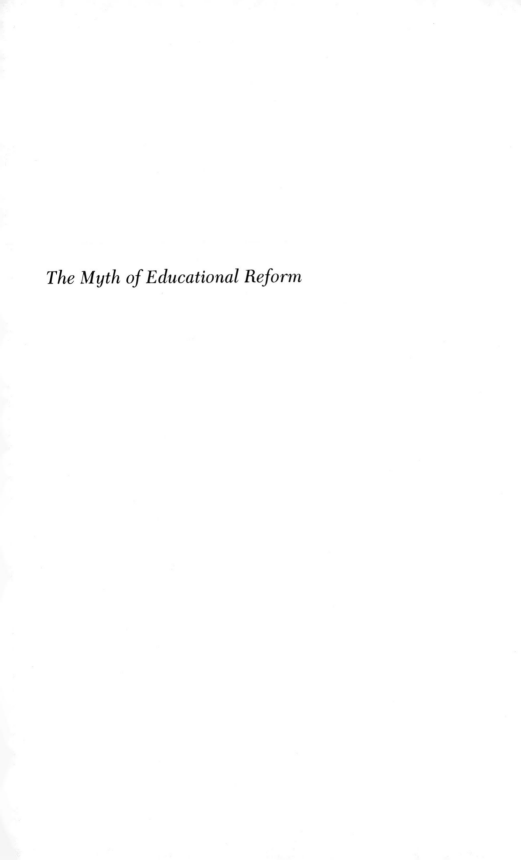

*The Myth of Educational Reform*

# 1

## School Reform
## and Institutional Life

### Introduction

The 1960s were a time of ferment for most institutions in American society. Schools were asked to respond to the social and political issues that commanded the nation's attention: the civil rights movement called for improved education for minority children, and political changes created a demand for schooling that could help establish a sense of community and of moral cohesion. When criticism of the ability of schools to solve personal and social problems undermined faith in the existing institutions, educational reform became a potent symbol for responding to the nation's social predicaments. The call for reform is a way of asking that institutions be rededicated to ideals to which people are deeply committed. The act of reform, in contrast to mere change, is an act of social commitment and reaffirmation.

Individually Guided Education (IGE) was a relatively comprehensive, sustained, elementary school reform effort developed in the 1960s. Its designers argued that conventional school practices had rendered instruction routine, trivial, and ineffective, that children were classified merely by age and through norm-referenced standardized testing, and that teacher responsibility for what and how to teach had been reduced or eliminated, with mechanical professional work as the result. Furthermore, educational practices had removed parents from any meaningful relationship to the school. Individually Guided Education was created by a government-sponsored research and development center to respond to these criticisms.

The designers of IGE used a systems analysis approach to coordinate organizational, instructional, and curricular aspects of the school in a potentially efficient and rational system for making school programs more responsive to individual variations in learning. As instituted in the elementary school, Individually Guided Education's reforms extend beyond the systems analyses and management procedures of its program: IGE is a complex social invention intended to enable its users to respond to the changing problems of schooling. Implicit in any such response, however, are values and assumptions about social change and control which remain tacit, even as concrete proposals to intervene in the social world are developed. To understand Individually Guided Education these tacit assumptions and values, which define the reform and make it feasible, must be systematically investigated, and the relationship of the reform technologies to the ongoing norms, beliefs, and values of schooling must be made explicit.

Our intent is to make problematic the assumptions and procedures of Individually Guided Education: to describe the implicit as well as the explicit learning which occurs when students, administrators, and teachers respond to an educational reform, and to examine how the technologies of IGE are incorporated into the continuing social and political context of schooling, and thereby receive meaning. Our investigation provides a framework in which more general theoretical questions about the assumptions, implications, and consequences of institutional life and change can be raised. We will discuss school interactions, work patterns, and the relationships between schools and their communities to illuminate the rules, social values, and interests that influence different school practices.

The particular processes of adaptation and response of the different schools investigated in our study revealed broad patterns of schooling and social life. And each school used the reform technologies in a way which responded to its unique social situation. Schools did not merely adapt the program, making modifications to reach the same goal; rather, they revised both the technology and its espoused goals. Such revisions helped to conserve quite different institutional conditions—in each of the schools a different style of work, conception of knowledge, and professional ideology was maintained, and in each school these reflected (or were reactions to) particular social values and interests found in the larger social/cultural community.

These findings raise substantive questions about the way in which reform is conceptualized and planned. The model of change underlying the

IGE program, which assumes that a well-coordinated and well-orchestrated effort to improve the efficiency of instruction can produce reform, in fact lent credibility to and often justified the very school practices and values the program was intended to change. Conventional school practices not only channeled reform thought and action, but also reinforced and legitimated existing social values concerning authority and control.

Ironically, most discourse about schooling obscures the relationship between reform and the underlying social values of institutional life. A method of occupational thought has developed (what Feyerabend [1978] calls "professionalized incompetence") in which the social assumptions, priorities, and implications of school practices go unexamined, while the rituals and procedures of school life become the center of public and professional debate. The ethical and political underpinnings of pedagogy remain concealed beneath a seemingly neutral concern for change and the change agent, and any modification of behavior or attitude is treated as a substantive outcome of schooling. The capacity of educational technology to sustain or modify fundamental human purpose seems no longer relevant. Filtered out of the discourse is schooling's essential nature as a socially constructed institution which mediates particular cultural values and human interests.

This investigation of Individually Guided Education, reform, and institutional life does not present a conventional evaluation: we neither establish a set of explicit criteria and apply them to some outcome (such as achievement) nor do we describe the extent to which IGE is "successfully" implemented. We have chosen instead to study six elementary schools whose programs had already been identified as exemplary.

Our research was a four-year project. Our first concern was to place the IGE program in a general context of school reform and institutional life—to establish the program as a particular case of educational change and reform from which theoretical insights could be derived. We then sought to understand what the planners of IGE had written about the program; our intent was not to use the definitions and categories of the planners in our field research, but to understand how the program had emerged historically, and what assumptions and implications about educational practice underlay the thinking of its designers.

To gain firsthand knowledge of how practitioners around the nation talked about and implemented Individually Guided Education, we initially paid two-day visits to each of seventeen model IGE schools. From these schools we selected five in which, in the second year, intensive case studies were carried out; a sixth school was added to the investigation in the course of the field work. Each school was visited for data collection on at least three separate occasions (for a discussion of methodology, see Appendix A).

The last two years of the project involved analysis and writing. Part 2 of this chapter concerns the problems of reform in an institutional context; we make explicit the questions, issues, and assumptions about institutional life that guided our analysis and subsequent interpretations of the six schools we investigated. Chapter 2 discusses IGE as a social invention; we consider the planners' purpose, probe beneath formal descriptions to examine the beliefs and assumptions about schooling, learning, and social change that shaped their effort at reform, and explore the social context and climate of opinion that was crucial to the genesis of Individually Guided Education. Chapters 3 through 6 present the findings of the investigation. As our research progressed, we had encountered fundamental variations in the conditions and social implications in the six schools studied, as well as different institutional responses to the technologies of IGE; to describe these variations and their significance, we created three categories: technical, constructive, and illusory schooling. The categories are related to Wittgenstein's concept of family resemblances; the schools in each category have overall similarities and overlapping characteristics, but the categories should not be considered as qualitatively identified or determined.

The interactions, events, and language of the technical schools are described in chapters 3 and 4, with chapter 3 presenting the schools and the IGE program as they were perceived by the participants, and chapter 4 considering the underlying institutional patterns of work, conceptions of knowledge, and occupational ideology (professionalism) that give coherence to the three technical schools. In chapter 5, dealing with constructive schooling, and chapter 6, which concerns illusory schooling, the focus is more precisely on institutional analysis. In the final chapter our discussion relates the three institutional configurations to the ways educational reform is conceptualized, implemented, and researched, and examines assumptions about the nature of school change as a neutral, technical endeavor.

## Elements of Institutional Life

Before discussing schools as institutions into which reform programs are introduced, a comment on methodology is appropriate. Analyses of research often separate discussions of reform and institutional life from discussions of methodology, making the choice of investigative procedures seem a purely technical act. We believe, in contrast, that problems of methodology cannot be considered adequately without referring to the questions, theories, and intellectual traditions that make particular investigative strategies plausible. Data and descriptions of social conditions are not presented in a vacuum, but are inevitably tied to theory. A study of educational reform, therefore, involves the complex and profound relationships of reform, institutional life, and methodology.

The problem of integrating these three dimensions in research is apparent when we begin to assess the effects of Individually Guided Education. One approach to studying IGE would be to adopt the point of view of the program's developers. The research problem then would be to determine whether the claims and objectives of the program had been successfully realized in the schools. Studying a program from its developers' point of view necessarily requires adopting their assumptions, language, and goals, and using research concepts and techniques that are responsive to the developers' definition of purpose. This approach is often used in program development to test and refine the technologies of reform.

A second approach might incorporate the perspectives of those who use a program in a school, with the researcher inquiring into how students, teachers, and administrators view its effectiveness. Criticism or accolades would emerge from their testimony. This approach helps program developers as well as practitioners, for it may reveal interpretations and practices not foreseen in the program design.

Taking a third approach, the researcher would maintain skepticism toward the assumptions, intentions, and practices of the reform program, remaining detached from official definitions of social conditions and neither accepting nor rejecting them as the inquiry is begun. Recognizing that results are not automatically attained as planned, the researcher keeps in mind that practical endeavors often have unanticipated and unintended effects.

We have used the third approach in this study. In doing so, we have felt obliged not to discount the developers' and users' goals and testimonies; rather, we make these, as well as the language, customs, and traditions of school practice and reform, the subjects of inquiry. Our intent is not only to describe the perceptions and actions of people in schools; we are concerned with the underlying assumptions and social values implicit in school practices, and how they affect the realization of reform technologies. The everyday activities of schooling and its reform are placed within contexts of larger social, intellectual, and ideological concerns. The questions that have guided our investigation are: How are school programs actually used? What social values and meanings do reforms and their technologies generate as they are used in schools? What are the assumptions behind and the implications and consequences of using reform technologies in day-to-day schooling? By adopting a critical stance, we can provide data helpful to those involved in program development and implementation.

We maintain a skeptical perspective by viewing school reform within a

context of institutional life. Schooling is seen as a socially constructed
endeavor characterized by specific patterns of work, conceptions of
knowledge, and occupational ideologies. Since social conditions and constructs reflect social values concerning principles of authority, legitimacy,
and control, the nature of these values cannot be taken for granted and
must also be scrutinized. Nor can we leave unquestioned how reform
programs change or sustain the particular social patterns and values found
in schools.

### Institutional Life as the Focus of Reform

Social institutions perform certain agreed-upon functions to achieve
social goals. The mandate or function of schooling is to provide a formal
social structure within which children are to prepare for adulthood.
Schools define and legitimize categories of competence in society, provide publicly acceptable classifications of people and knowledge, and give
access to valued positions in society. While it is important to recognize
that schooling is given legitimacy because it has a social mandate, that
charter cannot be taken for granted. Most Americans accept the mandate
on the grounds that schools should "prepare children for a democratic
society," or that people should "be taught to think for themselves," but
these slogans have many possible interpretations. Some may view the
school mandate as a call for providing individuals with opportunities to
develop their own intellectual capabilities, expressing a classic liberal
faith in the individual's ability to contribute creatively and imaginatively
to public life. Others may see schooling as preparation for entering a
social world already classified and organized according to certain occupational and status lines (Popkewitz 1981). Inherent in each interpretation
are different social values and implications for school practices that are
obscured by slogans about the social mandate.

The conflict between definitions of social purpose directs our attention
to a second aspect of schooling—the actual values and beliefs sustained in
day-to-day school life. Like all institutions, schools function according to
rules and procedures which give coherence and meaning to everyday
activities and interactions. Such rules and procedures are embodied in
regularized patterns of behavior, specific vocabularies (a child in school is
a "learner," his or her learning is "achievement," and so on), and particular roles (teacher, pupil, or administrator). So potent are institutional
patterns that the social structuring experienced in schools channels the
thought and the action of participants, giving definition and meaning to
both school reform and pedagogical practice (Popkewitz 1979). Institutional patterns, for example, evoke various theories, folk knowledge,
myths, and commonsense ideas which make a school's activities and the
roles and relationships of its personnel appear normal and reasonable

within their setting. Theories of teaching, learning, or administration are believed to be sensible because they are consonant with the background information people have about schools and classrooms. Similarly, the focus of and questions asked in current educational theories are seen as reasonable because they fit in with our beliefs about existing patterns of interaction.

While making this argument, we do not wish to present an overly socialized, deterministic view of the individual. Institutional life can respond to and be shaped by the people who participate in it. However, we cannot pretend that contemporary forms of social life are not potentially coercive. Our definitions of social conditions and our expectations are created by past and present patterns of action and belief which limit the possibilities for change, or at least restrict the options for making modifications.

## Surface and Underlying Meanings

Educational reform can be understood more fully when the surface and underlying layers of meanings in institutions are considered together.

The *surface* layer of meaning is provided by the publicly accepted criteria or standards by which people judge success or failure. A lesson objective or a team-teaching organization might provide such criteria. The *underlying* layer of meaning involves the socially accepted procedures, guidelines, and assumptions that provide people with a feeling of security within an institution, and that make the activities, interactions, and teaching/learning experiences in institutions seem plausible and legitimate (see Taylor 1977).

The relationship between surface and underlying meanings may be illustrated by an example. A teacher plans a lesson in arithmetic, writes an objective, constructs some materials, teaches, and then evaluates the lesson. She considers the lesson important for the students for a variety of reasons—she may believe that arithmetic facts are the basic ingredients of a mathematics curriculum and that they must be learned because they are related to previous and later lessons, or because students must know them to pass a standardized test. Such reasons provide the surface meaning, and may be offered to legitimate the lesson.

But surface meanings are developed and supported within a context of institutional patterns and beliefs which constitute the underlying meaning. The underlying meaning involves assumptions about the way children learn and develop, about the nature of knowledge, and about social order and control, and gives rise to rules that reflect these assumptions. In our example, rules and procedures existing before the lesson was given imposed constraints upon what was taught and how the teacher presented the lesson.

One underlying assumption concerns the nature of knowledge. Esland (1971), for example, identifies the epistemologies implicit in two dominant educational psychologies that guide classroom instruction. One, drawn from the psychometric tradition, assumes that knowledge exists outside the minds of individuals. A child is viewed as a "deficit system" to be initiated into existing forms of thought. Within this tradition teaching is concerned with the efficiency with which children master a specified range of solutions, and standardized testing is used to verify mastery. A second tradition, closely related to developmental psychology, postulates that knowledge results from participation in a community and in the problem-solving process. Instruction in this tradition focuses upon reasoning and cognitive development as they emerge from the classroom environment. The child is both an active and a passive agent: knowledge develops from interaction with the social situations in school and from negotiations between teacher and student.

The assumptions about the nature of knowledge and the role of the individual in society in these epistemologies become part of an institution's day-to-day life, and influence the way teachers interpret their roles as teachers and how children interpret their roles as students. These underlying assumptions are rarely examined or challenged; they are a taken-for-granted part of schooling.

Also incorporated into the underlying meaning are assumptions about how thought and action are to be categorized. In school, a child learns to distinguish and organize experiences through definitions of subject matter. For example, the act of reading may be classified as a form of knowledge, and as a result a child may spend two hours a day on reading *as subject matter*—practicing on worksheets, decoding sentences in books, or taking tests to assess reading levels. Other activities are classified under such headings as language arts, social studies, or science. These categories are only some of the many possible ways of organizing thought and action in schools.

The way a school organizes subjects also defines for students the legitimate forms for asking questions and documenting answers about both personal and public affairs. In social studies, for example, which provides students with an introduction to the study of society, the presentation of the content legitimates particular definitions and interpretations of social problems. Students are taught to use specific approaches to identify and answer questions, and in this way criteria for truth and validity are established. Yet these underlying aspects of instructional organization are often obscured by the everyday rituals, ceremonies, and language of school planning.

One might ask at this point, why are the underlying institutional structures of schooling a problem of educational reform? Schools are doing what they are supposed to do: transmitting culture and knowledge, and doing that as efficiently as possible. The task of research and reform is to identify the most efficient procedures to accomplish this end. This argument is incomplete and possibly misleading, for a variety of reasons. First, schooling does not just pass on culture: it modifies the content and spirit of culture, and those modifications have unanticipated and unintended consequences. Second, schools transmit some, but not all, aspects of our cultural heritage; inevitable biases and selection occur which can perpetuate inequalities and injustices. Third, the actual relationship between school practices and social commitments is often hidden behind the school's ceremonies and slogans. While everyone can agree to schools "meeting individual needs," offering "discovery" approaches, or providing "self-actualization," the words provide little information about how the enterprise proceeds.

*Elements of School Life: Work, Knowledge, and Professionalism*

Our understanding of institutional life and the effects of reform may be clarified by considering three important dimensions of schooling—work, knowledge, and professionalism—and the relations among them. Schools are places of work where students and teachers interact to alter and improve their world, establish social relations, and realize human purpose. Schools are also places where conceptions of knowledge are distributed and maintained; implicit in this discourse are ways of reasoning and communicating about social relations, social conditions, and social authority. Finally, schools are staffed by an occupational group whose activities give legitimacy to patterns of work and conceptions of knowledge. Often that group uses the label "professional" to establish its status, privileges, and control. The three characteristics of schools direct attention to the social assumptions and values that underlie school practices, and provide a vantage point from which to consider the authority, legitimacy, and social control that are maintained in the day-to-day activities of schooling.

*Schools as Places of Work*

The activities of students and teachers in schools collectively form a pattern of work (Popkewitz and Wehlage 1977). However, school work should be considered in relation to human work in general. Work is fundamental human activity by which people establish, modify, and carry out their social purposes. An important aspect of work is the relation of thought and imagination to the products of human labors (Braverman 1974): work not only affects the form of the material on which a person works, but expresses, in the shape given to the material, the realization of purpose and will. While we can view work as expressing human intent, we must also recognize that the structure of human activity delimits the adaptability of the world we live in and the possibilities for altering cultural and social conditions.

Work involves a developing interplay of activities, beliefs, norms, and social relations that is particularly important in institutionally defined situations. From an institution's structures emerge historically conditioned ways of expressing intent, establishing social relations, and giving form to the social world and one's own humanity.

The significance of the patterns of work in schools becomes apparent when we look at the initial experiences of students. An investigation of a kindergarten showed that children are taught particular distinctions between work and play (Apple and King 1978): work is what the teacher directs the children to do, while play includes those activities that are permitted only if time allows after children have finished their assigned work. Coloring, drawing, waiting in line, cleaning up, and singing were perceived by children as work, because these were actions they were told to take. The definitions of work had no intrinsic relation to specific accomplishments, but classroom work was related to certain social relations in classroom life: all work was compulsory and done simultaneously; identical products were sought, and the purpose of classroom work was always defined by teachers. Diligence, perseverance, participation, and obedience replaced excellence as evaluative criteria.

The preoccupation with standardization and control in schoolwork has been noted in many studies of classroom life. In a review of a 1970 Carnegie Commission report, for example, Stevens argues

most schools are preoccupied with order, control, and routine for the sake of routine; . . . students essentially are subjugated by the schools; . . . practicing systematic repression, the schools create many of their own discipline problems; and . . . they promote docility, passivity, and conformity in their students.

The teachers are said to be treated as subservient employees whose job is to take orders and punch the time clock every day, and whose competence is judged not by what and how their students learn, but by how well they control their classes. . . . Teachers assume that pupils cannot be trusted to act in their own best interests . . . and principals make similar assumptions about teachers. . . . Teachers become primarily disciplinarians, and discipline is defined as "the absence of noise and movement." . . . One result of all this . . . is to destroy students' curiosity along with their ability—more seriously their desire—to think and act for themselves. . . . It is not the children who are disruptive . . . it is the formal classroom that is disruptive—of childhood itself. (Stevens 1972:5–7)

The standardization and ritualization of schoolwork, some researchers argue, are related to an organizational need to process large numbers of students within a relatively confined space. Silberman (1970), commenting on the assumption that children should be "adjusted to fit the school," observes that elaborate sets of rules and regulations are maintained to cover almost all time spent in school, and that the rigidity of scheduling and lesson plans encourages an obsession with routine for its own sake. The teacher-student relationship is based upon institutionalized dominance and subordination which emphasizes conformity and silence. The organization of schoolwork, Silberman concludes, perpetuates uniformity and conformity that paralyze intellectual curiosity, severely curtail individual creativity and spontaneity, and reward acquiescence to authority.

Jackson's (1968) study of elementary classrooms also found the grouping and processing of students to be a major educational problem. The standardized and relatively unvarying social context a child confronts in school, Jackson believes, is a response to the crowded nature of the school. The teacher is a supply sergeant, dispenser of special privileges, official timekeeper, and traffic manager. For students, life in school means facing the inevitability of the school experience and enforced passivity. Typically, students wait, hands raised, for the teacher to check their work, and those who finish or have a question must wait for others. Little classroom time is spent trying to understand subject matter, and the need to control large numbers of individuals in schools produces a form of spectatorship in which students spend much of their time waiting for the teacher's directions.

Faced with schoolwork that is organized to process students efficiently, students may develop an "underlife" to meet institutional demands and make them tolerable. Cusick's (1973) study of student culture in a high school showed that students cared little about school activity, talked infrequently about schoolwork, and spent scant time in the productive work of learning. To make school life satisfying, they developed subcultural groups within the school that provided esteem and reward. In the context of the institution, these actions can be viewed as normal responses to a situation in which freedom is denied, activity is made routine, and no differentiation among students is made, regardless of class, curriculum sequence, or academic rank. The hierarchical arrangements aimed at processing numbers of students produced little teacher-student interaction to counter these subcultures or to bring about student involvement. Students were relegated to watching, waiting, following orders, and passively receiving knowledge.

In a similar ethnographical study of student subcultures, Paul Willis (1977) observed that, in an industrial area, students' experiences in part-time jobs and in social interactions in their homes contradicted the expectations and demands they experienced at a large secondary school. The students saw their school experiences as false. Willis argues that after rejecting the school's definitions of work and its criteria of competence and certification the students internalized and legitimized a notion of labor and social class that limited their options in society.

Because school work can not only define the possibilities of human creative activity, but can also provide opportunities for cultural development and social mobility, the institution's definitions of work are exceedingly important. The patterns of activities, social relations, and sentiments produced in schools must be clarified, so when the effects of reform are investigated we can question how reform technologies sustain, modify, or otherwise relate to these institutional patterns. The relationships between technologies of reform and other elements of institutional work should make the significance of intervention programs apparent.

### Conceptions of Knowledge

The authority of an institution to channel thought and to define human conditions has subtle implications for the way knowledge is conceptualized, and hints at the underlying patterns of thought found in schooling. Carl Becker (1932) suggests that rooted in the everyday life of each age are certain preconceptions, beliefs and value structures that give direction to social thought. The medieval assumption was that existence was a cosmic drama written by God, embodying a central theme and a rational plan. Men were to accept this plan as written in scripture and as interpreted by the church hierarchy. The subject of inquiry was the Bible, pedagogy concerned the examination of its text, and the function of intelligence was to reconcile experience with the pattern determined by God, rather than to inquire into the nature and origin of existence. These assumptions about the world were transformed by eighteenth century philosophy: the heavenly city was moved earthward, laws were said to be defined by nature rather than God, and the methods of science became the procedures of enlightenment.

Today a number of conceptions of knowledge compete for dominance in our schools, each rooted in different assumptions about our cultural traditions. The laws of God and nature, for example, are challenged by existentialists, liberals, and Marxists. From such a plurality of ideas problems of choice arise that are compounded by the institutionalization of education. Schools selectively impart cultural traditions and concepts of knowledge, and curriculum, instruction, and evaluation direct students toward specific uses of intelligence and a particular kind of reasoning about ideas and action. The concepts of knowledge that are distributed in schools thus become problematic when we view curriculum, instruction, and evaluation as having social as well as intellectual content. How history is defined, for example, imposes a particular mode of reasoning upon that discipline. A student may be led to conceive of history as a collection of objective, universally valid facts; evaluation measures the student's ability to identify information on a standardized test, or to observe examples of reasoning which apply the information "correctly." Alternatively, history may be conceived as a socially organized field of study; evaluation attempts to discover if a student can use those facts to give meaning to social traditions and to find solutions to social problems. In this way curriculum, instruction, and evaluation provide not only content but also the logic individuals are to use to think about and act on social issues.

Classroom ethnographies have revealed that schools impose conceptions of knowledge in which principles of authority, legitimacy, and control are implicit. Keddie (1971), studying the nature of discourse in an English high school, found that instruction frequently replaced what children had learned from everyday experience with esoteric academic language. For example, the teacher might reject a description of an extended family that was derived from the student's personal experience, and in its place ask the child to accept categorical definitions built around social science words. The stated purpose of such a lesson is to have pupils learn scientific categories as heuristic devices for inquiry, but what actually happens is that the student is taught to accept an imposed system of thought and abstraction as authoritative, and is subject to an imposed definition of "competence" (see also Stake and Easley 1978). Keddie also points out students in different tracks in the high school, while using the same material, were expected to learn different social science concepts, different practices of inquiry, and different definitions of personal competence.

That different kinds of knowledge are distributed in schools has broad implications. Young (1971), who views schools as institutions that distribute and maintain certain kinds of knowledge, argues that the essential functions of schools are cultural transmission and social control. He suggests that a school's methods of selection, organization, and assessment of knowledge often serve particular ideological functions. School instruction, for example, emphasizes knowledge that is literate, abstract, and unrelated to daily life. It also legitimizes the positions and privileges of those experts and elites whose knowledge is distributed by the school, and imparts a set of values regarding social and political arrangements in society as a whole.

The political content of classroom communication can be illuminated by looking at the curriculum content. Materials are not selected and organized outside of a value system, and the curriculum that emerges in the contemporary American classroom abounds with nuances of language that convey particular meanings. Anyon (1976) found that American history textbooks do not present dispassionate, "objective" views of the past, but maintain biases toward corporate business ideologies. She discusses at length the way in which labor conflicts and industrial growth are defined, and how labor problems are resolved through adaptation to the "system." The textbook discussions ignore systemic relations between social institutions.

Certain social and political values may also be embedded beneath a false rubric of inquiry. In an analysis of social science curricula (Popkewitz 1977), it is found that the social theories offered in a curriculum tend to support those existing institutions that emphasize social stability and the role of individuals as recipients of values. The way teaching is organized avoids making these issues problematic, and the aim of teaching is to replace students' commonsense ideas with the more esoteric knowledge of social scientists. The skepticism and tentativeness appropriately associated with inquiry is transformed into an instructional sequence in which pupils are to demonstrate the benevolence of ongoing student-teacher relationships and the legitimacy of professionals as definers of reality.

These analyses of curriculum materials and instruction suggest that all school activities impose styles of thought and concepts of knowledge. The issue raised by these authors is not how we can eliminate values and bias from school discourse; rather, it is how we can criticize and select among the cultural traditions and concepts of knowledge that are available.

Our discussion of school knowledge and work suggests that the criteria for the selection and organization of curricula have implications for the conduct of schooling, and that patterns of schooling are not self-contained: they exist in relation to larger social conditions, are historically rooted, and have developed from particular concerns and public issues of the past. That school ideals and practices have historical contexts is dramatically documented in Emile Durkheim's (1938/1977) study of the French secondary school. Changes in curriculum content and methods during the Renaissance, he argues, reflected profound social changes and conflict in European society. The development of an orderly economic life and a bourgeois class brought about a demand for educational systems that legitimized the new class. To provide the new class with the style and manner of the aristocracy, the older scholastic education was replaced with a curriculum based upon Greek and Roman classics aimed at fashioning writers, masters of eloquence, and accomplished conversationalists.

Reform in Jesuit educational institutions, also a response to social changes, was designed to prevent the spread of the heresies of the Reformation. Classical content was introduced to emphasize the virtues, vices, and great passions of humanity that exemplified the precepts of

Christianity. Individualization of instruction was used as a means of providing greater personal surveillance, while manipulation and competition were used to stimulate motivation.

The power of Durkheim's analysis lies in the relationship he establishes between school practices and social conditions: schools are socially chartered, and their reform is often related to changing social and political interests. His study also reveals how easily the past is made part of the ongoing life of institutions. As the social concepts and ideologies that underlie school practice become part of the routines of teaching, they assume an aura of tradition and normalcy which makes it difficult to detect them. Efforts to understand reform, therefore, involve consideration of how curriculum content, instruction, and evaluation give legitimacy to definitions of social order and control, and must confront the ideological question of whose knowledge is being distributed—what interests of society at large are being served or hampered by the knowledge imparted in school.

### Professionalism as a Social Category

Certain occupational groups—professions—at work in schools have the authority and the power to define pedagogical practices. Everett Hughes (1958) suggests that a profession should be viewed as a special occupation licensed to act upon clients in ways not permitted by other forms of social interaction. The label "professional" is used by occupational groups to signify a highly trained, competent, specialized, and dedicated group that is effectively and efficiently serving the public trust. But the label "professional" is more than a declaration of public trust: it is a social category that imputes status and privilege to an occupational group. In teaching, the label signifies not only technical knowledge and service, but the power of a particular group to bestow social identity ("students") upon its clients.

Berger and Luckmann (1967) view the creation of occupational groups to serve as "experts" as essential to the development of institutional life. Experts not only minister to the ongoing practices of an institution, but also have a legitimating function which enables the institution to survive. At the same time, various techniques of intimidation, rational and irrational propaganda, mystification, and manipulation maintain the special privileges and recognition of these experts. Legitimation is important for the experts, the institution, and those on the outside—the general public.

Historically, the professional sector of society has increasingly used prestige and status to expand its control over other sectors, and to maintain its power relationships. Bledstein (1976) holds that a culture of professionalism began to emerge in the United States after 1870 with the rise of a strong middle class, when groups of workers began to organize their occupations around "scientific knowledge." The appeal of this occupational orientation was that out of the many only a few, specialized by training and indoctrination, could enter the profession, but all were obliged to respect it. The social authority of the profession lay, in part, in its scientific claims, and in the assumption that only a few self-governed persons could exercise trained judgment in the field of expertise.

The helping professions, in particular, have used scientific technology and language to create a sense of awe among their clients and a sense of power among their members. Many professions have adopted therapeutic languages to orient and describe their activities. The terms used to describe forms of mental illness, forms of delinquency, and educational capacities imply scientific knowledge and are used to justify professional actions. To talk of diagnosis and give a technical name (dyslexia) to a child's inability to read, or to prescribe behavior modification for a child who does not behave, has a symbolic effect: each implies that the causes of the problem are known, and that all that is needed is the correct treatment. The application of deviant categories in practice, however, depends more upon the social situation and values in the school than it does upon any objectively defined criteria, and may involve highly unreliable diagnoses, prognoses, and prescriptions. The label "dyslexia," for example, involves the identification of no particular reading problem—it is merely the Latin term for the inability to read, whatever the cause. Professionally designated categories have a self-fulfilling function for both professionals and clients: they become part of an individual's institutional identity. Terminology may also be used as an aid to social control; the label "hyperactive," for instance, might justify giving tranquilizers to unruly children.

The purpose of therapeutic language in the helping professions, Edelman (1977) suggests, is political: it justifies the status, power, and authority of professionals, concentrates attention on procedures within the institution, and rationalizes failure in advance. Studies of schooling indicate that professionals use their power to preserve and expand control, and to resist adverse changes in power relationships. Howard Becker's (1952) investigation of parental involvement in Chicago schools found that teachers reacted to parents in ways that preserved their own control and status in the institution. The decentralization fights in New York City in the late 1960s and 1970s also reflected actions by teachers and administrative groups to prevent lay involvement in certain "teacher domains," such as hiring practices and setting standards for certification. One strike found teachers, administrators, and members of the central board of education allied against local school boards and parent groups in a professional effort to preserve the status quo.

Much of the bureaucracy that has crept into schools in recent years has further legitimized professional expertise at the expense of lay involvement. The use of technical language, increasing specialization, and hierarchical ranking of school personnel have made teaching seem esoteric and not amenable to outside influence. A study of a Teacher Corps project (Popkewitz 1975) showed that highly technical jargon set apart those who had been initiated (teachers, university professors, school administrators) from those who were outsiders (lay people from an American Indian community). Discussions about "competencies," "modules," "cycles," and "learning styles" made it necessary for the Indians to look to experts for interpretations of school life. While the technical language introduced a perception of efficiency and made it easier to deal with school failures, that language was actually devoid of content and helped to prevent any critical scrutiny of institutional priorities and beliefs. It also gave the appearance of reasonableness to the existing program which defined the school as a moralizing agency and imputed pathological qualities to the Native American community.

Some authors have argued that the culture of professionalism may have consequences for the capacity of individuals to provide for themselves (Lasch 1977). Individual ability and personal competence have been progressively diminished through schemes controlled, disseminated, and evaluated by particular occupational groups. To "educate" students for American life, school professionals have acquired mandates to teach children problem solving, values clarification, sex education, health education, safety education. and much more. These subjects reflect a professional definition of what kind of "help" should be given to people growing up and entering society. Such education often poses a contradiction: while the purpose of schooling is the introduction of certain forms of social and personal autonomy, it also introduces a form of dependency; people learn to rely on professionals to define and solve social problems. Psychologists give diagnoses and prescriptions for marital or family problems; urban sociologists issue guidelines for living together in cities; and educators define what knowledge, reasoning, and thought are taught to children in our society.

### The Resilience of Institutional Arrangements

The complex social and political arrangements of institutional life are not easily altered, and when we examine the context into which educational reform is introduced the assumption that reforms will be faithfully implemented can be questioned. Faced with reform, institutions exhibit remarkable resilience: innovations are first incorporated into existing patterns of behavior and belief, then used to legitimize ongoing patterns of educational conduct, while being identified in slogans to suggest reform.

Innovations cannot be treated apart from the uses to which they are put. Reforms are introduced into situations in which people have hopes, desires, and interests, and in which institutional contexts structure actions. Reform programs interact with school routines and assumptions, sometimes creating superficial changes, but leaving the underlying interpretive rules unchallenged. The introduction of new curriculum materials in Sweden, Great Britain, and the United States in the 1960s provides examples of how institutional constraints intervene to weaken reforms (Goodlad, Klein, and Associates 1970; Hamilton 1975; Kallós and Lundgren 1976; Sarason 1971). Many new science materials were put into classroom closets and are yet to be unwrapped. Teachers using "new math" materials applied the same teaching strategies they had used to present the "old" math. When the new curriculum was integrated into the ongoing activities of schools, the excitement, adventure, and intellectual curiosity that the reforms were intended to inject into school programs failed to materialize.

In the War on Poverty in the 1960s, efforts to improve relations between schools and communities of the poor had similar results. Since the poor distrusted professionals and felt alienated and disenfranchised, it was reasoned that their active participation in poverty programs would effect the distribution of community power and produce psychological changes that would eliminate the dependency associated with poverty. Reforms developed by welfare, economic, education, and political agencies were intended to provide the poor with power over the decisions that affected their lives and their communities. In reality, however, most reform programs limited the participation of the poor to advisory levels (Rose 1972). Procedures were developed that enabled existing community agencies to expand and to involve community representatives in "selling" the agencies' programs; in few cases were the reform programs used as originally intended.

In many cases reform activities take on ceremonial or symbolic functions. The rational approach offered by reform programs demonstrates to the public that schools are acting to carry out their socially mandated purpose, and the procedures and strategies of reform offer dramatic evidence of an institution's power to order and control change. But the ceremonies and rituals of the formal school organization may have little to do with actual schoolwork or with the teaching and learning that goes on in the classroom. The attention given to the formal organization protects the school from having its actual conduct questioned.

The legitimizing function of reform can be clarified by examining the symbolic nature of slogans. The terms "individualization," "discovery approaches," and "participation" are slogans, each of which symbolizes to educators a variety of emotions, concepts and values, just as terms like "democracy" and "national security" symbolize the values and aspirations of political groups. Slogans, however, are symbolic, not descriptive; they do not tell us what is actually happening. While some slogans accurately express the meaning of potential actions, others obscure the real activities and motives of the people involved. Medicare, for example, provides important benefits to both the doctors who participate in it and to the poor who are its publicly declared beneficiaries. As a reform, Medicare is "successful" in that it produces an aura of change without substantially restricting those who give direction to and gain from the existing organization of social affairs. Reform can be a symbolic act that conserves rather than changes.

The investigation of school reforms poses a special empirical problem for researchers and evaluators. The conventional wisdom assumes the existence of precisely defined variables, and the problem for conventional research is to choose which variable to manipulate; some form of testing is then done, and responses are compared to determine whether the strategies tested have been successful. In contrast, the problem for investigators of reform is to examine the meanings and interpretations that participants give to reform practices in schools, and how these interpretations relate to institutional patterns. We cannot assume that reform programs are used in ways defined in the program literature, nor can we assume that we know how people in schools actually construct and practice reform programs on a day-to-day basis.

The specific curriculum designs and organizational structures of reforms cannot be viewed as ends or results. Criterion-referenced testing, behavioral objectives, and mastery learning are technologies that are proposed in response to concerns about schools; the intent of such technologies is to change deeply held assumptions and institutional patterns. Educational planning must involve giving attention to the social, political, and educational complexity of schools, for when reform programs do not take into account the underlying patterns of belief and conduct, innovations may only rearrange the technological surface.

# 2

# Individually Guided Education as Social Invention

School reform was a prominent social issue in the 1960s. Talk of change was commonplace, and a variety of means were proposed to achieve the ideal of better schooling. Some saw new media technology as the solution to a number of educational problems, and envisioned schools where children would be taught by machines or television. Much publicity was given to national efforts to develop new curricula that would allow children to "discover" the "structure" of a discipline. Other efforts at reform were based on the social concerns that had forced the country to reexamine its collective conscience. Frustration over the perceived failure of the schools to educate black, Spanish-speaking, and other minority students led to the creation of alternative schools, which also attracted middleclass children, who were expected to benefit from new social relationships and authority patterns.

During this period of educational unrest, Individually Guided Education was developed. Herbert J. Klausmeier, a professor of educational psychology at the University of Wisconsin, and his associates believed that a number of school conditions prevented teachers from adapting "instruction to the needs of individual students" (Klausmeier 1977:3). They identified these "inhibiting conditions":

1. Students were required to adjust to uniform educational programs; adequate provisions could not be made for differences in rate of

learning, style of learning, and other individual characteristics of the students.

2. Students were instructed in age-graded classes, and all students in each class were expected to work toward the same instructional objectives, usually by studying the same graded basal textbooks and supplementary materials. Even widespread differences in reading rates had to be ignored because textbooks were adopted on a district-wide basis, and their use was directed by school and school district policies.

3. Students were given norm-referenced tests to measure intellectual ability and educational achievement; the results were generally ignored or used for categorizing and grading students, rather than as guides for improving their instruction.

4. Teachers were treated as if they were equally competent in all subjects and in the use of all media and methods of instruction; appropriate provisions were seldom made for differences in interests, knowledge, experience, and expertise.

5. Teachers were required to spend nearly all of their time with students, and had little time during the school day for planning and for evaluating instructional activities.

6. The principal tended to be a manager of materials and time schedules rather than an educational leader. Administrative procedures discouraged communication with teachers and cooperative planning and decision making.

7. The staff spent most of its energy in keeping the school going; little effort was devoted to the improvement of educational practice.

8. The staff of each school worked in relative isolation from the staffs of other schools; communication networks for sharing creative ideas, materials, and instructional approaches functioned only sporadically.

9. The typical school building was not well adapted for effective instruction; access to libraries and to audiovisual and other instructional materials was circumscribed, and space configurations impeded independent study and the effective grouping of students for learning activities.

10. Parents had only infrequent contact with schools, and that was usually negative; it was concerned mainly with problems of school finance or student discipline. The primary means of communication between the school and the home was through report cards or parent-teacher conferences, supplemented occasionally by school newsletters.

It was to these problems that work at the Wisconsin Research and Development Center was addressed, and it was out of this effort IGE was developed. This chapter examines the assumptions and priorities of the program's developers, and analyzes and interprets the literature written to explain the program. Whenever possible, the language of the developers is used to explore the program's intent and design. The examination provides a background to the subsequent analysis, in which the program is made problematic through an investigation of the patterns of work, knowledge, and professionalism found in six elementary schools.

## The Early Developmental Work
## of the Wisconsin Research and Development Center

In 1964, the United States Office of Education created a national network of research and development centers, intended to apply scientific and technological knowledge to educational practice. It was to be comparable to federal research and development networks already established in agriculture, space, medicine, and industry. Many believed that such efforts had produced long-term success, and that a similar effort in education would yield substantial results. According to Hendrik D. Gideonese (1968:157–163) of the Office of Education, a major concern was to develop an instructional model that would coordinate educational theory and practice into a total research effort. The importance of this model lay in the assumption that the "know-how" was available to make substantial and lasting reforms in the schools.

One of four centers created by the Office of Education to carry out programmatic research and development was the Research and Development Center for Learning and Reeducation at the University of Wisconsin. By 1966 one of two groups initially involved in the center had emerged to give it direction, and the name was changed to the Wisconsin Research and Development Center for Cognitive Learning. The purpose of the center was "to improve the efficiency of cognitive learning and to translate that knowledge into instructional materials and procedures" for use in schools. The first major effort of the center was Project Models: Maximizing Opportunities for Development and Experimentation in Learning in Schools (1966–1968). Project Models brought together experts in curriculum and academic disciplines, behavioral scientists, communication specialists, and representatives of local school systems and state departments of public instruction to develop and implement programs to increase the efficiency of learning in schools.

Although the specific focus of the center's work changed in time, its overall concern remained the extension of "knowledge about the processes of cognitive learning . . . and about the conditions associated with efficiency of learning in the cognitive domain" (Klausmeier and O'Hearn 1968:v–vi). Klausmeier set forth these principles as guidelines for the center: (*a*) "concepts provide much of the basic material for thinking"; (*b*) "concepts and cognitive skills comprise the major outcomes of learning in various subject fields"; (*c*) "the acquisition of cognitive skills enables man . . . also to generate new knowledge"; (*d*) "effective learning of concepts and cognitive abilities is related to conditions within the learner and the conditions within the situation"; and (*e*) "knowledge about cognitive learning concepts, cognitive skills, and conditions of learning generated by scholars requires validation in school settings" (Klausmeier 1968:147–48).

Using these guidelines as a foundation, the tasks of the center were defined as (1) the identification of the concepts to be taught and the cognitive skills necessary for utilizing them, and the arrangement of those concepts in a hierarchical order; and (2) the creation of "a rationale and strategy for developing instructional systems in the cognitive domain" that would enable children to learn those concepts and skills (Klausmeier 1968:148).

At the time that the center was formulating its tasks, there was considerable national debate about the nature of the concepts that children should learn, and about the "structure of the discipline" as a guide to curriculum development. Although one of the curriculum materials developed at the center (Developing Mathematical Processes) had its roots in structure of the discipline debate, literature about IGE does not address this issue. In the early publications of the Center curriculum experts emphasize the selection of research strategies to assess the efficiency of learning, rather than the question of what is to be taught or the rationale to be used in determining objectives (e.g., see Begle 1968). Readers are left with the assumption that what constitutes a concept or a skill can be agreed upon by curriculum specialists, and that no fundamental disagreements over curriculum content will arise that might prevent the implementation of IGE.

The planners at the center adopted a systems analysis approach to identify and to correlate the various organizational components of schools, and Romberg's discussion of the development of an instructional strategy was based on "systems" assumptions:

The word *system* . . . refers to a man-made controlled functional structure. *Man-made structure* means that the system has interdependent components which can be changed or manipulated. *Controlled* means that there is a feedback or monitoring procedure which can be used to manage this system, and *functional* means that the system is goal oriented with a stated purpose or intent. Minimally such a system has four basic components: input, mechanism, feedback, and output. The input is raw materials; the mechanism is the way in which the raw materials are transformed into the output; the feedback is the control process and the output is the same product reflecting the purpose of the system. (Romberg 1968:15.)

The systems approach provided a particularly useful perspective from which to develop an instructional model that included "all the objectives of education and all the groups of variables that may effect efficient learning" (Klausmeier et al. 1966:4). The instructional model provided an organizational system through which to identify goals and establish management procedures to guide students in their interaction with materials, equipment, teachers, and physical facilities of the school. The model also served to monitor students through assessment procedures in order to direct them toward appropriate behaviors.

The search for a mechanism to identify efficient methods of learning led to the center's first instructional innovation, the unitized school, which also reflected the researchers' interest in the psychology of individual differences. Children were believed to learn better in groups of peers organized around the information and skills to be learned rather than in groups based on age, IQ, or general aptitude. It was further assumed that there would be differences in the knowledge individual children brought to the learning situation, and in their ways of learning new material. The research problem, therefore, was to identify how to group pupils effectively and to manage their progress toward the predetermined objectives of the curriculum. The recognition that the typical classroom provided too small a sample for adequate randomization gave rise to the view of the school as a collection of children and teachers who could be reorganized efficiently into different sized groups: one teacher to one student, students working independently, small and large groups, depending upon the learning task.

As a result of these assumptions and design problems, "Research and Instruction (R & I) units were . . . established in 1966 in elementary schools in five Wisconsin cities. An R & I unit is staffed by a Unit leader, 3–6 certified teachers, and several paraprofessionals . . . This team is responsible for the education of 100 to 200 children perhaps from two or three grade levels . . . While the distinctive features of this organizational plan incorporate the better aspects of team teaching, the unit permits flexibility that is needed in randomization of teachers and students" (Quilling 1968:10). Klausmeier, Goodwin, Prasch, and Goodson (1966) claimed that the Research and Instructional Unit provides a "unique organization to carry out controlled experiments in any element of an instructional program . . . It is also the unit within the school in which to conduct research concerning a total exemplary instructional system—all the variables associated with subject matter, students, instructional staff, characteristics of the instructional group, instruction methods and learning procedures, media and materials of instruction, neighborhood and home conditions and services with a school system" (p. 4).

The unitized school and the randomization of sample populations were important to establish certain conditions for research, but it was equally important that they offer efficiency in instruction. "More vigorously than would be expected in the usual classroom teaching situation, the R & I . . . Unit attempts to get each child to learn as fast and as well as he can, to remember what he learns and to use it in achieving individually and socially useful goals" (Klausmeier et al. 1966:3).

In the unit organization variations in teaching came to be defined, not in substantive terms (varying what was to be taught), but in terms of the size of the group to be taught and the type of materials to be used. A teacher working with a single child was assumed to be teaching differently than a teacher working with a group of 10, and both worked differently than a teacher working with a group of 90. Similarly, the mix of teaching materials available—overhead projectors, worksheets, textbooks, slides, tapes, etc.—offered a variety of mechanisms for responding to different learning styles. In its definitions of variables, the unit system failed to distinguish among teaching procedures that emphasized lecturing to children and testing them, procedures that encouraged problem-solving, and those that used art as an alternative language. The failure to define these procedures as variations in teaching style may have resulted from early definitions of concept and concept attainment which stressed information acquisition and recognition rather than knowledge generation (see Frayer and Klausmeier 1971; Quilling 1968).

The Research and Instructional Unit did provide active roles for many teachers in schools involved in the center's initial project, and unit teachers were listed as co-authors in many of the center's technical reports. In many instances, research problems were defined by teachers, and the center provided technical assistance in designing, implementing, and analyzing the research.

The involvement of teachers in developing a more efficient instructional system is evident in the materials developed for the center's program. The Wisconsin Design for Reading Skill Development, a center-created management approach to teaching reading, was initiated by teachers in a Madison, Wisconsin, elementary school. They had suggested that a management system was necessary to monitor the mastery of reading objectives and skills, and to provide a mechanism for recording students' test scores. The Wisconsin Design was the result of a cooperative effort of teachers and researchers to identify a hierarchical sequence of all possible reading skills, and to offer "specific exercises and/or observations designed for use in assessing mastery or progress in the development of each of the several skills." While the program was thought of as a guide to be used within "the larger framework of the reading program and of the school's total instructional program," (Otto et al. 1967:1) the initial focus of the reading design was on specific skills that had been isolated in an analysis of reading behavior.

In contrast to the management approach taken in the reading program, the mathematics program (Developing Mathematical Processes), which was begun at about the same time (1967), was built around a problem-solving approach to help students discover basic principles of mathematics. This curriculum placed less emphasis on the management of students' learning and more on a developmental framework of mathematical activities (Romberg 1977). Despite the different assumptions underlying the Wisconsin Design for Reading Skill Development and Developing Mathematical Processes, both were seen as appropriate to the IGE systems approach to efficient and effective schooling.

By the late 1960s, research findings had accumulated and the various elements of the instructional and organizational system had been clarified. The Wisconsin Research and Development Center leadership believed it had developed and tested a product that was ready for implementation in schools. The new program was called Individually *Guided* Education to emphasize the importance of individual differences, and to suggest that the Wisconsin program was significantly different from the Individually *Prescribed* Instruction being developed at the University of Pittsburgh Research and Development Center. The term "guided" was to reflect a flexible, more varied system of instruction.

The crystallization of IGE into a specific system of technologies was catalyzed by factors beyond the Wisconsin Research and Development Center as well. When the federal agencies that sponsored research and development centers sought new funds, they presented to congressional committees and to accounting officers in the Office of Management and Budget tangible evidence of the fruits of the expenditures of past years. By the late 1960s and early 1970s, the work of the research and development centers could no longer be presented as "in progress"; products had to be created to meet the accounting criteria of the federal agencies. In addition, schools were asking for solutions to their problems, and wanted to place the new programs in their classrooms. To respond to the demands of the government and the schools, implementation literature and packages of materials were created by the research and development centers. At Wisconsin, the name of the Research and Instructional Unit was changed, first to Instructional and Research Unit and eventually to Instructional Unit, to indicate the shift in focus as the program matured.

A four-phase implementation strategy for IGE, formulated in 1971, was funded by the U. S. Office of Education. The four phases were "awareness of IGE, changeover to IGE, refinement of practices in existing IGE

schools, and institutionalization, more recently designated renewal"
(Klausmeier 1977:5). Change was considered a logical, sequential process. At the core of this strategy was instruction in the management and
implementation of IGE; teachers designated as unit leaders and principals were trained in the concepts and technologies of IGE, usually in
workshops and noncredit in-service courses. Although most early implementation training was directed at experienced teachers, a major component of the IGE strategy from 1972 on was the development of IGE
teacher education programs as part of the undergraduate certification
sequence.

### Individually Guided Education in the 1970s

By the 1970s, Individually Guided Education incorporated a number of
technologies by which school learning could be organized and evaluated.
The unitized school became part of a seven-component model which, its
designers stated, would create a new set of institutional relationships for
students, teachers, and administrators (Figure 2.1). This model persists in
the IGE program.

The components of the model are consistent with the early systems
approach that identified separate but interdependent elements of a functional school system. The first component is the unit, a nongraded group
of approximately 100 students, four teachers, a unit leader, aides, and
clerical help (Figure 2.2). The unit's main task is to carry out the second
component, the Instructional Programming Model, which is a sequence
of seven steps intended to provide efficient ordering, implementation and
evaluation of group and school-wide objectives (Figure 2.3).

Step one of the Instructional Programming Model (IPM) is to state the
educational objectives to be attained by the student population of the
building; step two calls for estimating the range of objectives that are
attainable by the several subgroups within the unit. The third step involves pre-testing students to assess their levels of achievement, using
criterion-referenced tests. Step four calls for setting objectives for each
child; given these objectives, an instructional program suitable for each
student is to be carried out during step five. The sixth step is the assessment of how well each student has attained those objectives. Finally, if
the objectives have been achieved according to the program, a reassess-
ment of the individual's learning characteristics is undertaken and the
student is sequenced through another IPM cycle. If the objectives have
not been achieved, remedial instruction is carried out.

The third component of IGE, Evaluation for Educational Decision
Making, follows the Instructional Programming Model closely. The five

Figure 2.1 Development and description of IGE.
Source: Klausmeier, Rossmiller, and Saily, eds., 1977: 11.

steps of Evaluation begin with formulating instructional objectives for the individual, and end with a judgment of the appropriateness of the objectives and instructional program for each individual. IGE planners have argued that to maintain a high quality educational experience for all students, regardless of wide differences in their characteristics and abilities, constant monitoring of individual student programs is necessary.

The fourth component of IGE is compatible curricular materials. The most important criterion of compatibility is that the materials can be taught within the Instructional Programming Model. To carry out the Instructional Programming Model, then, clearly stated instructional objectives, assessment and record-keeping procedures, a range of printed

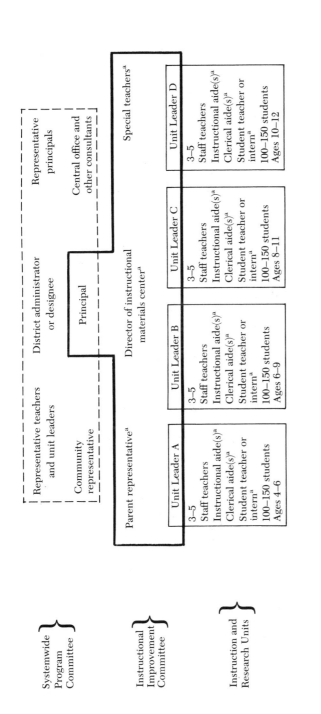

Figure 2.2. The multiunit organization.
Source: Klausmeier, Rossmiller, and Saily eds., 1977: 12.

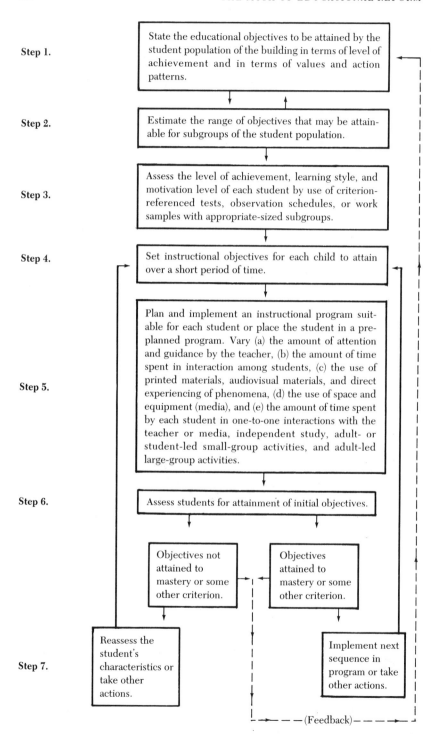

**Step 1.**

State the educational objectives to be attained by the student population of the building in terms of level of achievement and in terms of values and action patterns.

**Step 2.**

Estimate the range of objectives that may be attainable for subgroups of the student population.

**Step 3.**

Assess the level of achievement, learning style, and motivation level of each student by use of criterion-referenced tests, observation schedules, or work samples with appropriate-sized subgroups.

**Step 4.**

Set instructional objectives for each child to attain over a short period of time.

**Step 5.**

Plan and implement an instructional program suitable for each student or place the student in a pre-planned program. Vary (a) the amount of attention and guidance by the teacher, (b) the amount of time spent in interaction among students, (c) the use of printed materials, audiovisual materials, and direct experiencing of phenomena, (d) the use of space and equipment (media), and (e) the amount of time spent by each student in one-to-one interactions with the teacher or media, independent study, adult- or student-led small-group activities, and adult-led large-group activities.

**Step 6.**

Assess students for attainment of initial objectives.

Objectives not attained to mastery or some other criterion.

Objectives attained to mastery or some other criterion.

**Step 7.**

Reassess the student's characteristics or take other actions.

Implement next sequence in program or take other actions.

– – – –(Feedback)– – – – – –

Figure 2.3. The instructional programming model in IGE. Source: Klausmeier, Rossmiller, and Saily, eds., 1977: 16.

and other materials, and a variety of instructional procedures are all needed.

The fifth component advocates the development of home-school-community relations in which parents and other citizens participate in the resolution of school-related problems. The sixth component, a "system of facilitative environments" (Klausmeier 1977:20), concerns a network of agencies outside the school to assist the process of IGE implementation and renew institutional commitment to IGE: school district policy committees, state networks of participating IGE schools, teacher education institutions, the research and development center, and state education agencies. The seventh component is continuing research and development to improve both the theory and practice of IGE. The major responsibility for this lay with the Wisconsin R and D Center, where research, until the late 1970s, was concerned primarily with refining existing structures and materials, and with developing an IGE model for secondary schools.

Individually Guided Education, with its several components, is seen by its developers as a total, comprehensive system for the reform of schooling. The daily decisions of the teacher as well as the research of R and D Center personnel are aimed at introducing procedures and technologies that provide new patterns of educational conduct and new attitudes toward elementary education.

### IGE as a Persisting Model of Educational Reform

The IGE program embodies at least two attitudes found in the currents of American educational thinking. One of these is the belief that individualism is important, and that the development of individual talents and interests is a significant goal of education. The individualization of instruction can be seen as a contemporary response to the perception that schools have failed in their responsibilities to the individual. The second attitude involves the assumption that important social problems, such as the education of youth, are most effectively attacked through the power of scientific expertise.

IGE is unusually attractive to many school people because it links the appeal of individualism with the harmony and efficiency of scientific management. Systems management, behavioral objectives, and criterion-referenced measures seem to be backed up by research on individual cognitive differences and needs. The unitized school and the Instructional Programming Model combine systematically to provide for students who learn at different rates and at different times; by offering varied groups and materials as different routes to specified objectives, this system appears to be responsive to different learning styles. Giving teachers the decision over which individual objectives children should achieve is intended as a response to the cultural, social, and personal differences that children bring to school, as well as to the different interests and expertise among teachers. Individualism and scientific management blend to bring coherence to the social purposes of schooling.

The unitized IGE school has also provided a system through which teachers can respond to the new demands placed on them by increasing requirements for accountability and the specialization of teaching activities. Schools that have to account to federal and state agencies in order to qualify for funds to meet specific problems have expected teachers to produce visible results. At the same time, specialization has been taking place in various traditional subject areas, such as reading, mathematics, and guidance and counseling. Learning to read and to understand mathematics have been described in research as highly complex activities, which implies the need for specialists to deal with the subtleties of teaching in these areas. Such methods as team teaching and differential staffing have been offered to meet the need for specialists who can provide effective education. The teacher shortage of the early 1970s and the need to develop career incentives for more highly skilled teachers have also acted to change the nature of the teacher's job.

In further investigating why the marriage of individualism and science found in IGE has been so persistent, it is necessary to examine support given to the program by the R and D Center at the University of Wisconsin. An important part of the center's support comes from its research efforts. Between 1970 and 1980 hundreds of studies were conducted to investigate children's learning processes, organizational models associated with individualization, and the cost-effectiveness of school operations. Much of the knowledge gained was applied to the development of educational theory in order to provide a firmer scientific basis for making choices about schooling, and to give conceptual organization and refinement to IGE strategies. To supplement these scholarly functions, research is also directed toward the development of curriculum materials that are based upon the assumptions of IGE and especially its Instructional Programming Model.

The knowledge produced by and for the Wisconsin R and D Center also serves a political function, through research which examined the efficiency and effectiveness of IGE as it operates in schools across the nation. Such variables as learning climate, achievement, teacher satisfaction and professional development, and the cost effectiveness of the program are the subject of research reports and doctoral studies. These efforts support the center's commitment to implementation.

This commitment is also expressed through the center's efforts to organize and to assist state networks and state IGE implementors. A network is a formal group of schools whose staffs endeavor to develop their IGE program further. Implementors generally work within state education agencies to promote IGE and train school district leaders, teachers, unit leaders, and principals in IGE procedures. Regional IGE leagues are also organized; a league is a group of schools whose representatives assist other schools to institute IGE and to improve each school's program. A Research and Development Center implementation group trained IGE leaders at state and local levels. In 1974, the center helped to establish the Association for Individually Guided Education (AIGE), a national professional organization for people involved in IGE at state, university, and school levels, as well as at the R and D Center.

To assist the reform of schools through IGE, the Research and Development Center has developed an IGE Implementation Manual, a Performance Objective Resource File, and IGE leadership materials for principals, unit leaders and teachers. Undergraduate and graduate courses in IGE, and the use of multimedia instructional materials have been incorporated into a teacher education program. Since 1974 IGE workshops have been held around the country to aid implementation and to maintain communications among other research and development centers, the schools, and the Wisconsin Research and Development Center.

Each of these activities of the Wisconsin Research and Development Center legitimates IGE. The center has considerable intellectual and financial resources to support the program. The visibility given to IGE through journal articles, networks, associations, and national and state agencies argues for the feasibility of this comprehensive approach to schooling. Of course, the use of IGE in schools also serves to reinforce the legitimacy of the program and of the Research and Development Center.

### Assumptions about Knowledge, Work, and Profession in IGE

In considering the effects of IGE as a reform program, it is important to look beyond the language of individualized instruction, team teaching, and nongraded teaching units. The IGE model carries with it certain assumptions about the nature of knowledge, the most effective ways children can work to gain that knowledge, and the role of the professional in implementing the reform. IGE was conceived as a systematic attempt to reform schools; it was also designed as a comprehensive program affecting both agencies external to the school and structures within the school. There is a pattern, therefore, of interrelated assumptions that give IGE form and content. In this analysis of IGE we do not intend to accept or reject the assumptions of the reform program, but to identify them. In the final chapter we will return to these assumptions and analyze the reform program in light of the data presented from the six schools which were investigated.

The first assumption underlying IGE is that the *knowledge* which children are to acquire in school can be formulated in advance of instruction in terms of behavioral objectives, and that attainment of these objectives can be measured subsequently in terms of performance criteria.

A second assumption is that the *work* children do to acquire this knowledge can be structured by an Instructional Programming Model—a system of planned, sequential activities involving testing, grouping, instructional materials, and testing once more.

A third assumption is that the role of the *professional* is one of implementing the instructional program as it has been defined by IGE designers. Reform is considered to have taken place when the staff of a school manages instruction in accordance with the practices prescribed by IGE.

### Knowledge and IGE

Legitimate school knowledge, according to the assumptions of IGE, must be defined in such a way that it is measurable. Therefore the first task in developing an instructional program is to state learning objectives that permit attainment to be measured by explicit and public criteria. For example, a social studies objective might be to "show that you can make a list of questions to find out information" (Klausmeier 1977:57); a school-wide instructional objective might be "given a suburban school and children with above-average ability, 75 percent of the pupils might attain the objective by age nine, 90 percent by age ten, and 100 percent by age twelve" (Askin and Otto, 1972:8).

In establishing performance-based objectives as the basis of the school curriculum, the developers of IGE also see clear and precise measurement procedures as fundamentally important. Detailed and explicitly stated objectives "provide a clear indication of what is to be learned and imply how instruction may proceed, but they also require equally detailed and frequent assessment of children, extensive record keeping, and when children are grouped and regrouped for instruction alternative provision for early attainers and for late attainers" (Klausmeier, Rossmiller, and Saily, eds., 1977:69). Such detailed assessment is intended both to make instruction efficient and to provide for accountability.

Measurement of attainment is also intended to be coordinated with the instructional sequence. "Measurement plays a critical role in any school because staff and students must have feedback on the impact of instruction and the progress of students in the program, but IGE requires extra concern for the appropriate interpretation and use of measurement techniques" (Katzenmeyer 1977:151). Wiersma (1977) observes that employing the Instructional Programming Model involves the use of evaluation at every step.

Though a selection of measurement procedures are offered to assist teachers in evaluation, implementation literature claims that criterion-referenced measures in particular have "a critical importance to IGE" (Katzenmeyer 1977:152). Criterion-referenced measurements are related to the specific objectives of the curriculum. Instead of comparing the performances of all students in a group, the criterion-referenced measure provides IGE teachers with a mechanism for interpreting individual student achievement on a specific educational task: "a student obtaining a score of 90% on a test of beginning vowels by correctly answering 18 of the 20 possible items may be said to have mastered [the instructional objective]" (Katzenmeyer 1977:152–153).

The use of criterion-referenced measures of student performance responds to an important concern of IGE's developers. These measures demonstrate achievement in terms of absolute standards rather than by comparing students with one another. The use of norm-referenced tests that yield comparative measures is seen as a weakness in conventional schooling.

The kinds of knowledge capable of being defined in terms of prestated objectives that can be clearly and easily measured are limited; such objectives are appropriate to discrete factual knowledge and skills. Agreement must be reached by the school staff about what constitutes the knowledge and skills to be learned, as well as about the best way of measuring their attainment. The emphasis in IGE is upon knowledge transmission, skills which involve acquiring and remembering information, and on the use of knowledge by substituting equivalent terms for one another and by remembering relationships. The generation of knowledge is not discussed, nor is the learning of skills and attitudes appropriate for creating knowledge. The comprehension of relationships among items of information or skills may be identified as an objective in the Instructional Programming Model; but what is not identified as an objective is ambiguous knowledge, or learning that is incidental. Such learning is given no attention in the IGE literature.

In IGE literature the creative arts, the humanities, social education, and the affective domain are considered exempt from the closely specified objectives that are rigorously applied to other basic subjects. While these dimensions of instruction are valued in some of the literature, they receive little emphasis in discussions about the implementation of IGE, possibly because of the difficulty of applying management techniques to objectives in these areas.

*Work and IGE*

The kinds of work students may do is determined, in part, by the sequencing prescribed in the predetermined objectives. Sequencing is seen as a cycle; assessing the knowledge of each student in a group, instructing students through a set of prescribed materials in groups whose members have similar needs, and performing a final assessment to determine the achievement of the objectives. Variables in this cycle include the size of the group and the instructional materials used. IGE literature suggests that both shared and individual, variable objectives can be prescribed for students; that students can vary as to whether or not they master the objectives; and that the activities in a sequence can vary or be invariant, depending upon content or student characteristics.

Most IGE literature, however, concentrates on invariant objectives in which some identified level of mastery is set for all children. In the Wisconsin Design for Reading Skill Development, for instance, the objectives include different levels of skill whose attainment is considered invariant. Klausmeier states that "every student is expected to attain all the objectives within a given level to the same specified criterion of mastery before proceeding to the next successive level . . ." (1977:63). The sequencing of the Pre-Reading Skills Program is entirely invariant, and in arithmetic, ". . . because of the hierarchical nature of arithmetic skill learning, the units of instruction within various arithmetic strands usually follow an invariant sequence" (Klausmeier 1977:63).

This conception of curriculum implies a discrete and concrete structure of activities in which students can be closely monitored by teachers as they proceed upward through a hierarchy of skills. The work pattern dictated by this model requires students to be assessed in a skill area, to be divided into groups, to carry out predetermined instructional tasks, and then to be tested to determine if mastery has been achieved.

*Profession and IGE*

The role of teachers is carefully defined by the requirements of IGE. Since school reform is seen as a comprehensive organizational problem to be achieved through a systems approach and the technologies that professionals are to implement are designed to bring about the efficient achievement of educational goals, teachers are to become skilled as managers of the technology. Their tasks are to develop instructional objectives, to develop and use appropriate measurement tools to assess and evaluate student achievement, to select and sequence student activities and materials, and to work jointly with other staff members to maintain IGE procedures. A school is considered to be reformed to the extent that its professionals have successfully implemented and maintained the components of the IGE system.

## IGE as a Systems Approach to Reform

The IGE literature suggests the assumption that the school can contribute towards the egalitarian goals of a meritocratic society. This assumption is rooted in the liberal democratic theory which views the school as an objective institution that provides equal opportunities for achievement, and hence equal access to the social and material rewards of society. The IGE emphases on psychological traits, differences in learning rates and styles, and technologies to increase efficiency are based upon the belief that success is a result of ability and hard work, rather than accidents of birth or breeding. The function of the school is to increase the efficiency of the "delivery" system, thereby increasing all students' chances of success.

As a systems approach to the reform of schooling, IGE is intended as a comprehensive program coordinating research and development, teacher training, curriculum materials, school administration and district practices, and home-school relationships, as well as student and teacher behaviors. IGE's designers believe that by applying the principles of educational psychology through a systems approach the objectives, variables, and interrelationships of an educational environment can be known, and can be structured to yield efficient learning. IGE is assumed to be a universal model that can be applied to any and all traditional public school settings, and is believed to be a neutral, nonideological technology capable of reforming all elementary schooling.

While IGE is designed to enable professionals to guide each student toward maximum achievement, publications that describe the intentions and programs of IGE reveal some inconsistency. In some publications, learning is regarded from a behaviorist perspective, with the problem being to find the most efficient way to help students acquire a fixed body of skills and knowledge. In other publications, learning is held to be a constructive phenomenon, in which students must interact with their environment to create and invent knowledge. Nevertheless, predominant in IGE literature—especially in the implementation materials—is a behaviorist approach to the reform of schooling.

The assumptions underlying IGE are not new, nor are they unique to IGE. The search for more efficient management procedures in education dates back at least to the work of Bobbitt and Charters, and the accountability movement in contemporary education has strengthened the belief that management can be used in school reform. What is unique in IGE is the extent to which the reform has been systematized and provided with support through the many organized constituencies within school districts and states, through IGE institutes and networks, and through the collaboration of university and school researchers. The program has not only defined individual roles; it has also provided procedures and materials for instruction, program development, and organizational coordination. At the same time, IGE planners and developers have attempted to legitimate and support program activities through systematic studies and research.

In the following chapters we put aside the definitions, assumptions, and hopes of the IGE planners to inquire into the everyday patterns of behavior, the priorities, and the social values that are maintained or created as people in six "model" schools apply the technologies of Individually Guided Education.

# 3

## Daily Life and Public Language:
## Three IGE Schools

Among those schools found to have exemplary IGE programs, three—
Maplewood, Belair, and Clayburn[1]—share common institutional characteristics. Although the communities they serve display considerable
socioeconomic diversity, the schools are quite similar in the configurations of the work, knowledge, and professionalism they offer in their
implementation of Individually Guided Education. In this chapter we
describe and interpret these configurations from the perspective of the
public language used by the schools and formal organizational arrangements in the schools; in the next chapter the perspective shifts to an
analytic focus upon the institutional rules and meanings underlying those
configurations. With the descriptive perspective our intent is to illustrate
how symbolic forms are generated in ways that seem to give coherence
and provide legitimacy to schooling, whereas the analytic perspective in
the following chapter reveals how such forms actually obscure the underlying meanings and dynamics of life in the three schools.

The descriptions of each of the three schools that follow are intended to
orient the reader to the communities they serve and the daily school
activities of teachers and students, to identify the publicly expressed be-

---

1. The names that are used to refer to schools and people in this and subsequent chapters
are fictitious.

liefs and attitudes held by the teachers about IGE and schooling in general, and to indicate the public definitions that professionals give to the daily practices and technologies of IGE. In the following chapter, the perspective shifts. The objectives and conceptual categories of Individually Guided Education are not taken for granted, but are examined as part of the dynamic configurations of knowledge, work, and professionalism underlying school and classroom life. Chapter 4, then, uses the data of chapter 3, but makes problematic key elements of the social and intellectual contexts of these schools—elements that are accepted without question in the descriptive interpretation in chapter 3.

Geographically, these schools are widely separated: Clayburn is in the southeast, Maplewood is in the midwest, and Belair in the west. Clayburn is essentially rural, Maplewood is suburban, and Belair is in an urban area. One-third of Clayburn's student population is black, but minorities have only minuscule representation in the other schools. Clayburn is also the only school that serves more than a local neighborhood; some of its black students are bused across the county to achieve racial balance.

There are other differences among the three schools. Maplewood is solidly middle class, with few students from wealthy and poor families. On the other hand, nearly one-half of Clayburn's students qualify for federal educational assistance. Belair's students represent a range of family incomes, but of the schools we studied its neighborhood is the only one in which millionaires are reported to live. Information obtained from school personnel places Clayburn at the low end of the income scale and Belair at the top end, with Maplewood in the middle. It should be kept in mind, however, that Belair pulls students from the widest economic range, from welfare recipients to reported millionaires.

### Maplewood Elementary School:
### Serving a Suburban, Blue-Collar Community

Maplewood is a K–6 elementary school located in a small suburban community on the edge of a large midwestern city. The community underwent a growth spurt after World War II, when the move to the suburbs began in most metropolitan areas of our country. It is in the first ring of old suburbs, dominated by moderate-cost housing and mature shade trees. The teachers at Maplewood Elementary School describe the residents of their community as skilled and semiskilled tradespeople. It is essentially a bedroom community; many residents commute to work, and in many families both husband and wife are employed. Although teachers perceive the educational level of the community as only moderate, and the type of employment held by the fathers is ranked by conventional occupational ratings as not particularly high, combined family income is reported to be substantial. One administrator described the people as typical family-oriented Americans: "The people here vote liberal on economic issues but are conservative when it comes to traditional family values."

In general, community and parental concern for education is active and genuine. Participation in school affairs by parents, particularly mothers, is one of the most obvious features at Maplewood. There is an active parent-teacher association that receives credit from the school staff for carrying out worthwhile educational projects. Like many parents around the country, parents at Maplewood have high expectations for their children and for the contribution the school can make to their children's future.

Maplewood School is housed in a spacious contemporary building with an open plan featuring large instructional areas instead of conventional classrooms. Hallways encircle the instructional areas, which are all in the interior of the building; there are no windows to allow natural light into the instructional areas.

From the time the school was built in 1971, the intent was to have an organizational structure appropriate to the open plan environment. When the director of elementary curriculum in the school district became interested in IGE, he encouraged an elementary school principal to become familiar with the program. The principal became convinced that the school's physical structure and the goals of IGE were compatible, and recruited teachers for the new school by explaining the organizational structure and goals of IGE to the candidates. Those teachers whom he believed were interested in and capable of teaching in an open school with an IGE program were hired.

Administratively, Maplewood has three IGE units plus a kindergarten. Each unit serves two conventional age grades: the Primary unit serves grades one and two; the Intermediate unit grades three and four; and the Independent unit grades five and six. Each unit has about 125 students and is taught by a team of five teachers, one of whom is designated the unit leader. The units each occupy one of the large rectangular instructional areas that take up most of the space in the building. The school complex also contains an instructional materials center, a cafeteria, gymnasium, meeting room, teachers' lounge and administrative offices.

Unit areas feature moveable walls that can be used to create smaller compartments resembling traditional classrooms in size and shape. Although on occasion teachers choose to segregate a group of students for a specific activity, particularly if a high noise level is anticipated, the walls are generally folded out of the way. Portable tables in each unit can be arranged to seat four to six students apiece, or they may be pushed against a wall to leave an open area for activities.

To an observer one of the most obvious characteristics of Maplewood school is the continuous movement of students from teacher to teacher within the unit, and out of the unit to physical education, music, and other specialized instruction. To facilitate movement, each student carries a tote tray holding pencils, paper, books and personal belongings; trays are stored in a wall rack when not in use.

Within the unit, teachers are constantly active—collecting and distributing papers, checking student work, and presenting new assignments. This outward appearance of activity is not deceptive. Our conversations with teachers have repeatedly confirmed that hard work is needed to get the results they and the parents expect.[2] Teachers at Maplewood believe they have established optimal conditions for learning, and they view their instructional activities as implemenatation of the IGE program. In a survey of teachers' perceptions of the use of IGE technologies in schools, Maplewood ranked 8th out of 158 schools. Maplewood's teachers express a high degree of job satisfaction, in contrast to teachers in other IGE schools around the country.

In defining individualized education, the Maplewood professional staff has established sets of learning objectives that are the basis of the curriculum in each unit. Corresponding curriculum materials have been carefully designed to teach the objectives specified. Teachers systematically pretest all students on the sets of objectives, and subsequent instruction is aimed at mastery; mastery is defined as getting 80 percent of the answers correct on post-instruction tests.

An important dimension of IGE is the periodic grouping and regrouping of students according to their performance levels in each of the major subject areas: reading, language arts, math, spelling, and study skills. Regrouping occurs regularly at Maplewood. Test scores and achievement levels are recorded for each student, and careful records are kept of the student's progress toward the various sets of objectives. While some performance scores are now kept by a time-sharing computer program, the principal and staff eventually intend to record all achievement data through the computer. This will permit the maintenance of a semipermanent record for all students on all objectives through all grade levels, and will provide an accountability system to prove that the school has taught each student the basic skills. The computerized system also provides speed and accuracy in the grouping of students on the basis of their skills.

2. These comments are expressed in survey data regarding the teachers' perception of IGE.

The school's decision to computerize the recording and monitoring of student achievement is highly significant. It commits the staff to the kind of "systems" approach to instruction offered by IGE, and it commits the school to allocating resources to implement the system. Two Maplewood teachers have taken training in the programming and use of the computer, and the principal employs an aide to run the computer.

From the students' point of view, as well as the teachers', Maplewood is a good place. Casual conversations with students who have attended other schools almost universally result in testimony that Maplewood is better. Students like the freedom of movement that comes with open space and periodic grouping, and they see their teachers as fair and helpful. While they rate going to school somewhat higher than one would expect from children this age, these are still typical boys and girls, full of energy and almost certainly more playful and noisy in school than teachers like. They are probably less studious than ideal pupils, but teachers agree that this student population is likeable and relatively easy to work with. There is no great discipline problem, and especially in primary units the students seem both eager to please and responsive to adult directions.

The Maplewood staff was pleased with the results its students obtained on standardized tests of academic achievement. The principal showed us results from the Stanford Achievement Test, which was given to students in all of the district's schools at the second, fourth and sixth grade levels. The district's students scored above the national averge in all eleven test categories, and Maplewood scored above the district average by almost half a year at the sixth grade level. This was especially gratifying to the teachers because the youngest children's results indicated that they were below the district average. The implication for the staff was that the children started school with a lower level of achievement, but through the effectiveness of the school's program moved ahead of their peers in the rest of the district. Information about the achievement of Maplewood students was familiar to parents, and the reputation of the school in the community was favorable. In at least one instance it was reported that a family moved into the neighborhood so their children could attend Maplewood.

The principal is a dominant force in shaping the character of Maplewood school. He has a strong personality, an abundance of restless energy, and clear ideas about the way in which personality types interact in working situations. He uses a personality inventory to discover the attitudes of each teacher toward work and the extent to which a teacher strives for leadership. By using this instrument to match complementary personality types for teaching teams, the principal believes he has selected teams for each unit that are maximally productive. Teachers tend to accept this approach because they believe it has produced harmonious and effective teaching units.

The staff respects the principal and gives him credit for developing a successful school. Teachers see him as having high standards and expectations—sometimes too high. Teachers also mention that the principal, as a matter of policy, involves them in decisions that are considered the principal's prerogative in most schools. While this policy has allowed teachers to make decisions, their autonomy is not complete; the principal has often been heard to remark that "the decision is yours, but whatever you decide, it must be good for kids," and teachers have had to convince him that their decisions are appropriate.

For the principal, the ultimate educational authority is not the superintendent or school board, but the parents and the children. The principal indicated that he had gone "out on a limb" several times in the past to implement policies he believed in, and he had achieved considerable success in winning community support. This has made him the district's star principal in the superintendent's eyes.

The teachers report that one highly successful innovation at Maplewood is the extensive teacher aide program that employs mothers from the neighborhood. A sizeable budget allocation permits each unit to employ several paid aides on an hourly basis; other aides work as volunteers. This program provides the staff with much-needed labor to run ditto machines, collate materials, monitor and correct tests, and place student work on the walls for display. It gives mothers part-time employment on a flexible schedule. Mothers who observe the daily efforts of teachers and children often become boosters for the school and its programs, and can speak with authority about Maplewood.

## Clayburn Elementary School:
## Serving Rural, Agricultural Communities

Clayburn is a southern rural school located ten minutes' drive from the nearest community. The road to the school passes small plots of okra, small plantings of cotton, and fields where a few cattle graze. Pecans provide an important cash return for some residents in the area, including families with only two or three trees in their yard. At the main crossroads people frequently linger and pass the time of day at small gas stations and grocery stores.

The roads are sparsely dotted with homes whose outward appearances contrast affluence and poverty. The economic standing of many families in the district is low, and the principal has pointed out that more than 50 percent of Clayburn's students are eligible for federal Title I support (assistance for families below the poverty level). More than half of the low-income students are black, and many of these are bused from the other side of the county to create racial balance in the county schools. Usually black children walk from cabins and white children from ranch homes to board the buses bound for Clayburn. About one-third of the teachers are black, and many of them commute from a large city about sixty miles away.

In the school's kitchen, cooks prepare and package a breakfast each morning for many of the children. Teachers join the children for breakfast in the schoolrooms.

Individually Guided Education had been used at Clayburn for only a year when our study was made, but staff members reported that they had been working toward individualization for a year before they had heard about IGE. When a curriculum consultant with the district office who had worked with the Wisconsin R and D Center sent a circular about IGE to the schools, Clayburn's principal saw that the program was consistent with many of the things the school was already doing, which the principal termed "individualizing," "having continuous progress," and "meeting children's needs." The program was instituted at Clayburn to give the school's procedures coherence.

The school's two buildings show wear and tear, although attempts to keep them in good repair are evident. A rectangular building housed seven traditional classrooms when it was built in the early 1950s; a square building without interior walls was built more recently. The summer before Clayburn became an IGE school, the principal received permission from the local school board to remove the interior walls from the original building to create two open-space areas. He argued that the remodeling would help teachers to individualize their programs and to implement IGE. A wing that was added to the original building in the early 1960s has deteriorated considerably, and on rainy days wastebaskets are used to catch water dripping through the roof; the recording of one of our interviews was difficult to transcribe because of the sound of water falling into the baskets.

There are approximately 300 students at Clayburn, ten teachers, one reading specialist, and a librarian-materials specialist. The school is divided into three teaching units, each with a unit leader. The older building houses two primary units for children from grade levels one to three; the newer building houses a senior unit for grade levels four to six. The teachers have specialized in subject matter, and students move from teacher to teacher for instruction in different subjects. On entering the buildings, observers see children working at their desks in an environment that is disciplined, orderly, and humane. Children seem to feel secure in knowing what they are to do, and whether they have done their assignments correctly.

The curriculum, unit organization and physical arrangements of Clayburn school support the principal's deep belief in the value of an individualized learning program. To increase the efficiency of unit management, he designed and built some of the school's wooden furniture. Study desks with high sides were constructed along the side of one room and partitions were raised on long tables to provide spaces where children could work quietly and without distraction.

Instructional materials complement these physical modifications and make the individualized program more efficient. The principal designed the mathematics program to provide a "systems" approach, using ideas from several commercial programs. He organized the materials by levels of difficulty, developed worksheets for skill practice, and produced learning packages for each program level. A chart in the teachers' resource room lists the audiovisual projectors and related equipment available for children to use individually. A mini-computer in the senior unit enables children to practice arithmetic. It paces them as they respond to arithmetic facts, and rewards them by displaying the percentage of problems correctly answered, along with a smiling or frowning face to suggest whether the child has done well. Each unit also contains an electronic question-and-answer machine for student use. All of this equipment is intended to allow children to work individually and at a pace consistent with their skill development.

A brief look at the pattern of work in the senior unit illustrates how Clayburn school is structured to achieve this goal. After breakfast, the children in the unit take a mathematics skill test, which may be given orally by the teacher or delivered by a commercially produced recording. When the recording is used the teacher walks around the room to monitor the children's responses. After the test, students work on their individualized programs, which are organized by level of achievement and designed so that each child works alone. The student proceeds through the materials packaged for each level of achievement until difficulty arises or the time has come for the post-instruction test; the child then goes to the teacher for help or directions. Instruction is organized in this way for most subjects: students pace themselves through different levels of mathematics, language arts, and reading. The teacher's normal interaction with students involves correcting work, giving help, and directing them to the next level of materials.

The maintenance of the program is dependent upon a number of parents who work as teacher aides. The parents administer and record tests, sometimes prepare and run off worksheets on the ditto machines, and often have specific responsibilities within the units to monitor children's work.

The Clayburn principal is a forceful administrator. He expects to make the final decisions and to be responsible for final approval of any action taken by the school. His deep commitment to an individualized program leads him to be involved in all aspects of the school program. He spends weekends at school constructing individual cubicles for students, devising management schemes, and creating materials to enable children to work independently.

The unit leaders and teachers are responsible for ensuring efficiency in pacing children through the instructional systems and maintaining discipline in the classes. While some teachers feel that the individualization of instruction required by the principal needs some modification through group work, the teachers accept the principal's directives and his view of the IGE program as a beneficial instructional practice.

Most of the teachers at Clayburn see themselves as successfully implementing the model of Individually Guided Education; when asked if they are utilizing IGE, they respond affirmatively. A national survey of teachers' perception of IGE implementation ranks the school 21st out of 158 schools canvassed (see Appendix B). The school staff believes that IGE is contributing to student achievement by making the curriculum coherent and systematic in the basic skills of reading, language arts, and arithmetic. Although Clayburn pupils have scored among the lowest in the country on standardized achievement tests, the principal is quick to produce data showing how well the students perform on standardized tests in comparison with students of other schools in the district. Clayburn's achievement test scores in both reading and arithmetic have been below the 10th percentile nationally, but in the air is optimism and confidence that improvement is being made in the education of Clayburn students.

Discussions with parent aides in the school and officers in the school's parent organization suggest that members of the community strongly support the school program. The parents believe that the IGE program provides a consistent and efficient approach to teaching their children. Children also talk about the special program they are getting at Clayburn, and those who have attended other schools compare it positively.

### Belair Elementary School: Serving an Urban Community

Belair School is located on the edge of a large city in the western mountains. The building is situated on a hill in a neighborhood whose streets are lined with upper-middleclass houses. Most of the children attending Belair come from middleclass and upper-middleclass families. A small group of students are from a low-cost housing project within the school's boundaries, and according to the principal about 20 percent of the students come from low-income or welfare homes. Nevertheless, the student population is essentially homogeneous. Most of the students belong to the same religious group, and almost all are white; there is only a handful of black, Hispanic, and Native American children. All of the professional staff are white.

Belair was the third school in the school district to adopt Individually Guided Education. The district superintendent of schools had learned about IGE through his involvement with the U.S. Office of Education, and had encouraged elementary school principals to use the program because he believed that it would result in more effective management. Even though Belair is an older school with a conventional classroom design, when a new principal was needed the superintendent sought an administrator who would implement IGE. The previous school program, as described by the current principal, was chaotic; parents were unhappy and the superintendent wanted a change. The IGE program, according to the principal, has produced a much more coherent and systematic program which is supported by parents. Belair's current principal and his staff have participated in statewide implementation workshops, and the principal has visited the R and D Center in Wisconsin and has written implementation materials for other schools.

The school building is an older bilevel structure, with separate classrooms approximately 30 feet square. The building has been remodeled to create an entryway leading into an open instructional materials area containing books, cassette tapes, film loops, and other equipment. An administrative wing includes a large teachers' room. There are separate gymnasium and cafeteria areas, and classroom space permits instructional units to be formed by clustering students and teachers.

Belair is organized into four units in each of which four to six teachers work with up to 150 children. The units are: kindergarten and first grade, second and third grade, fourth and fifth grade, and fifth and sixth grade. Each unit leader was appointed when the school first adopted IGE, and has remained in that position.

The atmosphere at Belair is one of businesslike activity. Students and teachers look busy. Demands for order are usually made in quiet, crisp voices, and these requests are rarely ignored by pupils. Children seem relaxed with their tasks, and while giggling and whispering go on, order is well within the limits imposed by teachers.

A school day at Belair begins with 30 minutes of silent reading, followed by the movement of students into groups for reading and language arts. These groups are organized according to ability, and are usually assigned for the whole year; a few children may move to different ability groups, or to other teachers who may work more effectively with them. Most of the morning is spent on spelling, language usage, grammar, and reading (reading stories and answering questions from a commercial reading series). Once or twice a week, after taking tests from the Wisconsin Design for Reading Skill Development, pupils are assigned to work in task groups. Pupils return to their homerooms for social studies, science, or more language arts work at the end of the morning. After lunch pupils are sorted into ability groups again for math, and most move to different teachers for an hour's work. The rest of the afternoon is taken up by work directed by the homeroom teachers.

In addition to skill work, some time is spent on art, which is almost always done with preprinted patterns (coloring outlined objects, for instance). Most creative writing, such as "news stories" written by fifth graders, is done as an exercise. Work in science and social studies emphasizes transmitting information, often through the use of worksheets; although older pupils do "experiments," these usually illustrate predetermined principles and have known outcomes.

Throughout the school the criteria for success are public—completed assigned worksheets, movement from one level to another, and completed readings. Completing the assigned work takes just enough time and effort to challenge most children; the brighter ones put out periodic bursts of effort to keep up with requirements. The work assigned to low-achieving children permits them to experience the satisfaction of achievement.

The level of cooperation and the organization of work at Belair seem to make teachers feel secure, and the highly specific tasks make it easy to keep pupils busy and in order. As in the other schools, teachers cite these reasons for employing the IGE program. Pupils seem to feel secure too, because they know what they are expected to do and can easily tell whether they are doing it. The pupils in this school are highly successful on standardized achievement tests, scoring near or above the 90th percentile on reading and math. They were the highest scoring students we studied.

The Belair principal is a dominating instructional leader who expects to make the final decisions and to be responsible for final approval of any action taken by the school. Nonetheless, the Instructional Improvement Committee has considerable authority, and the principal leaves the details of implementing policy decisions to the unit teachers.

The teachers at Belair believe that the school's structure and routines carry out the intent of Individually Guided Education. In a survey of teachers' opinions about the extent to which IGE has been implemented,

Belair ranks 6th out of 158 schools—the second highest of all the schools we examined.[3] Clearly the teachers see their practices as consistent with the main features of the reform program.

### A Common Meaning for IGE: The Differences Dissolve

In spite of the demographic and physical differences among Belair, Clayburn, and Maplewood schools, we found them to be alike in their understanding and implementation of Individually Guided Education. In a survey designed to measure the extent to which IGE technology and principles are perceived as operational by a school staff, teachers of all three schools saw themselves as implementors of a school "unit" organization characterized by a flexible separation of children into multi-aged groups, team planning of the curriculum, and teaching activities appropriate to a range of student interests and abilities.[4] Teachers in these schools identified the Instructional Programming Model as a second key feature of IGE: they perceived themselves as formulating objectives for students, establishing record-keeping procedures to monitor achievement, and providing a set of instructional activities to guide students of differing abilities toward the achievement of individual objectives.

In each of the three schools, observers found that the procedures of Instructional Programming were central to the organization of curriculum and instruction. Teachers determined student "needs" according to pre-defined curriculum objectives, sometimes taken directly from a commercial textbook series and at other times synthesized from several commercial sources. In some curricular areas objectives have been made uniform throughout a school district, and often the choice of objectives had been influenced by standards or criterion-referenced tests established by the state educational agency. But in all three schools the specific objectives chosen must include skills and knowledge that can be measured by performance standards and the spirit of the curriculum clearly involves stating in advance objectives which can be easily tested in the classroom.

This type of curriculum organization is an application of the Instruc-

3. It should be recalled that in selecting the six schools for this study, use was made of a survey instrument sent to 158 schools that identified themselves as using the IGE program, at least in part. Results of the survey enabled us to rank the schools in terms of the teachers' beliefs about their success in implementing IGE, as well as their understanding of and agreement with IGE's principles. These self-report/self-perception data, along with other information, were used by the research team to decide which schools could be termed "exemplary" models of IGE in use. Each of the schools we chose to investigate ranked high in two crucial areas: the perceived extent to which IGE had been implemented, and the staff's agreement with certain statements about conditions important to the success of IGE. For further discussion, see Appendix B.

4. See Appendix B for a discussion of the questionnaire.

tional Programming Model "systems" procedures to children's work. In each of the three schools, packets of materials are provided for each level of objectives; packets contain worksheets and workbooks for use by individual students or groups. Students in the same classroom may work at different levels; teachers monitor students' progress, and evaluate their proficiency through posttest instruments that measure the attainment of stated objectives.

The teachers at Maplewood, Clayburn, and Belair also share certain beliefs about individualized schooling. For example, they agree with the following statements:[5]

Children have both the competence and the right to make significant decisions concerning their own learning.

Children will be likely to learn if they are given considerable choices in the selection of the materials they wish to work with and in the choices of questions they wish to pursue with respect to those materials.

Prior to instruction, each student's level of achievement, learning style, and motivation should be determined by the use of criterion-referenced tests, observation schedules, or work samples, in order to assign tasks with which they can succeed.

The assent of the teachers to statements of this kind is significant, because these statements could be seen as inconsistent or contradictory. It requires a particular orientation to schooling to combine belief in the first two statements about children with belief in the last statement about teachers. The view that children have both the "competence and right" to make choices and decisions about their learning conflicts, potentially, with the view that teachers must plan in advance the students' objectives and must assess such factors as "learning style" and "motivation." Views of schooling that emphasize the "natural" tendencies of children and views that stress the systematization of learning are not seen as inconsistent when teachers have developed practices and an institutional language to guide their work.

That there is apparently little or no conflict in beliefs felt by teachers in these schools may be a result of day-to-day activities that give special, but acceptable meanings (from the teachers' perspectives) to the rhetoric professionals use in talking about IGE. An example is provided by the way teachers define the "significant decisions" that students can make. Students may choose between reading a book or using a tape to achieve certain objectives, and since these options are available to students, the teachers believe that they are, in fact, allowing the students to make a significant choice. Potential conflicts in beliefs about IGE are generally

---

5. Taken from IGE Evaluation Phase I: General Staff Questionnaires. See Appendix B.

resolved by allowing institutionalized rhetoric to function apart from individual actions. This point will be explored more thoroughly in the next chapter.

## Pupils at Work:
## Answering Questions and Practicing Skills

For the most part, the work that children do in the three schools is standardized in the sense that all students move toward common sets of objectives, use similar materials, and engage in similar activities to achieve those goals. While students move through the curriculum at different rates of speed, and sometimes utilize different activities and media, a standard set of routines for all students may be identified.

In the three IGE schools described, pupils' work activities are organized around worksheets, workbooks, and oral responses to explicit, unambiguous questions. This kind of work is done by children of all ages in each of the schools on almost any day. Visitors to classrooms find students practicing skills of computation, word recognition and comprehension, and language usage; or they may be writing answers to questions about facts. These are exemplified in the following description:

> Two ditto sheets are passed out—one with an outline map of the world, and the other with some questions. The children have to locate the places on the map, continents and oceans. There are 29 children in the class.
> Teacher says, "Let me ask a few questions before you start, what are the names of the lines going north and south?" The children don't give the right answer. She says, "No, no, direction lines. We've done this before. What would you call them? Do you remember what it is? Ah, yes, it's prime meridian," she says. "The lines are called meridian."
> "Can anyone tell me where the lines go through? What piece of land?" One child says, "Africa." "No, no. Another piece of land," she says, "one that's more important." The child says, "England." "Yes, it's England. England has a lot of ships," she says, "and it all started there. That's why it's zero."
> "Can anyone remember, does anyone know the difference, the number of degrees between meridians? Fifteen degrees, that's good. Oh, lovely," she says, commending the children.
> She starts handing out the worksheets 1A and 1B. Then she turns the map on the side and shows where the labels have to go. Next she gives directions to the class. "Put your hand on it so no one will get mixed up. Put an E where East is. Put a W where West is. I'll give you five minutes to label the maps. Where do we live?" A child says the name of their state. "No, no. We live in America," she says.

While the work—and even the options—in all three schools are standardized, from time to time students successfully develop their own options in the course of meeting objectives. For example, to fulfill the objective of writing a newspaper story, one student decides on her own to write about Susan B. Anthony's work for women's rights. In another situation, all students in a Maplewood class are to draw a bicycle (a bike has been brought into the classroom as a model); however, one pupil comes to the teacher and asks, "Can I draw a semi-truck?" The teacher answers, "No, you can't." The student returns to his seat and begins to draw. He is obviously drawing a semi. Later we observe that the drawing of the truck has been pinned on the bulletin board, where drawings are displayed that have met the requirements of the lesson. In these schools, the use of standardized materials and assignments is routine, and deviations from them or the use of alternative suggestions by students stands out.

While similar work patterns are asked of children in all three schools, the patterns are not identical. At Clayburn, for instance, the Instructional Programming Model is interpreted to mean that each child will work independently of all other children whenever possible. This requires that pupils teach themselves by proceeding in trial and error fashion until a worksheet is completed. The teacher then corrects the worksheet and directs the child to the next task. When self-instruction is unsuccessful, the pupil asks the teacher for help. Sometimes many children have their hands raised or line up at a teacher's desk for help, particularly when a new or difficult task is encountered. This situation is most noticeable at Clayburn, where an extreme definition of individualization is used, but it can also be found at Belair and Maplewood, which rely more on group work.

Managing an IGE systems approach to education requires considerable time and effort for testing, recording scores, and grouping and regrouping pupils. Pupils participate in managing the system in interesting ways. At Belair, four pupils are observed correcting tests from a program of the Wisconsin Design for Reading Skill Development; the test scores will be recorded to monitor achievement and to place pupils in appropriate levels for skill development. At Maplewood, children select cards containing lists of words to be mastered at their own spelling levels. They pair off to drill, and when one of the partners thinks the words have been learned, the test for the appropriate level is obtained from the teacher and the student takes the test. On passing the test, the student goes to the next level. This type of management system keeps all students busy until they have completed the last level in the series.

That students are busy managing their work does not mean that these schools are grim or joyless places. Most teachers are tolerant of a certain level of noise and childish foolishness, and there are times during the day—most often during music or art—when fun is expected. But students generally accept the tasks they are asked to do, and they know the consequences of success or failure. Almost all students can accomplish their tasks if they invest some effort, and few of the tasks are ambiguous enough to create apprehension. While there is concern among students for achievement as measured by standardized tests, trying hard and looking busy are highly valued by teachers and can bring some measure of recognition and success to every pupil—even those who are not achieving their objectives.

There are children who fail to commit themselves to the system, or who will not participate in it as this example from Belair shows:

10:00—Six children (fifth grade level) leave for another room to be tested in study skills. Two groups working in the unit remain (fourth grade level). James is in one of these groups. He uses up five to six minutes looking for his discussion unit (a sheet with exercises to be completed). The teacher asks, "Will you be a good citizen?" "I'll try to be," he says, going for a drink; searches the back of the room for his discussion unit (they are kept in the front of the room). He turns to the observer and says, "Can't do a discussion unit if I can't find it. Got to do it or I won't get a good grade, will I?" He doesn't seem to be concerned. He finds a child at the front who shows him where the discussion units are. He takes one to his seat, stopping to chat with a friend. It is 10:16 when he begins his work.

But resistance is the exception rather than the rule, and most students find satisfaction in completing the specified tasks. Those who are academically able and who move rapidly ahead of their peers can occasionally persuade a teacher to let them have free time to read in an instructional materials center, or, in one school, to use a computer terminal to practice skills. For the majority who maintain normal speed and progress, there are diversions such as the popcorn machine provided by one teacher at Belair, or outings during school time at Maplewood. Outings for canoeing, skiing, and visits to nearby cities are provided in one Maplewood unit for all students except those who have not "worked up to their ability," or who have been disruptive in some way. Few children are excluded from these attractive activities.

In many ways, these schools are like other schools that one might visit in the United States. However the unit organization, the detail given to instructional systems and mastery learning, and the work options available give emphasis to the incorporation of the IGE program.

## Professional Life in the Technical Schools

In each of the three schools teachers lead similar professional lives. Each school is organized into IGE units in which four or five teachers are responsible for the instruction of about 100 pupils. The teachers in each unit meet at least once a week to manage the curriculum, make decisions about the placement of children, and plan activities; curriculum planning in the strict sense of that term does not occur.

In all three schools the unit leaders join the principal in an Instructional Improvement Committee meeting once a week. Details of school management are taken up, special events are scheduled, and decisions are made about implementing a curriculum for a holiday or preparing for statewide achievement tests. At the meeting, unit leaders can represent the interests of teachers to the principal, and decisions made in the meeting are passed on to teachers by unit leaders. Unit leaders say they prefer speaking out in Instructional Improvement Committee meetings to taking part in full school faculty meetings. These procedures result in a constant flow of information to and from the administration.

The teachers' main classroom task is managing the curriculum and the students. While some teachers suggest by their language that they view themselves as clinicians who diagnose and prescribe for individual students, this analogy cannot be taken too literally. More typically, teachers think in terms of students who share deficiencies in certain curriculum areas, and the teaching team organizes them into groups based on "learning needs" or general achievement levels. Individual instruction is not the usual procedure, except at Clayburn. Even at Clayburn, where individual pacing is stressed, student-teacher interactions are normally confined to short conversations in which instructions about what to do next are given, or student work is corrected. In all three schools, much attention is given to keeping accurate records of student achievement data, and the accumulation of data is seen by teachers as one of IGE's most significant innovations.

The physical pace that teachers in all three schools maintain during the day is demanding, and frequently the number of meetings, student conferences, and record-keeping tasks is almost overwhelming. Teachers do a variety of managerial tasks, distributing and collecting materials, gathering and recording data on student achievement, and organizing time, equipment and space. They constantly need to coordinate their plans with those of other personnel.

Nevertheless, responses to a job satisfaction questionnaire suggest that teachers at Clayburn, Maplewood, and Belair are generally satisfied with their jobs.[6] They like the way they relate to their colleagues and their students. One apparent reason for this high level of satisfaction, which emerges from both teacher comments and observations, is that the unit

---

6. On "job satisfaction," the three schools were ranked by their teachers in the top third of 158 schools studied; Belair ranked 44, Clayburn 38, and Maplewood 17. See also the following chapter.

organization provides a welcome opportunity for adults to talk with one another during the day: the isolation of the self-contained classroom is replaced by a cooperative relationship among colleagues who share common problems. The opportunity to socialize with adults may also relieve tensions arising from interaction with children.

Teacher satisfaction may also be related to the use of the Instructional Programming Model. IPM provides a professionally accepted method of making decisions about what to teach: it provides organizing techniques and precise procedures for teachers and students during the instructional process; it gives teachers a sense of professional respectability that may be absent in less precisely defined teaching roles; finally, Instructional Programming yields tangible results—student progress toward clearly defined objectives—that are satisfying to most teachers. In some cases, the reward also comes from parents who see evidence of student progress through the hierarchy of skills and lists of objectives.

## IGE as Public Language

Data gathered at Maplewood, Belair, and Clayburn indicate that the daily routines and instructional practices in these schools are given coherence by five educational slogans which teachers identify with their support of Individually Guided Education. The slogans are *individualization, continuous progress, meeting children's needs, positive self-image,* and *accountability.* These words provide the public language through which teachers and administrators discuss school conduct, justify program planning, and give coherence to the reform program itself.[7] The words in effect hold the promise that the quality of schooling will improve. They establish a mood with which both parents and professionals can feel comfortable, and with which they can affiliate particular pedagogical practices.

Individualized education at Maplewood, Belair, and Clayburn refers to certain facts and prescriptions about schooling. Students are said to differ in many ways, including their academic abilities and psychological characteristics; the most frequently mentioned variation in school ability is the rate at which a child acquires a skill or body of information. Continuous progress is tied to the commitment to individualization. All three schools organize instruction into a system of objectives, learning materials, and evaluation procedures. Objectives and materials are arranged in hierarchical levels that embody all the knowledge and skills a student is to know upon completing the school's curriculum. Continuous progress in meet-

7. The social function of educational slogans—their systematic ambiguity and reference to different and possibly conflicting interests—is discussed in Popkewitz (1980).

ing the objectives is obtained by steering children from one level to the next, from simpler to more complex objectives and materials. Each skill or area of knowledge must be mastered because each is necessary preparation for subsequent levels of the curriculum. Individualization and continuous progress are closely linked ideals.

The phrase "meeting children's needs" is heard repeatedly in conversations with teachers at the three schools, and is accepted as a goal of schooling. The phrase has a consistent meaning in these schools: needs are the students' deficiencies, which can be measured by tests of skills and knowledge provided by the instructional system; to meet these needs, teachers determine each student's deficiencies, then eliminate them through appropriate instruction. Some teachers recognize psychological and emotional deficiencies as student needs. These are determined by observing students as they interact with their peers and adults as they respond to the demands of the school. Such needs are met by counseling, increased or decreased work demands, values clarification, and disciplinary strategies.

Related to meeting children's needs is the goal of helping each child to develop a positive self-image. To accomplish this, the teachers believe that school should be a supportive and pleasant place. They attempt to create a warm environment in which humane relationships between adults and students and among students is stressed.

Finally, teachers believe that a school should be accountable. The teachers are committed to precise, observable, and publicly stated learning objectives. They believe that it is important to state in advance what is required of pupils, how requirements are to be achieved, and what standards are used in judging achievement. By committing themselves to the Instructional Programming Model, the teachers at Maplewood, Belair, and Clayburn accept the necessity of constantly measuring and recording student performance. These records are available to parents, and form the basis of accountability to the communities.

The five slogans provide an emotive language. The words incite enthusiasm among teachers and provide a feeling of unity about the tasks to be confronted in school. The language also gives coherence to the values and ideals that teachers see in the IGE reform program. At one level the slogans can be viewed as systemmatically ambiguous: the slogan "to meet children's needs" or "to be accountable" tells us nothing about the particular course of action that is being called for, but does call attention to some general and ambiguous purpose that people feel has been neglected in school. At another level, the slogans can be seen as the basis of particular practices, the underlying assumptions and implications of which need to be explored.

The foregoing discussion has treated the components of schooling and of IGE as independent elements, and has described them in the language of the three schools studied; it has considered them without reference to the social structures in which they exist. In the next chapter we go beyond these surface characteristics to examine the underlying assumption about work, knowledge, and profession as they are found at Maplewood, Clayburn, and Belair. What are the norms, beliefs, and patterns of conduct that give meaning and interpretation to life in these institutions? How does the overt public language of the professionals translate into patterns of social interaction and social value?

# 4

## Making Schools Efficient: Technical Schooling

All schools have educational technologies. At Maplewood, Clayburn, and Belair, however, techniques have become the ends of school activity rather than a means of instruction, and technology provides an independent value system that gives definition to curriculum, classroom activity, and professional responsibility. While these three "technical" schools differ in some of the formal ways through which they organize instruction and in their physical arrangements, all three incorporate IGE technologies into everyday activities and make technique into a value.

To explore the effect that these technical school values have upon the school experience, and how IGE technologies create and sustain a *social logic* that gives credibility to the interactions and structure of schooling, we will examine five important elements of technical schooling: (1) a curriculum development process dominated by the assumptions of rational planning, and resulting in a professional search for efficiency which emphasizes intellectual certainty and standardization; (2) the organization of classroom discourse, schoolwork, and social interaction in such a way as to sustain and legitimize routines and technical procedures; (3) the creation of a warm, supportive psychological environment that makes it pleasant for pupils to participate in the routines of school life; (4) the assignment of peripheral status to ambiguity, creativity, and nonstandardized learning, which are not institutionally sanctioned even when

they are personally valued by teachers; and (5) professional and community support of standardization and efficiency as normal and reasonable
values in the conduct of schooling.

The five elements in this list, while not exhaustive, are mutually
supportive; for instance, the organization of schoolwork and the curriculum assumptions sustain each other.[1] The five elements emerge as significant in creating a socially derived set of norms, beliefs, and patterns that
give coherence and credibility to the ongoing events in the schools and to
the reform program. The interaction of these elements can be viewed as
producing a logic for action that emerges from the social patterns found in
the daily life of these schools and is in contrast to the meanings conveyed
by the schools' public language and formal organizational characteristics.
As we examine some of the "world-shaping" elements of technical schooling, we will also note incidents of resistance in which teachers and
students have deviated from the rules or created work situations to
ameliorate the pressures of institutionalized routines.

### Curriculum Development: Creating a Management Scheme

An important part of teaching in an IGE school is to sequence the work
students do so that teachers can manage pupil activities and monitor their
achievements. These management procedures are often justified by reference to broader, more abstract educational purposes, such as enhancing
achievement, learning, or developing conceptual thought. In the practice
of the technical schools, however, the criteria for establishing procedures
arise from questions of how social relations and work within the school can
be made more efficient. The emphasis on efficiency is found in the development of school curriculum.

*Setting up Hierarchies: Standardizing Curriculum*
The designers of the IGE programs established guidelines for efficient
curriculum development. They hoped their instructional technologies
would stimulate thought about what ideas to include in schooling, but the
implementation literature does not provide much assistance in making
that link: it discusses the procedures to follow, but fails to explain how
content and goals are to be chosen and related to achievement objectives.
For example, Step One of the Instructional Program Model calls for
school staffs to "state the educational objectives to be attained by the
student population of the building in terms of level of achievement and in
terms of values and action patterns." The guidelines do not expand upon
what is meant by "values and action patterns," and IGE literature gives

---

1. The technologies of IGE will be considered in relation to other institutional conditions
in chapters 5 and 6.

most of its attention to achievement objectives and evaluation by pre-instructional and post-instructional tests.

Not unreasonably, teachers and administrators have interpreted the Instructional Programming Model mainly as a management scheme. The purpose of curriculum planning is seen as identifying and arranging explicit and measurable objectives. At Maplewood, Clayburn, and Belair, we found that the search for a standardized, objective curriculum was carried out in different ways. Sometimes teachers themselves took responsibility for identifying objectives and choosing appropriate instructional materials; sometimes the objectives and materials were selected by a curriculum specialist in the school district or by the school principal; in other cases, objectives and instructional materials were adopted from a commercial textbook series. No school staff used only one of these approaches; instead, there tended to be an eclectic pattern of use for each strategy.

A good example of a teacher-created curriculum was found at Belair. One unit leader, looking at several commercial math textbooks, identified the various computational skills that were taught for each grade, then chose as learning objectives skills that had measurable outcomes ($2 + 4$ *is* 6). To enable students to find instructional help and examples, each skill was cross-referenced to the appropriate textbooks. The objectives related to the skills were then organized into a logical sequence—one digit addition came before multiplication, for instance—and the sequence was divided into levels; each level presented a number of related objectives and criterion-referenced measures for evaluation.

For each of the skills defined as an objective, the Belair teacher put together a packet of materials to permit self-instruction. Typically, a packet contained a pretest, a transparency or an audio tape explaining the skill to be learned, a posttest, and a folder in which all test scores could be recorded for the entire level. A student was to practice the skill on dittoed worksheets, which might have been taken from commercial resources such as a workbook or an instructional program kit; sometimes the teacher created a unique drill based on the requirements of the skill. The posttest determined whether a pupil was ready to move on to the next skill objective, or had to repeat the same instructional unit with a new packet.

Teachers from each of the four units at Clayburn, meeting to develop a language arts curriculum, examined all of the language arts manuals available. From these, they derived a list of objectives for the language arts curriculum that referred to skills such as use of margins, and mastery of spelling rules and punctuation. During subsequent meetings, the list of objectives was put into a logical sequence and disseminated to the rest of the staff.

These examples of teacher-created materials and objectives, however, were the exception rather than the rule in the three technical schools we investigated. Teachers and administrators usually bought commercial materials that provided ready-made management systems and instructional materials. As one teacher at Clayburn confessed, "The objectives that we have in reading are the Scott-Foresman objectives. In math, they are the ones from Silver-Burdett, right straight from the manual . . . There are 107 . . . skills. That's what they are tested on." Another Clayburn teacher, when asked how she went about choosing objectives, replied, "Most things are in the book. I may pull out one thing or another that isn't, but generally it's in the book." This approach to choosing objectives was popular in all three schools.

The teachers at the technical schools have interpreted individualized education as a systematic way of responding to children's lack of specific information or skill. No curriculum or instruction is considered appropriate unless precise, measurable objectives are stated. Instruction can then follow the test-teach-test routine. If a commercial textbook series already presents criterion-referenced objectives, teachers are relieved of the burden of having to create their own.

By requiring curriculum design to be guided by criterion-referenced objectives, the technical schools have limited the kind of knowledge that enters the curriculum. Because the skills needed in reading, mathematics, and the language arts were most easily reduced to discrete and measurable steps, curriculum content of this type occupies most of the school day. The mathematics curriculum, for example, consists of learning computational skills in the smallest possible steps, such as addition and multiplication. Reading stresses such skills as the identification of initial sounds or the location of facts within a paragraph; the language arts emphasize correct word usage, spelling, penmanship, and the physical organization of the written page.

Planning in the technical schools proceeds from the assumption that learning is a smooth progression, with simple learning preceding more complex learning. This assumption has supported and justified the consistent, standardized curriculum. At Maplewood, a teacher created a language arts program by establishing seven levels of skill, all of which are commonly found in commercial materials: main idea, topic sentences, order in the paragraph, closing sentences, mechanics of a good paragraph, theme and report writing, and creative writing. Following this plan, creative writing was not offered until the previous six skills had been mastered. Some students did not reach the levels of creative writing and report writing in all of their elementary school experience, and many pupils did not write stories or essays until grades five or six.

The high priority given to learning discrete skills has necessarily limited planning for other types of educational experiences in the technical schools. One principal said that after children had learned all the required skills, time could be provided for problem-solving activities, or for satisfying their interests and curiosity. Another principal commented that there was no time in the school day for any learning but that defined in the learning systems.

While the skills of reading, mathematics, and other disciplines are vital in any educational curriculum, the relationship of these skills to larger intellectual acts is also vital. Learning how to think about human problems with mathematical insight and making cognitive sense of other people's written words are as desirable as adding, multiplying, or blending consonants. Nevertheless, the technical schools prefer to use materials containing management procedures related to more discretely defined skill objectives, even though there are curriculum programs available in mathematical reasoning and interpretive and creative reading. Curriculum design in these schools isolates skills from purposes and, in the process, narrows the apparent goals of teaching.

One possible effect of the technical "world view" is that critical and analytical thought may be replaced as educational goals by mere concrete objectives. Concepts are generally viewed as linguistic devices that can give coherence to the world we live in, express complex thoughts in succinct form, and serve as heuristic fictions to stimulate curiosity and imagination; "energy," "ideology," and "socialization" are concepts of this kind. In the technical schools, however, concepts are reduced to discrete, manageable technical steps related to the mastery of skills. A teacher at Belair observed that the complicated mathematics skills program he had developed reduced mathematical concepts to those tasks required in the behavioral objectives. According to an observer, he argued that "no separate set of behavioral objectives is needed beyond the 'concepts' which are organized in a systematic and hierarchical order. 'The behavioral objectives are the concepts,' he says. The concepts to which he refers are computational skills of mathematics."

### Creating a Record System: Evaluation as Central to Instruction

As interpreted by the technical schools, individualized instruction necessitates continual testing and recording to discover and keep track of students' individual needs. Once objectives were set and mastery criteria specified, record-keeping procedures had to be created. In each of the schools, keeping records of skill achievement was a major task because, without accurate and easily obtainable records, neither the teacher nor the student knew exactly what to do next.

Each school and most units within them maintained large poster boards that listed skills across the top and student names in a column down one side. The resulting grid displayed the objectives mastered by each individual. Maplewood was also perfecting a computer program for monitoring each pupil's test scores and record of skill achievement over the six years of attendance. While providing accountability by indicating what the school had done for each child, the major purpose of the computerized achievement record was to permit teachers to identify students who had common deficiencies in skill areas. All students who had not mastered a specific language arts skill could then be grouped for instruction; math and reading groups could be similarly formed. Except for occasional student art work, these record charts dominated the walls and bulletin boards of the classrooms.

Since test results are recorded, testing is an important component of the record-keeping systems in technical schools. Testing to evaluate instruction was extensively used at Maplewood. Pretesting to discover which skills mastered in the previous year had been forgotten over the summer began in the upper unit in September, and, with a review of previously mastered materials, took until the end of October to complete. By November, new skill objectives began to be introduced. With this emphasis on testing to determine the needs of the students and the success of instruction and learning, it was very likely that on any given day each teacher would give or grade at least one test.

At Clayburn the emphasis was also on testing. The reading program was designed to require pre- and posttests at least every 10 days, and the results were used to identify groups of students with common deficiencies. In the mathematics program, the work done in between pre- and posttests was usually carried out on worksheets that resembled tests.

In all three schools, considerable time and effort was expended in keeping records, although at Maplewood aides were responsible for correcting many of the tests and maintaining records of students who had mastered the corresponding skills. Maplewood teachers reported that the system would have collapsed if it were not for the aides who handled the record keeping. At Belair and Clayburn, most record keeping was done by the teachers. A Clayburn teacher commented on the time consumed by this activity: "I spend an awful lot of time in math on mechanics, on the record keeping, on moving them along, checking them in, [seeing] that they have this amount of work done correctly and then moving on to a test. . . . [It] may . . . take me the first 15 minutes of each class period just getting those problems solved before I'm able to go on to helping them understand something they need."

Occasionally the record system itself broke down. Once at Maplewood it was discovered that the computer program cards had been incorrectly punched and some data had been lost. Since the original tests were still available, volunteers—the "Thursday morning moms"—had to be called on to correct the cards.

In some instances, teachers resisted the routine produced by the testing programs. Some, who found that test results did not coincide with their own judgment, relied on their judgment rather than test scores when assigning a child to a group. In one situation at Maplewood, the sheer volume of testing and record keeping proved overpowering; after children had left the room following a test, the teacher threw the tests into the waste basket. She was obviously embarrassed when she realized that the observer had seen her, and explained that she was so overwhelmed with tests that she couldn't bear to correct them.

In most situations in the technical schools, however, testing and record-keeping procedures guided the formation of groups, dominated curriculum choices, and gave organizatin to instruction. The effort expended in testing and record keeping also yielded positive results in the area of school-community relations. Parent-aides from the community often did the record keeping necessary to keep the system functioning. Aides also administered tests to groups, gave make-up tests, graded, and recorded results. When testing became so voluminous that the available labor could not handle the work, volunteer parents were occasionally asked to come in to copy materials or mark and record grades.

To the community, record keeping showed that the school was providing necessary diagnoses and prescriptions and was therefore accountable. One principal commented that the ability of a school to demonstrate the concrete levels of accomplishment and test scores for an individual child showed parents that the school was responding to the particular needs of a child.

### The Psychology of Instruction: Children as Deficient

A corollary to the standardization of curriculum is an instructional psychology which assumes that children are deficient in skills and knowledge. Teachers refer to a lack of mastery (usually less than 80 percent correct on a pretest) as a child's deficiency. This view of children is related to the organization of teaching around measurable, hierarchically sequenced objectives. A significant part of the teacher's job, once a sequence has been packaged, is to administer tests that identify those parts of the curriculum that a child has not mastered.

The developers of IGE rejected the concept of deficiency. They spoke in more positive terms, calling for an identification of "children's needs." The notion of deficiency, however, has been adopted by teachers and administrators in the technical schools as a synonym for "children's needs," and classroom procedures support the view that children are in a state of continual deficiency: teaching and learning are seen as an endless process of correcting the deficiencies indicated by the latest pretest.

The psychology that views instruction as a remedy for deficiency is captured by the phrase "diagnosis/remediation." While the IGE planners never use this phrase, many teachers in the technical schools talk about meeting children's needs by diagnosing and remedying the deficiencies in their students' cognitive or affective make-up. The diagnosis is provided by a pretest; remediation is found in the curriculum packets related to the objective in which a child is found deficient. The medical analogy created by the "diagnosis/remediation" language reinforces the deficit concept of instruction: the locus of deficit in schools is the individual child, and the teacher's role is to eliminate whatever personal pathology is identified (cf. the discussion of deficient culture in the chapter on illusory schooling).

To summarize, in technical schooling, management is the central concern of curriculum development and efficiency is the controlling criterion for curriculum design. Consensus about educational goals is assumed, and the professional obligation is to provide efficient implementation and evaluation.

## Classroom Discourse:
## The Effects of Management Orientation

The social and material organization of the technical schools sustains and gives legitimacy to the standardized curriculum, and day-to-day life in the schools reinforces routine and standardization. Teachers persistently discuss the techniques and procedures that would best convey the predetermined system of objectives and tests to the pupils, and the management of material and human resources is the focus of professional decisions. The procedural language used to manage the program becomes central to how students define their interests and achievements.

To illustrate these consequences of management orientation in the three technical schools investigated we will look at several aspects of daily classroom interaction between teachers and students. What activities occupy children and teachers during the school day? Among those activities, what tasks are considered educational? What is the nature of classroom interaction? What do teacher-pupil conversations emphasize? What does responsibility mean for students? Finally, how are the activities and procedures of technical schooling reflected in the language used by teachers and students?

### Work on Worksheets: A Filling-in Syndrome

There is a striking similarity in the nature of the daily work done by all students in the three schools. At various times during the morning or early afternoon, the odds are overwhelmingly in favor of finding a pupil completing a worksheet concerned with questions of fact or practice exercises. An observer would be less likely to find pupils reading books, especially without worksheets to guide reading and test understanding, and even less likely to find a teacher explaining to a group of pupils what the dimensions of a problem are, or to find a group exploring ideas through discussion.

Worksheet instruction is related to the deficit concept of children and curriculum, and is made plausible by a system that defines learning in terms of concrete steps, answers, and scores and the repeated practice of skills identified as lacking. Worksheets provide a technology by which teachers can standardize the practice needed to master each skill, and they can be duplicated for all students and made available when the individual child is ready to tackle the related deficit. Worksheets can also become a mechanism of social control when the routines of worksheet instruction become ritualized.

In the classrooms we observed, the work of teachers and students between pre- and posttesting was related to preparing, filling in, and grading worksheets. For each identified skill several packets of worksheets were provided; each packet differed in detail and offered various ways of practicing the skill. These variations allowed students who had failed to master a skill to use a new set of drills in preparing to take the posttest again. One teacher at Clayburn, referring to the use of the kits to give children further practice, commented that "I go back and just work and work and give them extra games and worksheets to go with their deficiencies. Then after two weeks, I let them go back and take the test over."

The repetition and routine involved in worksheet instruction provided students with a feeling of satisfaction and security. They could immediately get a "grade" and find out whether they could move on to another objective or level; the criteria of success seemed clear and unambiguous. Since many of the worksheets were similar and none was exceptionally difficult, the children could be held responsible for doing the work. Worksheets made it possible for pupils to carry on some activities without a teacher's direct involvement, allowing the teacher time to correct papers or to work with an individual or a small group in need of special help. Worksheets also enabled teachers to determine how children were progressing in meeting deficiencies.

Two incidents highlighted the degree to which teachers in the technical schools relied on worksheets. When the principal at Maplewood warned teachers that a budget cut made it necessary to conserve ditto paper, unit leaders expressed dismay at having to tell their colleagues that they might have to reduce the number of worksheets. At Belair, a new student told one teacher that he had never done worksheets in his previous school—

he had just read books; upon hearing this account, another teacher remarked, "I can't imagine teaching that way."

In theory, variations in the nature and use of materials are provided to allow for the different "learning styles of children." In technical school practice, however, variations in instructional procedures were restricted to different sized work groups, and alternate materials were limited to programmed machines and media-related activities that supplemented worksheets.

### How to Succeed: Try Hard, or At Least Look Industrious

The emphasis on skill practice in the technical schools gave rise to several norms of classroom interaction. Students were considered successful if they looked busy, seemed industrious, and were trying hard; sometimes trying hard was more important than the quality of work produced. It was also held that the more time spent on learning something, the more effective that learning would be. This "time-on-task" norm carried no implication of quality or optimal time: working hard would pay off. Closely related to this norm was the value placed on quantity of output.

The value of looking industrious or of appearing to spend time on a task emerged in a variety of ways. In a school in which one primary unit had its reading period interrupted by its recess, the principal complained to an observer that the unit had 15 minutes less reading instruction than other units, and that if one added up the minutes lost by the end of the year "you [could] see how far behind they will be." This principal also rated teachers according to how hard their pupils seemed to work, and how many hours before and after school teachers stayed in the building.

In another technical school, teachers reported feeling positive about children who worked hard and scored well on mastery tests, and those who did not score well but worked hard. However, teachers found it difficult to view positively children who did well but did not seem to show any overt effort. In at least two schools, children were allowed or denied participation in reward periods (free time, special times) on the basis of how hard they tried.

Students who failed to look industrious presented a greater problem to school staffs than students who simply failed to achieve. The teachers in one Maplewood unit cited Dave as a boy who had not become "an independent learner":

He is not especially disruptive, but rather fails to participate in the systematic curriculum. Dave will not proceed through the various levels of math, spelling, and language arts skills. This is disconcerting to the staff because Dave has considerable ability. One of his teachers reported that he has a "very high IQ," and commented in front of Dave and the observer, "this boy will make a million dollars some day, he's so smart."

Dave's reluctance to participate in the normal flow of classroom activities made him a conspicuous anomaly. Although he sometimes scored well on standardized tests and read well above his grade level, his unwillingness to work up to his ability classified him as a failure.

The emphasis on working hard was reflected in the physical surroundings in the classrooms. At Maplewood children in the second and third grade unit were observed using cardboard folders to create isolated working spaces on a table. At Clayburn the principal had built wooden dividers to provide individual work spaces on tables. The assumption was that the less social distraction, the more efficiently a child could work at a task.

Instructional and evaluative procedures in the technical schools emphasized the number of worksheets completed and the scores obtained on posttests. Quantity was not related to any criterion of quality. The intellectual content, reasoning, and forms of expression a child used in solving a problem were not included in any measures of achievement.

The emphasis on looking industrious and on quantity produces its own contradictions. In a system in which learning is structured according to a sequence of hierarchical objectives, the child who attains the objectives has nowhere to go. The defined objectives create a *ceiling* to a child's work. In recognition of this ceiling, teachers in the technical schools organized activity in two general ways: older children became tutors to younger children; and when children completed a specific level of objectives and were waiting to be pretested for the next level, each child was given an opportunity to take part in activities such as reading and drawing that were unrelated to the specific mastery sequence. A teacher commented that she did not believe it was valuable to assign more of the same kind of work to children who finished fast: "Why punish them for being better workers?" The paradox of these schools is that if you work hard and succeed, you reach a dead end.

In significant ways, looking industrious had become a criterion of competence and achievement in the technical schools. Yet the opportunities for teachers and students to manipulate the system are limited. As more than one teacher stated in informal discussions, the day is well planned for children and teachers: for children, the plan of the day is to complete as many assignments as possible; for teachers, team planning, regrouping procedures, and testing programs create a constant flow of things to be done.

## Classroom Interaction and Efficiency

Pliant physical arrangements, the regrouping and movement of children, and the professional language of individualization suggested that student-teacher interaction in the technical schools varied and was flexible. However, close scrutiny of the interaction in the three schools revealed expectations, values, and patterns of conduct that limited the flexibility and the nature of both classroom and professional discourse. While worksheet-oriented learning and student grouping were intended to enhance self-instruction and self-pacing, these curriculum practices at the same time reduced teacher-student interaction to the procedural level. Under this system, teachers were required to interact with students only when pre- and posttest results were evaluated, and when directions had to be given for using the next worksheet or packet of materials.

Typically, a teacher's instructional role involved managing students by directing them to appropriate worksheets, tapes, kits, or games. The goal of efficiency governed the organization of student movement and student-teacher interaction. The management orientation gave legitimacy and predominance to those forms of interaction designed to reinforce efficiency operations.

The following observation illustrates the kind of interaction teachers normally had with students during class time:

The observer approached Mrs. Grant while she was teaching math. "You're set to add," she said, looking at the machine one child was working on. She walked on to another child. "You're on a different set of cards, and you only have three minutes to work with this." She turned again to another child and looked at his workbook. She said something to him. The child didn't seem to understand. She then said, "How many sixes go into twenty-four?" She watched the child write and said to him, "Do another and then call me when it's over." (Clayburn)

In this and other situations, teachers limited conversation to checking work and assigning worksheets. A line of children in front of a teacher's desk, waiting to have their papers checked and their test scores recorded, was not uncommon. The conversation between teacher and pupil was typically shorthand limited to questions about completion or assignment of worksheets or tests.

The type of interaction between teachers and students also had consequences for student interactions. The norm was that children should do their work and interact with each other as little as possible.

1:13 The teacher says, "Everyone put their heads down. There's too much visiting. I don't want anyone to talk to his neighbor." Heads told to come up. Work went on.
1:20 Pupil says, "Bill is not carrying." The teacher says, "That's his problem, Mark," (turns Mark's head around) "and not yours." (Belair)

The fragmented style of interaction in these situations was intentional because the teacher would like to see students as independent learners. Independent learning was defined as being as self-instructional as possible. In describing a math class, one teacher indicated that the 30 students were divided into three groups. "There are two dependent groups and one independent group. The purpose is to make them more independent so they can do it themselves without any formal teacher" (Clayburn). At Maplewood the upper unit was called "Independent." Independence, one teacher replied, meant:

Kids should be responsible for their own education. When we come into an area like this, the kids should get to work on their own. They should follow instructions on the worksheets or books and proceed without having to be told. "I don't think we're there yet, but we are making progress."

Self-instruction imposed a severe strain on pupils who had to depend on learning from instructional materials by trial and error and by continual practice, with corrections provided by the teacher. When this procedure failed, or if a pupil had little confidence in working alone, the teacher was there to help. Having many pupils asking for help at once, often about the same problem, placed a strain on the teacher as well.

Where the program was completely individualized, as at Clayburn, children were often seen with hands raised, waiting politely for the teacher's help. One observer recorded that

the child in front of me is working at a dittoed sheet. The sheet has equations. She writes "6." She looks at me and says, "Is that right?" I help her with it by working with some clothespins she has. After I show her how to do it, she changes her six to a four and goes on to another example on the worksheet, which had been incorrect. Later, I looked at her paper again. I noticed that 14 of the 20 which she had completed on her second try were incorrect.

To the extent that the interaction between a teacher and students who were moving through a common body of objectives was entirely individualized, a difficult load was placed on the teacher. A Clayburn teacher commented:

I think that this program, as it has been set up, . . . is completely individualized. No two children are working on the same page, at the same book, at any one time, unless it [is] just an accident. I think it has its advantages and disadvantages, and the disadvantages are that it is very difficult for me to explain so many times over the same concept, when they are coming up to a new concept and they need teacher help with it. It is very difficult for me to get around and help all of them with it, and then I have to re-explain it so many times that I can't really give the amount of time explaining that concept that the child needs. . . . Sometimes I get really frustrated, oh gosh! 15 kids out of 30 need help right now, and all of them on a different subject. If I don't help them right this minute, they're going to waste half the class. So I try to tell them to skip over that problem and go on to the next one, until you finally get your turn. . . . That works sometimes, and sometimes it doesn't . . . the assignment sheets that they may be on may have two or three of that same [kind of problem].

While both the principal and this teacher did say that "no two children are on the same pages," observers in the school found that in fact children frequently were doing the same pages. But the isolation imposed on the children by curriculum procedures prevented them from cooperating to get their work done. Isolation was useful for maintaining discipline and control, yet the school's rhetoric about independence neglected to point out the element of control in this system.

### A Language of Procedure

One result of the managerial emphasis in the technical schools was a functional definition of responsibility as "maintaining the systems." This concern with procedural and management problems introduced a language of procedure into the discourse of teachers, students, and administrators.

At Belair, a typical discussion in Instructional Improvement Committee and unit meetings concerned how much time to allocate to a given topic in the curriculum, when students should change groups, where the groups would go during particular time blocks, who would take responsibility for gathering teaching materials or organizing packets of worksheets, what changes should be made in schedules or room assignments, and when specific tests should be given to assess certain skills. The notes of an observer at a Maplewood unit meeting recorded similar discourse:

Unit 3 meeting: Unit leader goes over notes from Instructional Improvement Committee (IIC) meeting; state IGE meeting is coming up; teachers are to share rainy day activities; teachers are asked if they want to visit other schools; the administrative schedule for the Instructional Media Center (IMC) is presented. The unit's math assessment test is discussed; teachers are encouraged to remind students that some problems are "plus" and other "minus." Discussion results in agreement that the test is to find out individual achievement, and that no help should be given to students. These tests will identify needs and lead to prescription. A teacher demonstrates how a steno pad is used to keep a running inventory of spelling words for each child. Another teacher says, "I'm glad you showed me that, Fred. It's been so helpful." After some additional minor conversation the unit meeting breaks up.

In both of these meeting descriptions a language of procedure clearly dominates, rather than a language of ideas. This procedural emphasis was also found in other school contexts. Pupils and teachers talked about school work in terms of page numbers, columns, and letters, rather than in terms of ideas or skills. In some children's conversations, the importance of test scores outweighed the consideration of the ideas being studied. The task was to get a mastery score.

A new child came over. "What do I do after B–2?" he asked. The teacher said, "Go into the purple book." (Belair)

The children talk about mastery. One child said, "I have to make one more to pass. I got 34, not 35. In the computer," he said, pointing to the child next to him, "he got 100." The other child said, "Yeah, I got 100." The child next to him said, "I got 25 wrong." Next to him a child looked at me and said, "I'm learning a lot. I was a B but now I'm up to an A." (Clayburn)

A student who lacked the skill to get a mastery score might be allowed to fantasize:

A child came to show the teacher her work. She had done the mastery test and said, "Look, I got 96." The teacher commented to the observer, "There's no way she can get 96 because she doesn't add or multiply." The pupil sits down with a level-three book. She quickly thumbs through it, as though she's trying to look industrious, but she doesn't know how to read it. She looks up at the observer and says, "I finished the book. I made 100 and nobody helped me." (Clayburn)

Some teachers who recognized the inconsistencies and limitations they faced in the technical schools expressed themselves in the language of procedure:

Classroom management is fine, but I want to be more than just a manager all the time, you know. . . that's just not the whole story. Last year it was a big thing that the room was so organized and managed that I could leave for an hour and my kids were great, they were occupied. . . . I did not think that was great. It was fine for it to be organized, but I still needed to be there, because I think they need the interaction [with]somebody on some of those skills. They could still learn, I mean they could still pass the test, but they . . . didn't get the depth they needed on some of those skills. (Clayburn)

The managerial nature of discourse limited the range of teachers' decision making, and left them little or no professional autonomy over the nature and character of their work. For children, a concern with scores on tests and levels of achievement replaced insight into the ideas offered by the curriculum. As IGE was originally designed, the language of technology was planned as a tool, an aid to the teacher's and student's assessment of progress. The designers viewed the language of systems as coexisting with a language of ideas. In practice, this coexistence has never developed, and the language of procedures has become legitimized as the substance of the curriculum itself.

## A Supportive Environment:
## Psychological Management and Stability

It might be assumed that the limited nature of work and the procedural quality of the discourse in technical schools would create a cold, mechanical environment, but the facts are quite to the contrary. An abundance of evidence concerning student-teacher interactions supports the claim that teachers make a substantial effort to create a reasonably pleasant school environment for students. A supportive environment is justified by the teachers' belief that schools should enable children to develop what they call a healthy self-concept. For many parents and teachers, the idea of school as a warm, pleasant place is an end in itself.

A pleasant and supportive atmosphere has been sustained in the technical schools in three ways. First, certain subject matter that has not been defined by levels of mastery has been identified as different from the regular and important work of schooling. Most art, social studies, science, music, physical education, and a variety of activities such as values clarification and sharing time fit this description. These activities are seen as secondary and, like recess, provided a break from the routine skill work of schooling. "Affective domain" activities allow students to express their feelings and opinions about a host of personal, family, and social topics. These opportunities, one teacher said, were to show students that teachers are open to children's views and take them seriously.

A second way in which teachers have created a supportive atmosphere is by verbally and physically showing appreciation and affection for children. Observers frequently heard teachers say to a child, "You have really improved this year in math. You are terrific when you put your mind to it." Some teachers give a child a hug and whisper a compliment. The words and gestures are almost routine in two of the schools, and in the third, it is continually emphasized that caring for children is valued by the staff.

Psychological support is also provided by reward programs. The Three Star Program at Maplewood, for example, is designed to reward students who observe certain norms—students who show responsibility, work independently, follow directions, and do assignments on time and, as teachers say, "up to their abilities." The rewards for making the Three Star list include outings which take place during school time. Teachers consider these outings as opportunities to show that they are real people who care about their students, and to show friendship, trust, and affiliation.

The pleasant psychological climate of these schools can be considered as complementary and necessary to the structure of curriculum work and interaction. Since the repetitive quality of tasks done by teachers and students, accompanied by a norm of industriousness, can be psychologically draining if not debilitating, some safety valve is needed. Reward periods or slack periods are a form of psychological release during which a commitment to work can be renewed and stability ensured. The psychological ties developed with the teacher during nonwork activities often enable children to accept the necessary routine work.

A relationship between supportive environments and the procedural emphasis in instruction is grounded in the school reform effort. In the systems approach of IGE, schooling is defined by various elements that are interrelated but analytically separable in research and practice. This distinction enables researchers and participants to treat instructional technologies and humanizing school conditions as separate in everyday life, as well as in logic. In the IGE model, it is possible for a teacher to value both personal relationships and a depersonalized curriculum without having to consider how the two are related or what contradictions one value may pose for the other.

### Creativity: Inventiveness as Serendipity

Since the management orientation to school work filters out activities for which the criteria of success or achievement are ambiguous, and since activities that do reflect analytic, synthetic, and creative thought are mainly by-products of school routines, one might ask, What creative outlets for children exist in technical schools? Do they have opportunities to engage in higher levels of conceptual thought or problem solving? The answer to these questions is yes, but that answer must be considered in the context of institutionally defined knowledge and work. When creative thought is expressed, teachers respond positively, but institutional patterns preclude that value from being given a consistent place in the instructional program.

The emphasis on worksheets in Maplewood, Clayburn, and Belair limited any sustained inquiry or examination of issues in depth. The instructional task was to eliminate students' particular deficits, and there was little, if any, opportunity for refining or going more deeply into the knowledge offered. Once a child had answered a question or marked the correct box on the worksheet, the work pattern required the pupil to go on to the next task or test, or move on to the next objective. The allocation of classroom time limited opportunities for more flexible forms of interaction: there was no time to wonder, to reflect, or to probe.

Instances of genuine intellectual challenge were offered by specific assignments, often in the language arts and sometimes in mathematics. Assignments with potential for creative responses were routinely reserved for the abler pupils. In one school higher achieving children who had finished their skills assignments were permitted to write short essays on the topic "My toes are terrific because . . ." The writing seemed clever and free to the observer.

While work that was ambiguous in nature was neither sought nor systematically developed, teachers recognized its value and rewarded tentative explorations, challenges to incomplete or faulty logic, and genuine intellectual inventiveness when they occurred.

8:30 A sixth grade teacher brings a small handmade book to show other teachers. It was done by a sixth grader, including words and illustrations. It is hilarious. Each page has a single sentence beginning with the word "fortunately" or "unfortunately." The book tells the story of an unlucky English knight who helps subdue the "semi-barbarian Welsh." His teacher and the other teachers who see it appreciated its excellence. The principal happily comments on the student, "You know, he never takes a conventional approach to any assignment." (Belair)

In interviews, teachers talked about how they would like to challenge children to be more creative and thoughtful, and in some cases, about how limiting a curriculum based on skills alone could be.

That teachers value problem-solving activities poses a major contradiction in the technical schools. School expectations and tasks channel activity toward practicing skills that can produce competent functional behavior. The daily organization of schooling is intended to identify and eliminate deficits, and the rhythms and pace of activity often limit the time pupils can spend on a topic and prevent their delving into it more deeply. For pupils, their work is not a search for ways to invent or elicit meanings from their experiences. Yet when children's educational activities go beyond these routine tasks, teachers do recognize that the efforts have value.

Although the IGE program gives value to flexible forms of interaction and in-depth analysis, the procedural emphasis in these schools leaves little time for sustained discussion about the ideas being studied. The instructional model of IGE refers to "variant" objectives (those curriculum purposes which can not be precisely stated, measured, and hierarchically ordered), but the references are not specific and are not accompanied by suggestions for action. In the technical schools, specific and clearly articulated objectives receive most of the attention of the staff and the administrator. The resulting limits on school activities and interactions minimize analytic, synthetic, and creative thought.

Designating creative work as enrichment and separating it from other learning has several possible consequences for the way children view knowledge. First, children may come to view creative and intellectually demanding responses as distinct from, less valuable than, and worth less time than other school activities; critical thinking becomes a form of recess from the important work of schooling—it occurs after the regular schoolwork has been done, and it is not integral with other activities. Second, the relationship of analytical, problem-solving activities to the skills upon which they depend is not systematically taught or developed. Third, if education is viewed as a progression from skills to divergent thinking, the less capable child is made to feel inadequately prepared for critical thought, is thus permanently deficient, and is discouraged from engaging in higher forms of mental activity.

## The Social and Professional Setting:
## Belief in Efficient, Rational Schooling

The institutional values of the technical schools are justified and supported by professionals in the schools and school districts, who view them as responsive to the values of the surrounding communities. Teachers' perceptions of community social and cultural backgrounds—and in one instance the religious background—give credence to technical definitions of education. In addition, what parents expect of the schools supports the emphasis on skill development and social control. Furthermore, professional ideologies in school district administrations and in other educational agencies sustain the emphasis on efficiency and management in schooling.

Socially and culturally, the communities in which each of the technical schools is situated are quite different from one another, as we have noted. Clayburn is a rural school in a southern community where numerous people work in small service-related businesses and agriculture. When our observations were made, approximately 50 percent of its students came from families that qualified for state welfare, and of those receiving aid more than half were from poor black families, some of whom lived in rural shacks that had no running water. Maplewood is in a suburban community outside a large midwestern city. The typical parents were skilled blue-collar workers. Most of the children lived in modest, comfortable ranch-type homes and the community streets and lawns were generally well cared for. Belair is located in a medium-sized western city. This community is unusually homogeneous, ethnically and culturally, for its size, and most pupils in the school are white and belong to the same religious denomination. The values, attitudes and interests of this cultural religious group had a significant impact upon the major social, educational, and political institutions of the area, and technical schooling conformed to the hierarchical relations maintained by church authorities. At the time of observation, many of Belair's children came from upper- and middle-income families, although 20 percent of the school population was from lower income families. A drive around this community revealed both affluent and more modest middleclass neighborhoods.

At two of the schools, Maplewood and Clayburn, the teachers interpreted the social and cultural values of the community as providing a mandate for teaching functional literacy. Both teachers and administrators in these schools believed that the communities would not support instructional emphases on subjects other than the basic skills of reading, mathematics, and writing considered necessary to participation in society. The superintendent of the Maplewood school district characterized the members of the community as "salt of the earth," hard-working, hard-playing people, for whom snowmobiling takes precedence over the symphony. The superintendent continued,

The importance of this style of life is that when students do not have enough affluence to appreciate the arts, the school program must limit itself to 'survival skills.' . . . I'm a great supporter of the arts and I believe that those are the things that provide lasting impact upon a civilization. If you can't read, you can't write, you can't verbally communicate or communicate in a written form, you're not going to have much appreciation for the arts. And, you know, you can teach a kid, you can teach a youngster all about the finer things of life, but if he can't go and read a program, he isn't going to wind up as an adult enjoying those aspects [of life]. He is going to be too busy trying to survive. . . . a certain level of affluence has to be attained before one can begin enjoying the finer things in life.

There is irony in the superintendent's reference to the community's lack of affluence, since its blue-collar workers were not poor: in many families both parents worked and the combined income was high. The superintendent's comments, however, are important for they justify pedagogical emphasis as related to some perception of social class.

At Clayburn teachers and administrators justified functional literacy as a goal by pointing out that the cultural background they thought to be necessary for school success was lacking in the community. The home background of the pupils helped to define what was appropriate in a school program. One teacher related the nature of classroom work to the lack of educational experiences the children brought to school:

[It's] not that they don't care [in the homes], but that they don't know. They are not as concerned with education. Maybe they are not educated themselves. The kids are not read to, there are no books in the home. . . . They have never been to the city. We took a group to the city and they went crazy last year. . . . You know, just experiences. They just don't have any experiences. They are just not exposed to a lot. . . . We've tested many that we thought were really going to be low and they had normal intelligence. They just haven't had the experience.

The teachers believed that the only thing the school could effectively teach children from such a background was "survival" skills. The

Clayburn program consisted of the continual teaching and reinforcing of reading, writing, and arithmetic skills. The principal commented that there was no time for children to make choices in the instructional program. The children had to spend all their time practicing the skills identified in the curriculum system if they were ever to catch up. While this definition of "cultural lack" contains a tacit reference to some desired cultural experience, that other culture is never made explicit except when it is said that there are "not enough books in the home."

At Belair, a set of factors different from socio-cultural class seemed to promote technical schooling. Children in the school from all economic backgrounds shared the same cultural-religious affiliation, which also permeated community institutions beyond the school. School and home were in close agreement about the purposes of schooling since professionals and parents generally shared the same cultural-religious orientation. Requests from the school for parent cooperation acquired extra legitimacy because of the relation of the school mandate to established religious institutions, and because principals were often members of the clergy.

This overwhelming cultural homogeneity created a sense of discipline within the school. As in most religious groups, there were strong pressures to accept prescriptive patterns of action and belief as they had been established by a hierarchy of church authorities. Self-discipline and self-control were personal virtues that were rewarded, while cooperative obedience to the rule of authority was the rewarded social virtue in all community institutions, including the schools. This is not to suggest that in regard to schooling there were no differences in perspective or disagreements about policy and practice. Before implementing IGE, Belair was reported to have taken a laissez-faire approach to teaching and learning; some teachers followed a prescriptive academic curriculum, and others a loose classroom organization within which children made decisions about what (and whether) to study. Although this loose approach generated criticism from parents, the present carefully controlled and monitored system has community support, according to the principal.

The professional perception of community characteristics affected areas beyond basic conceptions of schoolwork and knowledge. Close observation of values clarification exercises that were conducted in at least two of the schools under a variety of labels showed that they were meant to give children "correct" values for behavior: children were urged to obey social rules, work hard, refrain from smoking, and obey parents. Career education activities focused on occupations similar to those of the children's parents. In a Career Awareness Week at Clayburn workers were invited to talk about their jobs, and students dressed up for role-playing exercises. "Every day I have to set up a different program," the principal observed. "And when I run out of people to come, then I get the parents to come and patch up. The parents come in and they speak to the children. Then we have a day where the child can come dressed [for an] occupation, what he thinks he would like to be. . . . a policeman, nurse, fireman, telephone man, anything . . ."

The intent in this instance was not to explore the full possibilities of work in the community, and the study of occupations was restricted to those that required functional literacy, and, typically, minimum educational attainments. Problem-solving ability or the "arts" was not seen as an asset in these occupations.

Among the professionals at Clayburn and Maplewood there was optimism that within the context of technical education children would indeed learn the necessary basic skills. In part, their optimism was derived from the perception that the parents were mostly hard working and productive members of society. The professionals had no reason to believe that, with precisely the right training, the children would not also be able to achieve in school and in later life.

Concern for skills was not merely a fabrication of the professionals in these schools. Parents believed the technical school was fulfilling its mandate.[2] This support was built upon a belief that achievement in school is related to later success.[3] The rituals and ceremonies associated with learning the technical skills provided evidence that the school was doing all that could be done to meet the parents' expectations.

In discussions about schoolwork with parents two themes predominated: first, parents wanted the emphasis in schoolwork placed on learning and practicing the basic skills (reading, writing, and arithmetic), and they defined student achievement as achievement in these subject areas; second, parents wanted their children to learn to take responsibility for their actions and behaviors. Social responsibility was defined as self-control and the ability to work independently. When asked what the most important objectives for students were, one Clayburn parent responded that "The main thing would be to teach the child[ren] to be responsible for their actions and behavior and learning. I want them to learn reading and writing and arithmetic. Mainly reading to me is the most important, but at the same time, I want them to learn social skills. I want them to learn to get along and to take responsibility for their lives and for their

2. The evidence of how parents perceived the schools comes from interviews with PTO officials and parents who had worked in the schools as teacher aides and volunteers, and from observations of school activities in which parents participated (PTO meetings, conferences, and general interactions between parents and teachers).

3. The relationship of school achievement to success is viewed as simple because of a variety of social and cultural factors that influence success in an occupation (see Collins 1979).

work habits and so forth." The social skills emphasized in this conversation reflect the values of the Clayburn instructional program. The parent accepted the school's definition of responsibility as "good work habits" and "getting along" and perceived that the program at the school provided those basic educational and social skills the children needed.

Parents valued the elaborate record-keeping procedures at the technical schools as appropriate to the emphasis on skills. The records provided parents with a precise language for articulating what happens and why, and test scores gave parents confidence that the school was doing what it was supposed to be doing. A parent aide at Belair, for example, believed that the school's system of reporting specific achievement levels enabled teachers to know more about each child's achievement and needs than before the system was used. This parent thought highly significant the clarity of reporting and the resulting precision with which a teacher could respond to questions about a child's abilities and accomplishments.

Professional ideologies in which the task of schooling was defined in terms of management and efficiency provided still another source of credibility and support for the technical schools. In school district administrations, the classroom management procedures and emphasis on efficiency in these schools was seen as an extension of district programs to develop consistency and standardization. Districtwide objectives, criterion-referenced measures, single-reading textbook series, and curriculum management systems had all been introduced in at least one of the districts. The superintendent in another district viewed the development of a standardized and consistent program in all district schools as essential to good school administration, and compared the school district to a football team in which an individual school was one member of "a system" which fit into a "structure systematically." He argued that allowing schools to go their own way produced "fragmentation and disorganization," and that just the opposite is needed: "Uniformity can produce greater results." The system idea, he continued, makes sense for the internal organization of each school "because things can feed into one another and make for a better organization." In this view, providing a rational procedure and consistent rules can ensure quality control in all the schools in a district.

At the district office of the county in which Clayburn is located, school management appeared to be important. The curriculum coordinator said that the district was beginning to develop a comprehensive management scheme which would include many of the instructional procedures at Clayburn, and that management systems of instruction were being introduced districtwide through an adaptation of the reading textbook. The record-keeping program at Clayburn was also an example for the district:

it "shows what the school is responsible for." As evidence of high regard for the program at Clayburn, the curriculum coordinator commented that the Clayburn principal was one of only two elementary principals retained since the hiring of a new superintendent a few years before.

Professional agencies outside the Clayburn school district also gave credibility to the school's program. The state department of instruction regularly used criterion-referenced tests to determine the level of achievement in schools throughout the state. In practice, this state policy gave legitimacy to instructional practices which aimed to improve test scores. The instructional program in Clayburn was designed to ready students for the criterion-referenced test and, as the actual test date approached, all school activities were designed to provide test practice. The principal had children take tests similar to the state criterion-referenced tests, used a stopwatch to time the children, and then graphed the results to see how children were scoring. To the principal, the tests results were important for school credibility. The local paper printed the results for each school, along with statewide results, to give the public evidence of the efficacy of school programs.

At Maplewood and Belair standardizing curriculum and rationalizing instruction were also given credence by agencies outside of the schools. The superintendent in Maplewood's district considered the school as a model for other schools to emulate, and Maplewood's principal and staff gave workshops and talks to other district personnel. The state department of public instruction financially supported the school's computer program. At Belair the principal received strong support from the superintendent's office, and also had backing—including a grant—from state officials.

Pressures and counterpressures for interpretations of schooling that were not technical arose within each district and community. At an evening PTO meeting at Clayburn, a few parents seemed dissatisfied with the school's definitions of responsibility and schoolwork. Some teachers complained to the superintendent about the limited educational experiences provided for children by the school, but to no avail. In none of the three schools did such disagreements receive sustained attention or result in action.

In summary, it can be seen that technical schooling is sustained by both internal and external factors as a plausible way to educate children. Teachers perceive that the social and cultural life of the community gives them a mandate to focus on basic skills, and parents expect schools to emphasize basic skills and social discipline. Professional ideologies supply a technical definition of educational problems. Together, these influences give credibility and legitimacy to the programs in the technical schools.

## Conclusions about Technical Schooling:
## Public Image and Social Control

In this concluding section, we will examine the effect of the public image provided by IGE and the form of social control underlying technical schooling. Each is important to understanding the assumptions and implications of the three studied schools.

The public image of IGE as it is applied in the technical schools is one of a comprehensive system of schooling that meets the broadest range of children's needs.

Parents, administrators, teachers, and children concur in this view. Teachers occasionally complain about the problems entailed in coordinating the IGE program, but such criticisms are more like fleeting thoughts than serious challenges. IGE is responsive to important interests of the professionals and the community.

To parents concerned about skill mastery in the basics, IGE offers a logical, sequential approach to teaching basic skills. Parents are generally satisfied that the technical schools are providing a proper curriculum that serves the interests of their children. Parental approval is evidence to teachers and administrators that the schools are responding appropriately to the community mandate.

It is important to both the community and the professionals that the basics are taught in a manner which implies efficiency and effectiveness. Like most institutions in our culture, the technical schools wish to embody these values. IGE's hierarchical curriculum, supported by elaborate record keeping and hardware, suggests not only that everything important is being systematically covered, but also that each child's progress can be documented. Parents, children, and teachers have clear goals, procedures to follow, and criteria for measuring success. The system provides a link between the good intentions of the schools and the procedures and information that indicate their accomplishment.

IGE also provides professionals in the technical schools with a common structure that gives order and identity to their work, and contributes to their esprit de corps because they see themselves working with the latest in educational technology. Staff members in an IGE school have a cooperative system with a shared language, set of procedures, and goals. No longer is each teacher isolated in a single classroom: teachers interact regularly with other adults in planning school affairs and resolving problems. Professionals in the technical schools see IGE as a cooperative effort that is more effective than any individual attempt to improve the quality of education.

The IGE system gives an explicit structure to students' schoolwork. Its

formal organizational characteristics and tasks enable students to understand easily the procedures for completing a sequence of skills. They can
see that work is being accomplished and that the knowledge specified by
the system has been acquired at the end of their efforts. All of this takes
place in a relatively noncompetitive environment; institutional approval is
explicitly given to the notion that students achieve at different rates.

Finally, IGE has general public appeal because its public language—its
slogans—refer to important values. The humaneness of individualized
schooling and the rationality of public accountability bring two competing
and sometimes contradictory demands to bear upon schools. The incorporation of IGE technologies into the technical schools seem to demonstrate successfully through daily classroom procedures and achievement
measurements that the kind of schooling it fosters is good for the affective
and cognitive needs of students.

The processes of legitimating institutional patterns, the strategies of
change, and the definitions of social relations achieved through the manipulation of symbols and work that are characteristic of IGE in the technical schools also exert a form of social control. In school children learn not
only skills, but ways of thinking about social events, and patterns of
working that establish relationships between the world and the individual. To understand the full meaning of Individually Guided Education
in technical schooling we must examine the kind of social control that was
realized in practice. We will consider (A) the nature of the control that
resulted from conceptions of knowledge and work prevalent in the technical schools, (B) the social function of the systems used to rationalize and
legitimatize institutional patterns, and (C) the obscuring of social and
political issues that resulted when problems of technique were emphasized.

### Control and Conceptions of Knowledge and Schoolwork

The effect of viewing technologies as the ends of schooling was to alter
social relations by defining the content and nature of schoolwork in such a
way that individual control over ideas or work was denied. This interplay
between technologies and social meaning can be illuminated by describing six factors involved.

First, professionals searched for the most efficient ways to process people. For example, a teacher at Belair spent a major part of his time planning improvements in record-keeping procedures for children's math levels.
The emphasis on processing people resulted in an unusual definition
of responsibility. For teachers, responsibility did not mean considering
what was appropriate to teach and how best to teach it; rather, responsibility meant structuring objectives, keeping proper records, and insur-

ing an orderly movement of children. In these schools, the unit planning time and decision-making process of Individually Guided Education came to be used in a way that denigrated the knowledge and work associated with teaching. For children, responsibility meant learning and obeying the rules of the classroom, listening to authority, and striving to master predetermined objectives. Responsibility was operationally defined as accepting dependence upon others for ordering activities and thinking about intellectual problems, rather than taking charge of these issues in any manner. The criteria of teachers' and principals' success in all three schools seemed to be related to the degree of planned control that could be exercised over children's progress.

Second, "excellence" was generally achieved by looking busy (process), or by producing in quantity (outcomes). These criteria often applied to both teachers and students. The definition of a better teacher in one school, for example, was one who spent more time before and after class preparing lessons and keeping good records, and who kept children looking busy. For children the ability to look industrious was important, and achievement was often judged on the basis of hard and continuous work rather than on the quality of the results.

Third, knowledge was standardized. All ideas and skills to be learned were presented in a discrete and sequenced form. Ordering knowledge in this way enabled teachers to devote full attention to the procedures of implementation. The standardization of ideas was demanded by the process of social control.

Fourth, the standardization of knowledge reduced the curriculum to learning which could be measured. "Understanding a story" meant being able to respond to five questions which had precise, unambiguous answers that a child could identify on a dittoed sheet. The learning that resulted from these procedures offered few opportunities for children to pursue ideas. To master an objective related to counting, for example, a child might have to identify numbers in order—no time to raise questions about numbers, or to pursue an interest in the origins of numbers. Once the objective was mastered, a child was expected to move on to the next level, not to follow an intriguing idea further.

Fifth, the emphasis on preplanning and measurement eliminated from consideration the serendipitous, accidental, or problematic processes of instruction. Many valuable learning experiences arise from children's interactions with materials, people, and events. If a child enjoys the alliteration in a poem a teacher can capitalize on that interest when planning further activities. Similarly, a lesson on computing change may raise questions about currencies in other countries and how they differ from ours. Opportunities for learning such as these were observed in the technical school classrooms, but the emphasis on technical mastery limited classroom exchanges to short, utilitarian interactions serving immediate goals. Serendipitous learning was improbable in the technical schools.

Sixth, breaking learning down into a sequence of objectives to be mastered created a division between the conception and the execution of work. Earlier we argued that a fundamental aspect of human work is the interplay of practical skills, situational factors, and creative conceptual thought. The conception of work contains the creative power by which people shape and fashion the objects of the world to improve their usefulness. In technical schooling, the separation of the conception and execution of work was a result of the fragmentation and oversimplification of human activities. Each element of the system was defined for the learner in isolation, distinct from the logic which might guide or tie activities together. The consequence of this separation was that teachers and students lost control over their work.

The separation of conception and execution found in the technical schools coincides with fundamental changes that have occurred in the structure and function of work in western industrial society (see Braverman 1974; Noble 1977). The purposes of management and administrative perspectives that underlie the division of individual labor, which was originally developed to promote labor-saving devices and management control in the economic sectors of society, are incorporated into instructional programs in schooling. In reflecting on these changes from a historical and social perspective, Braverman argues that such management perspectives work to destroy the self-organized and self-motivated community. Work becomes dehumanized and new forms of social control are introduced. Labor is subdivided so that the individual no longer has a conception of how the separate elements of the work process relate to the total product of labor. This fragmentation of work alters the very quality of human life (Braverman 1974).

*Control and the Rational Systems of Institutional Legitimacy*

While the management system structures the nature and meaning of schoolwork, it also provides slogans and rituals that serve to create an image of institutional efficiency, consensus, and competence. This image is important for maintaining stability and legitimacy for those who control institutional life. Rituals and ceremonies deflect attention from the underlying values, assumptions, and implications of school conduct. In the technical schools, highly efficient mechanisms were developed for realizing stated objectives. In the language of the schools, these mechanisms were described in terms which suggested precise knowledge of student achievement and deficiencies, carefully sequenced instruction, logically arranged hierarchies of skills and knowledge, and the grouping of children by ability and interest, as pedagogy required. The image offered was one of a well-coordinated, rationally devised machine which compensated automatically for every variation in student potential and curriculum. This machine metered out the right instructional method and content to produce mastery of the specified curriculum by each student.

In daily life in these schools, however, many contradictions meant that such efficiency was often an illusion. The pretest was unreliable in some situations. Before students could move on to new objectives, they often had to wait a considerable time while tests were marked or new groups were formed. The quest for efficiency also hid the fact that a ceiling was placed on the learning of many students: brighter students mastered the limited objectives quickly, with little to challenge them beyond the mastery of each skill. Quantity, as a criterion of achievement, provided children with no place to go once that quantity was achieved.

In spite of the inconsistencies and contradictions teachers in the technical schools recognized in the management scheme, the symbols of a rational system conveyed a sense of competence and legitimacy that was important to both teachers and community and created a powerful form of social control over teachers. Evidence was found that some teachers thought privately about teaching systems other than those used in the technical schools. Administrative controls, however, reduced any overt conflict among teachers and administrators about what teachers should do, and the team approach required that cooperation rather than dissent be valued. In one school, a personality test used by the principal was meant to increase harmony and output by matching staff members with different but complementary personality types. In each of the schools, the principals made clear to observers that they fired or transferred teachers who did not accept the program.

The illusion of efficiency does help to provide institutional stability and consensus. Meyer and Rowan's (1977) work on organizational theory and Edelman's (1977) study of political symbols illuminate the importance of formal rituals and ceremonies in portraying efficiency in schools. They suggest that formal organizations reflect widespread beliefs about institutions as rationally organized activities. But this belief in the rationality of organizations, they assert, is a social myth which identifies the purposes of institutions as technical, and which specifies that appropriate means be sought to pursue institutional purposes. In schools, however, rational organization is difficult because of the uncertainty involved in both organizational technologies and environment. One way of responding to the threat of uncertainty is to create public rituals in which a display of technologies establishes the institution as appropriate, rational, and modern. The use of external assessment instruments such as criterion-referenced tests implies that an institution is rational because test scores appear to be objective evidence of achievement.

*Control and the Obscuring of Social and Political Issues*

The technical emphasis given to conceptions of knowledge and to work at Clayburn, Maplewood, and Belair obscured underlying social and political issues embedded in the process of schooling. By focusing attention on problems of management and of efficiency, the existing priorities, values, and patterns of social control remained unscrutinized. While the three schools responded to and were sustained by institutional, demographic, and cultural facets of their communities, the emphasis on technology appeared to separate education from other community affairs. School staffs operated as though there was a broad consensus about the goals of instruction, and teachers appeared to believe that the school mandate was unambiguous. Far from being a technical matter, however, the choices that have to be made in education involve substantive issues about social life and its interpretation, and they require debate. At this point we can only touch upon the substantive issues related to schooling and illustrate the poverty of professional dialogue in the technical schools; the last chapter returns to this subject.

Educators concerned with curriculum have long recognized that schools cannot respond to the vast array of cultural and social experience available. Significant debate has focused on how choices are to be made. Involved in the discussions have been ethical, epistemological, and political commitments. The relationships between world and individual in pedagogical practices, the kinds of citizenship toward which schooling should be directed, and the social values that should be articulated in curricula and in classroom organization are a few of the issues that have been addressed. Curriculum planners have raised questions about the consensus view of social institutions presented in most school materials, and how that view creates an image of stability which obscures the conflict that underlies social change.

Debate of this kind was stifled in the technical schools. By viewing teaching as a response to children's needs or a way to meet specific objectives, the presuppositions of the curriculum that defined needs and objectives were obscured. A view of the world was presented which crystalized social affairs and institutions, and which defined a passive role for the individual. To assume that there was a consensus about what is most worthwhile and to proceed "technically" was to hide the actual social values inherent in schooling.

The apparent agreement upon "ends" filtered out any discussion among professionals of the possible impact that their perceptions of the community might have had upon the definition of school purposes. Many of the expectations held by professionals in two of the technical schools were related to their concepts of social and cultural class. Their expectations could be summarized as follows: "While the American dream is to rise to be a millionaire, the reality for the children of this school is that they will probably work in occupations similar to their parents'. Further, while we might want to have them deal with the tentativeness of knowledge or aspects of 'high culture,' the lifestyles of their parents do not value this. As teachers, our first task is to prepare children in a way that makes the transitions from school to work easier. We can give children plenty of practical reading and mathematics so they will not be eliminated from jobs because of inadequacies in basic skills. We can also teach them the responsibility and discipline that are so important for holding jobs." This emphasis on functional skill, however, was not a fabrication of professionals. People in the community seemed to support what the schools were doing.

The third school, Belair, was an anomaly. Not only was the community fairly homogeneous in its cultural, social, and religious orientation, but the presuppositions of the church had filtered into the infrastructure of social and political organizations. The community surrounding Belair school was the most affluent of the communities encountered in our study, and the school's achievement scores were the highest. The norms of conduct maintained by this technical school were not in conflict with the norms and principles of authority of the religious community. This suggests that the ways in which the school defined adult-child interactions were consistent with the cultural and religious organization of the community as a whole. It does not mean that technical schooling is the only educational possibility in that community.

*Tentative Evaluations of Technical Schooling*

The combination of social factors that makes technical school practices legitimate is a historical question which cannot be addressed here. It is crucial, though, to consider our contention that the technical definition of the school mandate actually serves the interests of neither the community nor the teachers. The dissociation and fragmentation of knowledge and work in these schools produce a definition of professionalism that limits the creative and purposeful quality of teaching. Students are offered a mode of thought that cannot penetrate the complex patterns of communication dominant in contemporary society. Schooling is thus robbed of its imaginative and liberating potential. The emphasis on only the most limited skill acquisition legitimates a style of work which is fragmented, isolated, and unrelated to truly purposeful activity. This style of school work and reasoning, if internalized, imposes occupational limitations

upon the students: rather than offering options for adult life, this schooling legitimates the specific demands and expectations of the social and
cultural majority of the home community. It provides no means for considering new possibilities beyond those suggested by circumstances of
birth and community location. It also helps to perpetuate a false belief
that success in later life is directly proportional to success in basic skills
(see Collins 1979).

Many educational planners who argue for a technical orientation to
schooling see a need for a closed system in which skill development and
mastery learning are emphasized during the early grades. As a child gains
in skills, it is believed, the system can open up. Data from the technical
schools we observed suggest that this opening did not occur. Instead,
technologies and procedures were elevated to the status of values. This
orientation created its own set of priorities and beliefs that defined school
practices. In fundamental ways, technique became an independent moral
domain; it was the criterion for choosing curriculum, instructional processes, and evaluation.

In considering the social, cultural, and religious influences that legitimate the technical school program within the community, we do not
mean to suggest any causal relationships. It is not clear, for example,
whether the mandate for a technical conception of schooling comes from
existing community beliefs or from the definitions of educational practice
suggested to the community by professional rituals and ceremonies. In
Wisconsin, a legislative bill requiring objective assessment in schools
originated with groups within the state department of instruction who
advocated school accountability; the bill did not emerge as a result of any
grass roots demand for accountability. While we cannot establish any
causal links between the institutional patterns of the technical schools and
the surrounding communities, any adequate description of the patterns
must take into account interaction between the dynamics of schooling and
the professional and social concerns external to the school.

The very real political and social consequences of technical efficiency in
the schools cannot be denied: (1) Language and patterns of conduct gave
emphasis and legitimacy to certain pedagogical practices that limited action and reasoning, among both teachers and students. (2) The unfortu-
nate dissociation of purpose from procedure in the implementation guides
for Individually Guided Education gave credence to the beliefs and patterns of conduct found in these schools, and sustained certain principles
of authority, control, and legitimacy. (3) School staffs used the technologies to extend and to articulate an interpretation of schooling which was
different from the expressed intent of the IGE program. (4) The focus on
rationalization of procedures resulted in an administrative control over

teachers that limited both conflict and sustained discourse about alternatives. (5) Technical language and rituals drew attention away from any critical scrutiny of institutional beliefs, priorities, or practices. (6) Teachers' constant efforts to keep the system going restricted opportunities to modify it. (7) The psychological release mechanism built into the classroom drained off or channeled any discontent that might have been felt.

The question of who benefits from such arrangements is complex and involves a closer look at the relation between institutions, social forms, and practices of the profession. We will return to this question after examining constructive and illusory schooling.

# 5

## Exploring Ways of Knowing: Constructive Schooling

Two different approaches to pedagogy for elementary schooling were evident in the development of Individually Guided Education. One was behavioral, which conceptualized schooling through systems analysis, behavioral objectives, and criterion-referenced measures. Implementation literature of the reform effort, as we have seen, used the concepts and the procedures of the behavioral approach in explaining the program to schools. It was the IGE technologies that became the focus of the forms of schooling we have called technical. A second approach to the pedagogy of Individually Guided Education drew upon constructivist psychology. This tradition views children as capable of building knowledge through their encounters with the experiences of schooling. As the definitions and practices of schooling suggested by IGE literature were incorporated into the systems language of program implementation, however, the constructivist beliefs about pedagogy were filtered out of the program's focus.

When we visited Kennedy Elementary School we had already spent considerable time in those schools we have characterized as technical, and our experience had led us not to expect major variations in the way they interpreted and implemented IGE. It was with some surprise that we confronted a totally different set of institutional assumptions and behaviors at Kennedy. The term "constructive" eventually emerged to summarize the patterns of work, concepts of knowledge, and professional definitions that gave meaning and interpretation to this school situation.

The intent of this chapter is to examine the characteristics of constructive schooling and how they incorporate and express IGE technologies. After describing the Kennedy school and its community setting, we will explore the pedagogical language of constructivism in order to identify the assumptions that guided teacher actions. This language will be related to the constructivist school curriculum, in which problematic, aesthetic, and integrated knowledge were emphasized, and to the discourse of instruction in which interpersonal skill and control were stressed. The practices of constructive schooling at Kennedy were not without certain strains and tensions, two of which are identified and discussed: one conflict was between school district policy that promoted greater consistency in school practices and teachers and administrators who viewed that policy an intrusion on professional autonomy; a second conflict concerned internal pressures that produced what one teacher called "burnout." It is in relation to these internal conditions and external pressures, as well as the assumptions of the constructivists, that Kennedy's interpretation of IGE is to be understood. At the conclusion of the chapter we will attempt to relate the various elements of constructive schooling to the particular social situation to which it responds.

### Kennedy: Serving a Professional Community

Kennedy school is located in a university town on the edge of the foothills of a major mountain range. For years the community remained modest in size, and the university and agriculture were the mainstays of the town. Recently, however, corporate industry has discovered the area and the population has expanded dramatically. Much of the new industry uses advanced technology. In addition to the lure of jobs, a pleasant climate and recreational opportunities make the setting attractive. On several occasions people in the school system commented to us that new families were moving into the community because of its attractiveness even though the parents had not yet found employment. The conventional wisdom is that population and business growth will continue unabated in the foreseeable future. One new school opened in 1979, and the school district has been hiring a substantial number of new teachers.

The school district, which includes rural areas as well as the town, serves people from a range of economic levels. There is a low-income section of town in which a sizeable number of Mexican-Americans live. Evidence of conspicuous wealth is absent in the district, but in the 1970s the neighborhood in which Kennedy school is located developed into a middle- to upper-middle-income section of large split-level dwellings with two-car garages. The school's teachers suggested that many of the professional and business members of the community, including professors from the university, have chosen to build new homes in the neighborhood.

Kennedy school served approximately 500 children at the time of our observations. Teachers reported that the level of academic ability was above average. The principal showed us data from the Stanford Achievement Test which indicated that 12 percent of the second grade students were below average, 49 percent were average, and 38 percent were above average. While the overwhelming majority of the pupils were white, the student body included a few blacks and Asians as well as children from nations around the world. These children's families, teachers reported, belonged to the professional middle class which populates the neighborhood.

To meet the demands of the expanding population, Kennedy school was built in 1972. The brick building is placed on one corner of a large lot that occupies almost an entire city block. The well-equipped playground includes two baseball diamonds, and one section of it is designed to be used as an outdoor classroom. The school has a modern, open-plan design. The main hallway leads directly into a large, open instructional materials center housing the school library and audiovisual equipment. At opposite ends of this center hallways lead to two identical open-design areas that contain the teaching units in which screens are used to create separate teaching spaces. Doors lead directly to the playground from these units.

Although its open-plan construction makes Kennedy somewhat different physically from the typical elementary school, in many respects it resembled other schools in our study. The unit areas were lined with chalkboards and bulletin boards, and filmstrip projectors and record players were placed on carts for students and teachers to use. The open unit areas and the central pod enabled teachers to adapt space to the needs of different sized groups and to different kinds of activities, but teachers complained about architectural features that made it inconvenient to carry on normal business. Recent increases in the number of children intensified teachers' complaints about the acoustics of the building and the distractions of noise. Overcrowding produced other inconveniences as well. Teachers reported a shortage of storage facilities in the teaching areas; books and equipment were piled up because there were no book shelves or closets. There was only a single drinking fountain and sink in each unit, making it difficult for one group of children to use these facilities without disturbing another group. There were not enough coat racks for the children's cold weather clothing.

Teachers frequently told us that high levels of commitment and energy were demanded during Kennedy school's first two years as a program was developed to capitalize on the open-plan school. Much of the involvement, teachers recalled, was stimulated by the original school principal, who introduced them to Individually Guided Education, and whose ability to recruit and mobilize a staff that was willing to work hard on developing an individualized system was credited with setting the foundation for the school's program. This principal was successful in cajoling the school district's central administration into giving him extra funds to provide in-service training for new teachers. Money was allocated for workshops to help the staff implement IGE, and teachers were sent to regional IGE meetings.

After two years, the original principal left the school. Teachers believe that he left because of his "fights" with the school superintendent about the Kennedy school program, and his own "personality, which made him look for new challenges." A new principal was selected from the Kennedy staff, but this person has not had the resources to continue the in-service programs of the initial two years. When several new teachers were asked how they had learned to apply IGE, they reported receiving little, if any, formal instruction. New teachers now pick up the routines by talking with their more experienced colleagues. To teachers, Kennedy school appears to be running on the traditions and practices established in its early history. We will return to this problem later, but at this point we will try to discover what practices and traditions teachers referred to when talking about Kennedy school by observing a typical school day.

A day at Kennedy begins with students assembling with their homeroom teachers for announcements. In the lower grades, a teacher might use this time to read a story to the children (approximately 20) in her group. After reciting the pledge to the flag, students disperse with their tote bags of school materials to an assigned area within the unit to work on mathematics, science, or language arts. Students going to language arts are divided into small groups for at least part of the period, and two or three children from the special education class might join these groups. Children who are hearing-impaired wear special receivers, and the teacher wears a transmitting microphone. In the different language arts groups, some children may read silently from a text or a story, others may work on a writing assignment or answer a set of dittoed questions, and still others may discuss a story they have read with the teacher. Each small group eventually engages in all of the activities. If some students finish their work early, they ask the teacher for permission to pursue another activity, such as rehearsing a play or working on a science project.

Following language arts, students move to other areas of the unit and to different teachers, perhaps for mathematics. All students in the group might receive similar math instruction. At midmorning there is a recess. Sometimes this period is spent in "free play," with each student deciding what activity to pursue. On other occasions teachers organize soccer or softball games. Later in the morning time is set aside for art or music, and once a week high school students come to Kennedy to introduce fifth and sixth graders to French, German, or Spanish through a basic conversational method.

After lunch, which students eat in the school cafeteria or at home, time is planned to permit sustained activities in science and social studies. Some children work on such unit projects as building a cage for the chinchilla, while others work on research projects in the instructional materials center. Sometimes a film is shown. At 2:00 there is a period of uninterrupted, sustained silent reading. Other afternoon activities may include softball or soccer, a visit to the nature center, a field trip, or a bike ride. The day ends for the students at around 3:15; teachers stay until 4:00 to meet as a unit and to make plans.

Observers are not likely to see students at Kennedy taking tests to measure their achievement on specific skills or knowledge. Students are more likely to be seen filling out self-evaluation forms which are appended to the papers accumulated in a subject during a period of three or four weeks. These are sent home to parents to inform them about the work students have done.

In the following discussion, the language of constructivism will be discussed to illuminate the pedagogical ideology that teachers use to explain and justify the classroom practices observed at Kennedy school.

### The Language of Constructivism: "Kennedy Is a Kid's Place"

During the first years of program development at Kennedy, a song was composed by the school's music teacher to symbolize the educational climate the teachers hoped to establish. It was called "Kennedy Is a Kid's Place." In speaking to observers, "the phrase "Kennedy is a kid's place" was used repeatedly by the school's principal and teachers to convey what they believed was the school's unique quality. To the teachers, the words expressed an important tradition that emphasizes the interests, rights, and well-being of the students. "The school," one teacher said, "is not to be a place where adults can be comfortable at the expense of the children."

Although teachers in all the schools we visited expressed concern for the interests and involvement of students, the teachers at Kennedy used the language of "a kid's place" to organize and judge everyday practices.

This language referred to the relationship between work and play and to the importance given to children's development by the teachers.

One characteristic of Kennedy school was the organization of work around enjoyable activities: teachers sought out activities for the children that would both offer knowledge or skill and be fun to do. Beyond this, however, teachers also believed that school itself should be enjoyable, and that, from time to time, a break from the routines of the classroom was essential. Breaks were justified not only or always by need, but also by the conviction that a wide variety of experiences contributes to learning. Making the school a kid's place would have the ultimate effect of encouraging children to work harder and learn more.

The idea of fun activities at first might seem to signify a permissive or less-than-serious approach to education, but at Kennedy "fun activities" was a code phrase for at least three beliefs about teaching and learning that governed day-to-day decisions about the work children were asked to do:

1. Teachers believed that children have a right to enjoy life, and that teachers are obliged to make school an enjoyable place. When an institution demands that children spend a significant proportion of their time responding to directives from adults, the experience should not be unnecessarily dull, tedious, and repetitive.
2. Teachers believed that enjoyable activities are accepted with fewer reservations by children, and that children therefore respond to such activities with a more authentic engagement that provides greater potential for social as well as intellectual learning. In addition, such activities may result in serendipitous learning, which teachers value because it permits interaction between student and adult, and between one student and another.
3. Teachers believed that fun activities make it possible to broaden the range of activities appropriate to the work and knowledge required of students. This broad range of activities includes different kinds of intellectual experiences and the complex social experiences necessary for children's development.

In contrast to the view prevailing at Kennedy, teachers at the other schools in our study separated schoolwork from fun activities: "fun" was a break in the action much like recess. In one of the technical schools (Maplewood), fun activities were emphasized to the extent that they were offered as rewards to children who had "worked up to their ability" and had worked "independently" (that is, had not been a discipline problem). But while these activities (outings) could have been seen as either educational or recreational experiences, the emphasis was clearly on the latter.

While some teachers at Kennedy had a clearer notion than others of how fun activities related to school experiences, there was a general commitment to their use. Kennedy's teachers did not think it was necessary to justify all activities by specifically linking them to traditional learning objectives. The teachers defined many non-classsroom activities, such as softball tournaments, bike hikes through the park, and field trips throughout the city and county, as legitimate experiences within the school's conception of learning. At one point, forays into the park and to the local shopping center were questioned by the principal, who was under pressure from the central administration to provide strict accountability for student and teacher time. The district wanted all field trips to be planned in advance and to have specified and approved objectives. Teachers argued with the principal that fields trips were justified even if specified objectives were not provided in advance. The following exchange occurred in an Instructional Improvement Committee meeting when the principal read a district directive on the matter:

Principal: I frown on those [activities] that have no real academic purpose.
Teacher: What if going outside is part of your program? I agree that you have to plan, but it's unfair [to say] that if you can't have a clear objective you can't go outside. If you have objectives it's okay, without objectives it's not okay? Now it's not a place for kids if you can't do it without objectives. If you want to fly kites in the nature center, now you have to feel it's wrong. I object to that!

Several issues were joined in this brief exchange. First, this teacher spoke for those of her colleagues who believed that school should help students to achieve different kinds of objectives. She could invent some academic justification for going out to fly kites—students would learn about aerodynamics or wind currents—but why bother when it is not merely academic objectives that matter, but also learning to do things for their intrinsic pleasure, learning that school is a place of surprises and enjoyment? Second, these teachers believed in the value of spontaneity. Specifying academic objectives in advance makes every activity deliberate; students are prevented from acting on their impulses and learning when to trust or to question them. Finally, there was the recurrent theme of professional responsibility. These teachers believed that they should choose the activities to be pursued to achieve school purposes, and that such choices should not be made by "bureaucrats," who were separated from the school and its students, or by the principal, who was not part of day-to-day classroom life.

The slogan "Kennedy Is a Kid's Place" also expressed the teachers' belief that schooling contributes to the students' social development and maturity: school should be a place where adults and children interact in a responsive and humane manner about a wide range of concerns. As one teacher put it, "I do feel that kids . . . need to have some interaction with adults about things that are not necessarily academic."

This belief was reflected in a team meeting which was called to discuss the behavior of several girls from an upper unit. The teachers expressed the opinion that they had a responsibility to respond in a way that would promote greater social and emotional maturity for the girls. For one teacher, "the four girls [weren't] the issue. It's that they should not feel guilty about what they feel." Later on she explained her position: "I see the role of the teacher [as] becoming more and more [involved] . . . we are dealing with personal problems and the girls' situation right now . . . the kind of budding emotional development that takes place and the sexual development that takes place. Dealing with that if it needs to be dealt with and not putting it aside."

Among teachers of younger children, concern was expressed more in terms of a family relationship within the unit. A unit leader stated that an important goal of his unit was for children "to have a feeling of belonging to the family . . . children should feel comfortable with every teacher . . . within the unit."

The slogan "Kennedy is a kid's place" was used consciously by teachers as a reminder of the need to make children comfortable, to make learning enjoyable. One teacher recognized this social concept of schooling in her own way: "I'm sure there are plenty of other teachers and schools in the district that teach kids to read just as well as we do. Maybe it's that good feeling that you have with the kids that I'm really referring to. The good rapport: I think exceptional rapport. Feedback from people who substitute around the district is really positive in terms of what they say about our discipline, the kind of kids we have, their enthusiasm toward learning and toward school activities."

This statement suggests the importance that Kennedy school gives to integrating social expeiences with the more formal school work. The constructivist phrase "Kennedy is a kid's place" provides a rationale enabling Kennedy's teachers to justify the forms of curriculum maintained in the school.

## The Curriculum:
### Problematic, Aesthetic, and Integrated Knowledge

Constructive schooling, rather than emphasizing states of knowledge, pays attention to the ways knowledge is created. In the curriculum, relational ideas and the exploration of general principles and concepts are stressed, and skills are developed within that context.

For analytical purposes we can separate the kind of work and knowledge that occupied students from that which occupied teachers, but in actuality they are inseparable.

The commitment to make Kennedy a kid's place rested in part on the belief that different kinds of activities and experiences contribute to children's intellectual and social development. The resulting curriculum design provided a broad range of ways of knowing and learning. Kennedy students were continually offered experiences that included art, music, poetry, drama, logic, literature, science, history, and even controversial issues.

The variety of classroom work and knowledge at Kennedy shared three characteristics. First, the *problematic* aspects of knowledge were emphasized. Students were asked to solve some kind of problem: a difficulty to be resolved, a search to be made, or an answer to be found, invented, or discovered. Second, *aesthetic* forms of knowledge, in which poetry, drama, music, and art are used to produce and express understanding, were incorporated into schoolwork. Students were encouraged and even required at times to use these forms to depict their insights and experiences. Third, frequent efforts were made to *integrate* different kinds of knowledge and skills. Sometimes this meant interdisciplinary integration: art and literature were brought together, for instance. In other situations, different kinds of knowledge and skills were joined to produce more complex understanding: for example, math skills were used to calculate the per capita consumption of energy in a country. While from time to time we found examples of problematic, aesthetic, and integrative work at the other schools we studied, the persistence and pervasiveness of these characteristics was definitive of the curriculum at Kennedy.

Examples from the day-to-day activities at Kennedy may illustrate these aspects of the children's work. In some cases, a single activity exemplifies more than one characteristic. The strategy of one teacher for selecting spelling words for students integrated the use of basic skills with problem solving: "What I do is try to tie it to their reading program. For example, if we are working on phonics, I would say, 'find words with a long *a*.' We would take 10 words each week. . . . Each individual reading group gets [its] own words. They usually get them from their textbooks." The students were challenged to find their own words instead of having a standardized spelling list from a commercial series. This example also illustrates a belief among Kennedy teachers that routine work, such as spelling, should be integrated with other aspects of study.

Another example of the integration of routine basic skills into a problematic framework was provided by a language arts assignment. The teacher brought to class an editorial from a local newspaper which attacked the advertising of snack foods on popular children's Saturday morning television shows. The students were asked to write a response to the editorial, either agreeing or disagreeing with it. The substance of the response was problematic for the students, while the assignment also taught skills. Teachers helped children to use proper grammar, spelling, and punctuation in stating their arguments.

The combined interdisciplinary and problematic approach was also characteristic of Kennedy's treatment of subject matter. One social studies lesson combined geography, current social problems, and mathematics: students used maps to identify major oil exporting and importing countries, and their problem was to depict the oil exports or imports for each country on a graph. The students looked through a news article to find information about the number of barrels of oil traded. An observer reported that

the teacher encourages several students to go to the blackboard to draw a bar graph depicting the figures. The teacher suggests that another way of representing the export-import situation is to draw bars based on percentages. She indicates how they can do this. The students are busy converting barrels of oil into percentage figures for the major countries. Soon three students indicate they have worked out the figures; they go to the board and draw a graph (after several false starts) showing the percentage of oil imported by several large consumers (the U. S., Britain, Germany, France, Japan). Once the graph is complete the students discuss the political implications of this situation. The teacher asks: "What problems might develop between nations because of this sharp difference between who exports and who imports?" One student sees no problem: "We get their oil and they get our money." The teacher suggests that maybe the exporting countries might get together to raise the price higher than we want to pay. This, she continued, can create a possible problem.

A unit's response to an expanding chinchilla population also integrated knowledge and problem solving. For a number of years, an upper unit had kept chinchillas in the unit area. In the past year, however, the animals had multiplied and could no longer be housed in their cage. One of the units turned the necessity for a new cage into a scientific and mathematical problem, as well as a lesson in the craft of construction: combining an understanding of the habits and environmental needs of the animals with their knowledge of geometry and metric measurement, the children designed and built a hexagonal structure that provided a functional solution to the problems of both chinchillas and students.

This example clearly illustrates several aspects of the kind of curriculum experiences Kennedy provided for children. First, facts and skills are integrated and related to some problem. Second, children engage in a problem of discovery (how to design and build a structure), the answer to which is indeterminate but is within the students' capabilities and re-

sources; general principles and concepts must be understood and applied
to obtain a desired result. Third, the children's activities are to be fun.
Group activities help students to develop a sense of involvement and
purpose, enhancing both learning and social relationships among children
and teachers.

Similar activities were observed in one of the technical schools, where
they were used mainly with the ablest children in a unit and, in one
instance, with a small group of slow learners, possibly to motivate them.
The difference between the two institutional situations was that these
activities were available to *all* the children at Kennedy, and were expected to add to everyone's learning capability; in the technical school
most children rarely experienced this kind of approach. The integrated,
problematic approach was central to the work at Kennedy, while it was
clearly peripheral to the efforts in the technical schools.

At Kennedy skill activities were practiced from the perspective of
problematic and integrated knowledge. Teachers talked about the importance of drill, but it was valued only to the extent that it contributed to
the larger goals and purposes of schooling. During the school day groups
of children at times did drills to master specific skills. A teacher might be
observed organizing a computation lesson in arithmetic, and then giving
the children dittos for practicing the skill. Drills were also organized to
provide practice for memorizing spelling, as an observer recorded: "At
1:00, the children started a spelling lesson. There were about 30 children
in an extra large room reserved for the primary grades. The teacher put
on [the chalkboard] two groups of words, one for each of the reading
groups. The children were given a piece of paper to divide into four
columns. The words were somewhat unusual for a first grade—summer,
round, fold. The children copied the words and wrote them over again
four times."

The opportunities that Kennedy's curriculum offered to engage in aesthetic expression were also integrated with the teaching of conventional
skills and information. For example, in a language class the teacher gave
students "story starters" (sentences) that were to be continued, with correct grammar and punctuation. According to an observer, "the teacher
emphasizes the need to use their imagination along with the correct form.
. . . One optional starter which several boys choose is a brief description
of a boy climbing a mountain, dressed in appropriate climbing gear. He
has a rope around his waist and is making his way up the face of a rock
wall. From this beginning the student is to create a complete short story.
Presumably some kind of adventure ensues."

Aesthetic opportunities were similarly provided by one unit in which students were encouraged to present interpretive paintings, drawings, or other art projects as part of their book reports. As the children in one group got started on these projects, the teacher read and sang limericks to another group. The children seemed attentive, and after some discussion they were assigned the task of writing limericks of their own.

Kennedy's teachers recognized aesthetic activities as a legitimate part of schoolwork. Students were encouraged to write and perform their own plays and skits, and to view this as fun activity. While students viewed a play as a fun activity, it was apparent that they also took their dramatic efforts seriously. An observer who witnessed an impromptu rehearsal for a play written by a group of children noted that any suspicion that students might be wasting time and not taking responsibility for putting on a competent performance was "quickly dissipated":

The teacher gives the class an assignment and most begin working on it. A group of six or seven, however, ask if they can rehearse their play. She says "yes" and suggests they go outside so as not to disturb the rest of the students. I follow them out to the playground area, where there is a shady corner next to the building. They immediately begin taking positions and acting out a scene. There is some giggling and fooling around for a few moments and one of the girls sharply reprimands her peers, suggesting they have only a few minutes to get organized. One student doesn't know her lines and is told to memorize them. The director, who is also one of the authors, suggests some changes in how a character should react to a situation. While there is a no-nonsense approach [taken] by most of the students, they are obviously having fun. After about 20 minutes of rehearsal, they return voluntarily to the unit area. At 9:45 [the] students present their play to the two units in their section of the building. The title of the play is "Queen Mabel's Liberation Movement." The setting is in medieval times, but the theme of women's liberation is modern. It is something of a spoof on contemporary women's liberation, because the women in the scene try to stop the men from treating them as objects to feud over, but the women in making their point become very aggressive and start beating up on the men. One form of fighting is replaced by another. The younger children from the lower unit probably fail to grasp the point in the same was as the fifth and sixth graders, but with the various pratfalls and jokes the smaller children are entertained. Everyone seems to have a good time, and a sincere round of applause concludes the performance.

The inclusion of poetry in the curriculum provides another example of the importance given to aesthetic knowledge at this constructive school. Teachers read poetry to the students, and on at least one occasion students were observed writing their own poems. One teacher developed a technique for involving an entire class in writing a poem, which she called "fractionating." An observer described the process:

Sarah is teaching some kind of creative thinking. She is working with a branching diagram which takes students from word to word or idea to idea:

| SALT | Malt | | smooth | mica |
|------|------|---|--------|------|
| | | | | water |
| | potato chips | crisp | fish |
| | | | | burnt toast |
| | | ridges | mountains |
| | | | | orange peels |

They [students] decide they will write a poem about a horse using the following words which they came up with using the branching procedure: sour, song, water, mica, fish, burnt toast, mountains, orange peel. Some children work together calling out lines that are to be the poem. The teacher writes the poem on the board:

There was a sour horse who ate a fish, of course,
The fish tasted like mica
His song, in Italian, "I lika"
And said, "It tastes like burnt toast"
He smelled from mountain to coast
He ate an orange peel,
Turned on the wheel,
And drove into a post.

While the teacher in this incident permitted a good idea to lose its sharpness and accepted doggerel, certain social characteristics of the lesson are worth noting. The teacher involved the children in a cooperative activity, seeking to expand their communicative flexibility and competence, and the structure of the lesson required children to take initiative and to exercise control over the lesson material.

The most conspicuous of the aesthetic activities at Kennedy school was the production of the spring concert, in which every student in the school participated, including the hearing-impaired. The spring concert was presented in three parts, each involving children of different age groups acting out different themes and singing different songs. Kindergartners performed for their parents during school time. This event was well attended by mothers and fathers, some of whom took time from work to see their children perform. Teachers in the kindergarten unit were quick to testify that the children's experiences in these activities were every bit as important educationally as more conventional school work.

For the intermediate and upper grade children, large blocks of school time were set aside for rehearsing the songs and spoken lines of musicals. The story and musical arrangements for the upper grade performance were written by the music and art teachers, scenery and lighting arrangements were produced to accompany the singing, and poetry written by the art teacher was flashed onto a screen at the back of the stage at one point during the production. On consecutive nights the two upper units presented their productions in the school's gymnasium to packed houses.

Comments by parents filing into the gymnasium indicated enthusiasm about the students' productions, and teachers were proud of the approval parents gave this kind of school activity.

The involvement of teachers and students in aesthetic activities at Kennedy differed sharply from the concerns found at the technical schools. In at least two other schools investigated in our study, people with considerable talent in art, music, or drama were on the faculties. However, their talents were neither utilized nor rewarded, since aesthetics were relegated to a minor, even insignificant, role within those schools.

We have argued in this section that the institutional character of Kennedy is different from the other schools we observed because, in part, the conditions of work and concepts of knowledge are different. Schooling at Kennedy involves problematic thinking, aesthetic expression, and the integration of skills and knowledge in complex activities. This takes place in an atmosphere in which schoolwork is playful and active, and in which an ambiguous concept of knowledge emerges. A range of options in subject matter and method of presentation is available to teachers. Greater reliance is placed upon shared, cooperative educational tasks in which children have increased discretion. It is to this authority structure in the school that we now turn our attention.

## The Discourse of Instruction:
### Interpersonal Skill and Control

The pedagogical emphasis on breadth and depth of experience in learning corresponds to an emphasis on developing interpersonal skill and control. The Kennedy teachers provide students with a range of activities to stimulate such development. This requires a social setting in which children are allowed initiative and take responsibility for their own ideas.

The social processes of the Kennedy school involved teacher-student interactions in which students had some power to determine instructional practices and to make evaluations. Providing students with an active role in planning and interpreting school activities was a challenge to teachers. On one occasion, fifth and sixth graders were observed criticizing an instructional unit on "effective communication" that had been developed by a school counselor: "One boy articulates what appears to have considerable support from his peers: 'We already know how to do most of this; we should do academic work instead of this stuff.' Another pupil, who is recognized by the teachers as a student of considerable academic ability, asks, 'What subjects were cut because of this communication unit?' A girl stands up and addresses the teachers by saying, 'The teachers got more out of this than the kids,' and then looking at the counselor says,

'Your group was not very well organized.' " The evaluation session concluded with a student's comment that summarized the group's feelings: "the last week the kids lost interest, it was sort of boring." This remark received a sustained round of applause.

Such sessions in which students criticized instructional units were not daily events, but this incident exemplified the teachers' belief that student opinions should be taken seriously. The teachers solicited and valued student views on school matters, and they perceived students as having the responsibility and the right to criticize adults. In using such opportunities to evaluate teachers and the curriculum, Kennedy students exercised a degree of power, initiative, and responsibility that was absent among students in other IGE schools investigated.

The belief in student responsibility extended to the inclusion of controversial issues in the curriculum. In one instance, a teacher was interested in having two professors from the university come to the school for a debate on the ethical implications of a rodeo. Some students approved of the rodeo, while the teacher viewed rodeos as a form of cruelty to animals. This posed a dilemma for the teacher: she hesitated to stage the debate because she believed that the defender of the rodeo was less articulate than the "animal liberationist." The teacher believed that it was appropriate and desirable to expose the children to public controversy, but she was afraid that the match would look phony because of the unequal preparation of the adversaries. Complicating the matter was her desire to indoctrinate the children with the "right values," even though she also believed that to do so was wrong as a general policy.

That students should take initiative and responsibility for school activities seems to have been generally accepted by Kennedy's teachers and students. While children could be found who appeared to be unresponsive and uninvolved in normal school activities, in general students seemed to accept, even to demand, participation. The children's responsiveness to the demands made at Kennedy were influenced by experiences in their homes. During one lesson on reading scales on maps, the children commented on how they had seen their families use maps in their travels. One child had just returned from Korea; another had been to Mexico recently; another was going to go to France. They discussed the need for passports and the problems of travel in these countries.

In this incident the children drew upon their home and community experiences in a way which the teacher had not foreseen. The teacher responded by accepting those experiences and treating the children's verbal aggressiveness and self-assurance as appropriate to the conduct of the lesson. The incident illustrates the negotiated order in the school: students and teachers tacitly agreed on what school is about and how to act appropriately.

In pointing out the general responsiveness of Kennedy students, we do not mean to minimize the efforts of teachers who encouraged interest in a wide range of schoolwork. Nor do we wish our picture of the student body to suggest that these students had different abilities from those children that other teachers confront. Like the children in other schools in our study, Kennedy students sometimes made too much noise, fought on the playground, sulked, talked back to teachers, and forgot to bring their books to class. Some unit meetings had to deal with the problem of disruptive, withdrawn, and aggressive children. The general responsiveness of the students, however, must be seen in relation to the concept of Kennedy as "a kid's place": students responded not only because of who they were, but also because of the initiative and responsibility encouraged by teachers.

The emphasis on initiative and responsibility extended to attitudes and behavior patterns as well as to work. Discipline, one teacher commented, was not a matter of forcibly making children do things, but rather of ensuring that they understood the expectations and norms involved in schoolwork; the key word was expectations: "I want children to understand what behavior style is appropriate for working in a team." Discipline, in this view, refers to inner control, to attitudes toward schoolwork, and to behavior in which children exhibit responsibility and initiative.

Kennedy's concern with children's psychological states can be contrasted to the meaning of discipline found in the technical schools, in which children are asked to control themselves by conforming to the routines of the curriculum and demonstrating appropriate levels of effort and content mastery. A well-disciplined child in a technical school is one who can independently carry out the predefined tasks of instruction. At Kennedy, a more diffused expectation of control exists: childen are expected to confront a wide range of activities and social situations.

Writing a play, rehearsing it without supervision, and then performing before a group was an expression of the style of behavior Kennedy's teachers valued, as was the students' appropriately presented evaluation and criticism of the communications unit. This flexibility and spontaneity was attained by paying attention to the norms and beliefs underlying a child's patterns of conduct.

### The Technologies of IGE at Kennedy School

Within the set of beliefs, priorities, and patterns of conduct established at Kennedy, Individually Guided Education was given a special meaning. While teachers appeared to have adopted the main elements of the reform program, the technologies were used in ways that responded to the definitions and special requirements of the school. The organizational structures of IGE, such as the units, provided forums in which teachers could carry out their programs. Some form of the Instructional Programming Model was used in a few subject matter areas, but not to guide instruction. IGE's record-keeping procedures provided evidence that the school district's minimum objectives were being respected by the staff.

Unit meetings, so important in IGE design, were seen by teachers as opportunities to discuss curriculum issues and the children, as well as to consider administrative and procedural matters (the latter being the primary concern in technical schools). At one meeting, for example, teachers discussed whether or not students should feed live mice to a snake kept in their classroom for study. It was argued by one teacher that the children should feed live mice to the snake, even though this was unpleasant for some, because the predator-prey relationship was a fact of life. This point of view carried the day.

Similarly, Instructional Improvement Committee meetings were characterized by debate which reflected general concerns about school programs and policies. During the period of observation, heated discussions were held on the effects of school district policies, which one teacher felt were "eroding" the Kennedy traditions. The committee also helped to implement special school programs such as the Music Show or the Arbor Day celebration, coordinated curriculum activities across units, and integrated special education classes for the handicapped into the regular classes during certain teaching periods.

In walking around the school, observers did not see the prominent displays of objectives, the charts, and the record-keeping systems familiar in the technical schools. When one unit leader was asked how teachers kept track of student progress, he pulled data on student math and reading activities from his file cabinet; periodic entries had been made for each student, especially in mathematics.

The modification of IGE technologies by the Kennedy school staff can be illustrated by the teachers' use of objective-based curricula. The objectives, record-keeping, and evaluative aspects of the IGE program were used in the school, but were subsidiary rather than central in curriculum planning. Teachers understood the need for a series of measurable objectives to meet the district policies for each grade. The Kennedy teachers kept records for those curricular areas for which minimum district objectives had been established to demonstrate that the objectives had indeed been met.

While Kennedy's teachers did not minimize the importance of the specific skills and information to which the district objectives referred, they argued pragmatically that many of the children had these skills and that teaching could be concerned with other aspects of education. A kindergarten teacher said that she did not pay much attention to the district objectives because "the children in my class have already mastered the skills required of kindergarten before they enter the class. They learn them at home, so I can do other things that I feel are important."

The teachers at Kennedy adopted those IGE technologies, such as the unit structure, that enhanced the established educational values of the school. Technologies such as the Instructional Programming Model that might limit the school's instructional goals were used only minimally to inform instruction.

### Competing Professional Views:
### Local Autonomy and District Consistency

While the teachers in each of the schools we studied defined themselves as "professionals," the configuration of teaching practices and discourse found at the constructive school gave the term a unique meaning.

The interest at Kennedy in promoting student initiative and autonomy had its corollary in the work of teaching itself: teachers viewed themselves as having the responsibility to decide what knowledge was to be introduced into classrooms, how it was to be introduced, and when. The value placed on autonomy involved the constructive school teachers in a professional conflict with the district administration.

The teachers' beliefs about their professional obligations were articulated in situations in which they saw their "rights" being transgressed. In the Instructional Improvement Committee meeting discussed earlier, teachers used the principles implied by "Kennedy is a kid's place" to argue against restrictions on their freedom to take children on field trips. Kennedy teachers also resisted adopting materials or procedures that agencies outside the school, such as educational publishers or the district administration, had decided were appropriate for their students; they contended that it was their responsibility to decide whether particular materials should be used to provide intellectual and social development. Those commercial materials that were used at Kennedy were usually chosen because they could be adapted to the instructional purposes.

The teachers' sense of professionalism was dramatically demonstrated when actions of the central administration were perceived as limiting teachers' prerogatives. When the district administration announced a policy of enforcing student attendance at schools on the basis of neighborhood boundary lines, teachers and students were notified that transfers would take place immediately. At an Instructional Improvement Committee meeting at Kennedy, teachers condemned this policy on several grounds: less than two months of the school year remained; transferring students would be harmful because of the difficult transition they would have to make to new schools, teachers, and peers; and teachers themselves were in the best position to make judgments about student transfers. The teachers argued that they had intimate knowledge of the academic and personal characteristics of those involved in the transfer situation, and with one or two exceptions they felt strongly that the half-dozen potential transfer students would be better off remaining at Kennedy through the academic year. Teachers saw this situation as one that called for the kind of professional judgment that they were qualified to make. "Bureaucrats," one teacher said, "ought not to make decisions which involve professional judgment about the welfare of the students."

A number of the teachers were also willing to assert their professional judgment in the area of curriculum. The district central administration had instituted a policy of "consistency" in the curriculum, which entailed (among other things) the specification of common behavioral objectives that all teachers were to follow in developing the basic curriculum for the several grade levels. While in most respects the objectives were perceived as minimal, at least in terms of what Kennedy teachers intended to accomplish with their students, there was the spectre of the camel's nose in the tent. Teachers were concerned that the district would specify an increasing number of objectives to be achieved. The idea of a highly specified curriculum was offensive to the staff, because they believed that it was their right as professionals to make expert decisions about what educational experiences were appropriate for their students.

The principal was not unmindful of this conflict. She volunteered to observers specific instances in which teachers' fears were being realized. Kindergarten children who were able to read stayed in school longer than the traditional half-day in order to join a unit with older children of the same achievement level. Because none of the other district schools offered this program, the superintendent's office saw it as creating inconsistency within the district. A committee of principals in the district agreed, and in spite of the belief of Kennedy's teachers and principal that the program was a successful element of the school, it was dropped.

In another example of mandated consistency, the district required that all schools use the same reading program to ensure that students who transferred from one school to another experienced little discontinuity in reading. Most of the teachers at Kennedy objected to adopting a reading series which they believed did not allow enough flexibility. Teachers talked about their professional responsibility to decide what text materials were most appropriate. When the principal, trying to defend professional prerogative, wrote to the superintendent and to the board of education to protest the requirement, she was told by the superintendent's office that a principal should support district policy and that it was politically unwise for her to go over the superintendent's head by writing to the board. The principal stated to one of the observers, "I learned my lesson."

There were other instances in which the district office pressured the school to give up some of its autonomy in the name of consistency within the district. For example, teachers were told not to introduce instruction in handwriting until the second grade, regardless of the readiness of the children. In another situation, when teachers representing the schools in the district met on a regular basis to choose a single commercial spelling program, several Kennedy teachers objected to the idea and argued that many teachers had successfully developed their own approaches to teaching spelling; why was it necessary for all teachers to use the same books? The answer from the district curriculum coordinator again was "consistency."

The threat to professional autonomy felt by Kennedy teachers is probably genuine. The superintendent, in an interview with two members of our research team, spoke of "lighthouse" objectives—goals toward which all teachers could work—being established for the district. He saw such objectives as the next step beyond the minimal goals then specified for all students. The implication was that greater uniformity in the curriculum would result.

While teachers felt that they could get around the district requirements and retain most, if not all, of their professional prerogatives, the extent to which teacher autonomy had already been eroded was sufficient to chill the enthusiasm of some Kennedy faculty. Pressure from the central administration was a signal to the staff that their efforts to steer a course based on the principles which built the Kennedy traditions would continue to be seen as "inconsistent" with district policy.

## The Demands of Schooling: Teacher "Burnout"

The conflict between the policies of the district administration and the sense of professional autonomy held by Kennedy teachers, as well as the demands required to keep Kennedy "a kid's place," developed into a self-acknowledged "burnout" problem among the teachers. The "burnout" phenomenon was described as an inability of teachers to sustain the level of activity and commitment that had been shown during the early years of the school. The teachers believed that burnout was a result of the high level of cooperation and interaction required to plan and execute the kind of schooling espoused by the staff. One teacher described the problem this way:

The last two years, it was just too much of a hassle getting the teachers together to plan lessons and to plan time to make sure you still cover what the district wants you to cover for each grade level. . . . My unit is just at a point where pretty much everyone is on the same wave length as far as not wanting to . . . do very much that requires a lot of after school meetings or before school meetings. . . . We are just to the point where we are happy doing the least amount of things that require group planning.

In some respects, the decline in the amount of time and energy teachers were willing to commit to the school was related to the high level of commitment originally required to start up the school. Observers were told that the departure of the first principal and a turnover of teachers had made it difficult to maintain the early sense of tradition, values, and climate. The principal noted that several newer teachers recently had to be transferred because they were unwilling to invest the time and energy required at Kennedy.

Efforts to maintain the traditions of Kennedy through in-service programs, teachers reported, had become haphazard. "I've been involved several years with trying to provide in-services for new people coming in," one unit leader explained. "Each year the effort gets less and less. I don't really know why it gets to be less and less; you try to do something and it doesn't come off as effectively as it might. So you have less initiative to try a second time—the last couple of years the in-service [took] place simply within the unit."

Teachers attributed the decline of in-service activity mainly to the central administration's unwillingness to violate the district policy of consistency by spending money on a program that was unique to one school. No funds were set aside for training new teachers in the constructive interpretation of IGE, and the administrative leadership necessary to stimulate an institutional commitment to constructive schooling was lacking. As one unit leader put it, "the people that are in it from the beginning . . . get tired of always being the ones to push it again . . . So finally you just sit back too, which is too bad. You hang on to the things that really mean a lot to you . . . and try to see [that they] happen within your own learning community. I feel it [enthusiasm and drive] needs to come from the top. . . ."

The unit structure required considerable cooperation among teachers within and even across units. The teachers saw themselves spending more and more time trying to conserve what they had built and in working out conflicts with newer staff who were not as strongly committed to the original vision of the school. Instead of using meeting time to generate ideas for curriculum activities, which teachers considered the most exciting and sustaining aspect of their work, energy was drained away by the effort to maintain what had already been achieved.

The frustrations involved in constantly dealing with internal problems and interpersonal conflicts led one teacher who had been with the school from the beginning to request a transfer to another school within the district. She wanted a change of scenery and more personal autonomy, which she believed would come from a self-contained classroom; her desire for autonomy was expressed as a need to be free of constant coordination and interaction with other teachers. In an editorial in a newsletter which went out to the other IGE schools in the area she wrote that

many teachers *are* questioning. Many have burned out and have quit or transferred to other schools. I'm wondering if this could be averted by the recognition of where a particular staff is on the road to IGE. Perhaps a new understanding is needed for teachers who have been involved in IGE for some time, and who basically love the concepts but are beginning to hate the procedures. Or have some of you already done this?

Could we gain something by heeding the popular slogans on light switches brought on by [the] energy shortage? "Turn me off when not in use!"

It can be argued that the particular interpretation given to IGE by the teachers at Kennedy substantially increases the amount of intellectual and social effort required of the staff. The demands that accompany a constructive approach to schooling suggest that teacher burnout may be a serious problem. And at Kennedy in particular, the pressure from the district office for "consistency" make the survival of the school in its present form problematic.

## Conclusions:
## Professional Community, Constructive Schooling, and Social Control

How can we explain the existence of constructive rather than technical schooling at Kennedy? What elements give this style of schooling its coherence and purpose? One method of examination would call attention to those school variables which might influence programming, such as money spent, or the experience or educational levels of the staff. Comparisons of the various schools in our study, however, suggest that these differences are of little or no importance. A second method would focus on the "great person" theory and consider the drive, energy, and charisma of Kennedy's first principal as instrumental in developing constructive schooling. There is evidence that the teachers valued the former principal's leadership. Yet the principals of all of the schools in this study were

dynamic and forceful and had important roles in building the school programs. In each of the schools the dynamics of leadership created a different sense of purpose and different institutional conditions, and responded to different external pressures.

To reach an understanding of constructive schooling, we must consider
the relationship of Kennedy school to its community. This explanation
emerges phenomenologically. It is clear that the style of life and orientation of the community influenced specific patterns of instruction: parents
supported the instructional emphasis on multiple forms of knowledge
and their children's active participation in learning; teachers often took
the backgrounds of students into account when planning programs; children related their own experiences to the programs and, in some instances, took the initiative in determining programs. The relationship
between pedagogical practices and the community can be illuminated by
considering how work, knowledge, and professionalism contribute to social control in a constructive school.

Teachers at Kennedy believed that children learn through active participation in school affairs: students were encouraged to participate in a
variety of class and school activities that emphasized interpersonal skills
and strategies. Work that included plays, music, and art, as well as group
activities in social studies and reading, provided opportunities for children to take personal responsibility, initiative, and control in the instructional setting. This perspective of schoolwork created an expansiveness
and expressiveness in the school's social relations. In contrast, social relations in the technical schools were narrowly constrained by the focus on
the procedures of mastery learning and the hierarchy of skills and information that defined the curriculum.

The pedagogy at Kennedy stressed the ways in which knowledge is
created and principles are established; self-discovery and multiple ways of
knowing were emphasized. Students were offered a range of viewpoints
to social situations, and were expected to consider different kinds of
knowledge as well as different ways of knowing about the same object. It
was assumed that each individual actively constructed and altered knowledge, and was not just a passive receiver of ideas. Knowledge was treated
as permeable and provisional, ideas as tentative and often ambiguous.

The emphasis on students' responsibilities and rights and on personal-
ized knowledge had implications for professionalism in the constructive
school. Teachers exercised control to a large extent by appealing to student interests and by establishing norms of behavior and interaction. The
Kennedy teachers had a diffuse notion of competence, related more to a
developmental theory than to any fixed notion of achievement. Children's
activities were guided by emphasizing behavior appropriate to student

participation and verbal expressiveness, rather than by external forms of control. This is not to say that the teachers were unconcerned with formal academic achievement, but rather that they viewed and evaluated achievement in relationship to the other social and intellectual competencies stressed in the school.

The nature of the relationships between teachers and students also had implications for the nature of teaching itself. The kind and range of the decisions made by teachers at Kennedy were substantively different from those made in the technical schools. Many of the day-to-day choices at Kennedy concerned routines and instructional procedures as they did in the technical schools; however, at Kennedy classroom practices and curriculum choices were often related to a different ideological view of children's intellectual and social growth. The general pedagogical principles of this view resulted in more options for selecting, transmitting, sequencing, and evaluating the curriculum by both students and teachers.

At this point we can begin to relate the social conditions in Kennedy school to the community in which the school is located and to the form of social control posited by this form of schooling. The intellectual and social points of view found in the school are those of that substratum of the middle class represented in the professional occupations (see Bernstein 1977; Gouldner 1979). The societal position of these professionals (psychologists, sociologists, personnel directors, lawyers, and educators, among others) is related to the complex division of labor which has emerged in the last few decades: achieved rather than ascribed status is characteristic of this group. Their achieved status, however, is not derived from "craft" skills or from the ownership of property or capital; it is a result of servicing people through the creation and control of systems of communication. Words are the currency of exchange.

The expansion of this professional substratum has produced demands for a socialization pattern that enables individuals to take advantage of the diverse occupational choices within the group. Its emphasis on interpersonal control encourages facility with language and responsiveness to the subtle nuances of interpersonal situations. These abilities, which are necessary to enter the occupational stratum, are reflected in the flexible roles and ideas found in Kennedy school: knowledge and work are the property of the individual, enabling him or her to establish control in interpersonal relations and to maintain skepticism toward ideas.[1]

1. While skepticism and a reflective relationship with the social world are ideals of the new middle class, those ideals are not always realized (see Gouldner 1979; Popkewitz, Tabachnick, and Zeichner 1979).

The implicit assumption of the professional style of thought and action is derived from the Enlightenment's concept of the rational person. According to this assumption, rational discourse is superior to other styles of thought,[2] and a flexible and reasonable attitude toward words, customs, and traditions enables people to limit the impact of accidents of birth and social circumstances on life. It must be kept in mind, however, that the assumption that rational discourse is potentially liberating is the view of a particular social group—the professionals. While this perspective of rationality and reason enhances the prestige and privileges of the group, uncritical acceptance of that perspective means embracing not only its possibilities but its limitations and pathologies as well.

The language of professional discourse makes certain aspects of the social world visible and comprehensible, but obscures other elements and the particulars of daily life. The language is abstract, complex in construction, and self-reflective. Its flexibility permits different kinds of information to be related and analyzed through the development of generalizations or principles. The language of the middle class as a whole (including the professionals), however, is passive rather than direct; it shifts the focus of responsibility from the person to the object (in parent-effectiveness training, a person does not give a direct order, "You will put your coat on a hanger," but takes the passive voice, "The coat belongs on the hanger). This language structure avoids assigning causality and responsibility, and it abstracts everyday experiences in a way that obscures the meanings of partcular events. As it is applied in constructive schooling, this language, while legitimating the skills and sensibilities of intellectuals, denigrates the creativity, imagination, and craftsmanship entailed in some physical work. Problematic, aesthetic, and integrative elements are also important to the manual activities associated with working on automobiles, making furniture, and welding. The relationship between concept and execution is important in both mental and manual work because of its implications for the way individuals relate to the world in which they live.

By maintaining a form of social control that emphasizes monitoring interpersonal relations and attitudes, constructive schooling may provide a technology that, in fact, decreases the possibilities and options that can be actualized. With knowledge and work defined as the property of individuals, the pedagogic emphasis is upon children exhibiting the attitudes and emotions appropriate to learning; and participation and involvement

2. The idea of rational discourse has, in the past, included aesthetic forms; the contemporary distinction between science and art did not emerge until the 20th century merging of science and commerce (see Nisbet 1976).

are the criteria of performance and achievement; no longer are fixed standards to be used for judging competence, as they are in technical schooling. Children's activities are monitored to assess the underlying attitudes and emotions that give purpose to their intellectual and social activities. The teachers at Kennedy saw no dichotomy between children's social and intellectual development and gave serious attention to regulating and channeling social growth. In consequence, what had previously been private and closed to institutional scrutiny was made public and subject to teacher assessment and control: at Kennedy, all aspects of intellectual and social life were treated as part of the public concern of teaching. Reducing the private space in institutional settings like school can make it harder for an individual to withdraw, even momentarily, and can make norms and expectations more coercive.

Our analysis so far has considered the dynamics of the school-community relationship in terms of the influence of community expectations and norms on constructive school practices. The relationship at Kennedy contained other influences and tensions that must be considered. School district policies on standardization, by implication, limited the diversity of experience available to children. Within the school were teachers whose pedagogical beliefs coincided with those of the school district and conflicted with the dominant, constructive orientation of the school. These contradictory influences made debate, reflection, and controversy important elements in school life.

In saying that Kennedy responded to its community, we must be aware of the complex of competing interests that were involved. The cultural and social values of the neighborhood filtered into the school to give definition to the school mandate; other pressures from the school district competed in establishing the school's purpose and direction. At district curriculum meetings and school unit planning sessions, the conflicting ideologies of consistency and constructivism were articulated: the relationship of the Kennedy program to its neighborhood constituency was countered by the school district's call for consistency. Consistency resonates with broader social beliefs about cost and effectiveness, accountability, and back-to-basics (see the discussion of IGE development in chapter 2).

The relationship of Individually Guided Education to the conditions of constructive schooling can be briefly summarized. The aspects of the IGE program used at Kennedy were those which sustained the knowledge, work, and professionalism of constructive schooling. The unit and team-teaching technologies were employed as devices through which teachers could express school and classroom priorities, and respond to outside pressure for consistency. The Instructional Programming Model was not an integral part of the program; it existed as a symbol of change and effectiveness in the school, but its systems of record keeping and testing were not basic to the teachers' thinking and planning. Records were used to prove to others that skill development was being given explicit attention. The priorities, beliefs, and norms of Kennedy demanded a flexibility and ambiguity of ideas and work that made the Instructional Programming Model appear subsidiary and of minor importance.

The concrete ways in which the interests and orientations of the community and school district were mediated in Kennedy school is one of the major concerns that emerges in our analysis. Our data suggest that these interrelations are important. In the technical school it was evident that the relationship of pedagogy to external factors was significant, but that relationship was suppressed, to some extent, by the emphasis on the procedural aspects of school life. The language and procedures of technical schooling made pedagogical activities seem efficient, objective, and neutral in application. What we see in Kennedy is the confluence of contradictory forces which attempt to define and shape the school. The definition of schooling advocated by the central administration and the technologies of IGE were adapted in relation to the expectations and demands posited by the specific community in which Kennedy is located. Within the school, this adaptation was not without strains and conflicts.

# 6

## The Image of Substance: Illusory Schooling

In analyzing the institutional meanings of Charles Evans and Pierce schools, we discovered a series of anomalies, discontinuities, and contradictions. Much of the action in these schools created an image of rational, controlled, and productive enterprise, and their practices appeared to be governed by a wish to create a positive image: what professionals and parents want and hope for is actually happening. While in a few instances the image represented reality and could be substantiated by observation, in many other instances the image was void.

To a casual observer, activities in these schools conform to expected patterns: teachers print instructions on the chalkboard, plan and direct lessons; evaluate children's behavior, and explain pupils' accomplishments and failures to parents, district administrators, and the community. Visible signs and rituals celebrate the technologies of Individually Guided Education. Seldom, however, do these formal acts seem related to broader curriculum purposes, such as clarifying children's concepts, or to the teaching of skills. This kind of schooling cannot be described as either technical or constructive.

Work and social interaction at Charles Evans and Pierce presented fundamental contradictions. There were facts and subjects to be taught, but the rituals and ceremonies of the formal curriculum were unrelated to this content and therefore could not produce success for most pupils. The

121

social processes of the daily activities, however, did have substantive meaning. Teachers perceived the failure to learn as a result of conditions in the children's lives (broken homes, indifference to academic values, lack of educational readiness), which were believed to make achievement impossible for all but a lucky few. The shortcomings of the schools were attributed to the inadequacies of the poor and minority communities in which the schools were situated.

The label "illusory" applies to both the images and the details of life in these schools—the false impressions created by everyday patterns of activity, and the substantive values represented by these patterns of schooling. The emphasis on community pathology, pedagogy as therapy, and ritual gives these schools meaning different from those of the technical and constructive schools.

The first two sections of this chapter describe the physical environments and everyday activities of Charles Evans and Pierce schools. Then we identify the guiding professional ideology, which emphasized community pathology and cultural inadequacy and was linked to the discrepancies and discontinuities found in school practices. In the following sections we discuss Individually Guided Education as ceremony, curriculum as a form lacking content, and the language of illusions. Finally, parent-school relations are considered. Our discussion will attempt to relate the particular form that Individually Guided Education took in illusory schooling to the social situations in the schools. Our quest is not only to define the conditions of illusory schooling, but also to understand the dynamics that made the use of Individually Guided Education as a reform program a plausible and reasonable activity within these contexts.

## Charles Evans: An Inner City Elementary School

Charles Evans Elementary School is in a low-income area of a large city in the southwestern part of the United States. On three sides, the school is bounded by heavily traveled highways. Across the street at the front of the school are one-story, single-family frame buildings on tiny lots; the age of the homes shows in their sagging porches, but most have been painted recently and only a few show peeling paint. From the back door of the school one looks across asphalt play areas and a grassy playground through a chain link fence to a broad, busy street lined with low commercial buildings—mainly stores and a few warehouses.

Most of the children who attend Charles Evans live on the far side of an interstate highway that bounds one side of the school. Walking under the freeway to this neighborhood, one comes into an area of frame houses that have been converted into apartments and small, one-story buildings in various states of repair.

Surrounding the schoolyard on all sides is a six-foot chain link fence, topped with three or four strands of barbed wire. All school doors and the gates in the fence are locked during the day, forcing visitors to come to a single door.

The exterior of Charles Evans school is painted an institutional green, but inside, in bright contrast, the walls are painted in panels of different colors which are linked by a design of flying birds. Most of the older part of the school building, which was built in 1965, is divided into conventional classrooms that house primary grade units. An open-space instructional area was added in 1973 after the school decided to adopt Individually Guided Education; it houses fourth, fifth, and sixth graders.

Of the approximately 600 children who attend Charles Evans school 98 percent are black, and the remainder are described as Hispanic. Forty-six percent of the children qualify for Title I clothing allowance, and 98 percent qualify for free lunch. The school has an annual "mobility rate" of 27.7 percent, but only 10 percent of the children are absent during an average week. More than 90 percent of the teachers had spent at least two years at Charles Evans at the time the school was observed, but a lenient transfer policy within the school district had permitted a high turnover of teachers until the previous year, when the transfer policy was changed.

Charles Evans had become an IGE school six years earlier, with encouragement from the school district. One of the district staff members who was experienced in IGE had visited the school, described the IGE way of organizing a school for instruction, and presented films which showed the procedures in action. The teachers at Charles Evans then voted to adopt an IGE form of organization. During that year the principal attended several weeks of IGE training, and the following year unit leaders attended a two-week clinic in another school in the district.

To observers the teachers quickly volunteered their feeling of satisfaction with how the Individually Guided Education program had helped to bring order to the school. The principal remembered the early days of his term as a time when he had to deal with chaos and discipline. He and the teachers were proud of the businesslike atmosphere and the relaxed interaction among the children that had developed under IGE.

Teachers at Charles Evans say that IGE means they can organize themselves into teaching groups and are able to plan together. They have created five Instructional Units, each of which is cross-graded and is staffed by three or four teachers who work with from 60 to 100 children. Teachers go on to say that in IGE planning is based on pretest scores of students' skills in reading, language, and math. For instruction in skills, students are grouped within each unit according to ability levels. There is considerable movement of students in the intermediate and upper grades as they travel from homerooms to work groups within the open area;

students walk in lines in a quiet and orderly fashion. In the primary grades there is an attempt to group children homogeneously by classroom, and students do much less moving from class to class. Exceptions occur when groups of primary pupils go to special teachers for remedial instruction in reading, language arts, and math, or for work in special programs to motivate and instruct them in skills.

The day at Charles Evans begins with breakfast in the cafeteria followed by a brief stop at the homeroom for attendance-taking and morning announcements. Pupils in the open teaching area (fourth, fifth, and sixth grades) typically go quickly to homogeneous groups for reading instruction. Teaching stations in the open area are separated by movable bookcases and chalkboards, and the two units in the area are separated by a corridor.

The work that children are directed to do comes mainly from the teacher's manuals of various commercial reading series, or from the teacher's instructions that are provided by commercial programs in math, science, and social studies. Assignments, directions, and questions cover the chalkboards in the open area and the conventional classrooms. Each teacher leads three reading groups, moving from one to the other in turn. In working with a group, a teacher listens as each child reads a story in the reader, correcting mispronounced words or calling on children who raise their hands to correct their classmates. Reading aloud is followed by worksheet exercises that emphasize language usage or word attack skills.

Students return to their homeroom stations briefly at about 11:15 and move immediately to working groups for math. The change is made quickly because textbooks and other teaching materials are stored at appropriate teaching stations. Teachers who work with groups of top achievers in reading are likely to see quite different students following regrouping according to math achievement levels.

After lunch, afternoons are given to social studies or science, with some time kept open for finishing language arts and math assigned in the morning. Work in science and social studies follows a pattern similar to that in reading: students read paragraphs from textbooks, then answer questions written on the chalkboard, on worksheets, or at the end of chapters. At times they copy diagrams from their textbooks and label them.

Special teachers for music, physical education, and the library work with the classes throughout the week. Remedial classes, staffed by teachers who are supported by federal programs under Title I of the Elementary and Secondary Education Act, are also available.

While teachers at Charles Evans expressed satisfaction in the school program, they also indicated widespread disappointment that the scores of intermediate and upper grade students on standardized tests were so low.[1] These scores were below the tenth percentile when compared to national norms in reading and math.

### Pierce School:
### Serving a Low-Income Population in a Small City

Pierce Elementary School is situated in one of the older parts of a small midwestern city. The city is surrounded by gently rolling hills, and a wide, shallow river meanders through the town and the countryside. Leaving the interstate highway to drive to the school, one passes a large shopping mall and enters a business district of two- and three-story shops and small businesses. Pierce school is several blocks to the south of the business district, its back to the river.

The homes within walking distance of Pierce are mainly small, one-story bungalows and two-story frame buildings. Some have been divided into duplexes to accommodate people looking for inexpensive housing. Professional staff in the school commented that 20 or more years ago the area around Pierce was considered the roughest part of the city, but they say it is "much better" today. Most of the homes appear to be fairly well maintained, though a few are in poor repair. The area might be categorized as predominantly lower middleclass. Teachers report that a fair percentage of area families receive welfare of one type or another. Pupils at Pierce school are a racially homogenous group: more than 90 percent are white. Teachers say that "a high percentage" of the pupils come from single-parent homes. Approximately 50 percent of the school population qualifies for free lunches. Of crucial economic importance to the city and to residents in the Pierce attendance area is a giant national corporation's large factory, which employs half of the working parents of Pierce school in its semiskilled production line work.

Pierce school is a big brick rectangle, typical of the schools built before 1930. The building sits on a small knoll, with a large asphalt playground behind it and a grassy area beyond that sweeping down to the river. There are two main floors of separate classrooms, with a cafeteria below. A high central corridor on the main floor has an Instructional Materials Center and a gymnasium at its end. When IGE was first implemented some years ago, a few walls were removed to allow greater flexibility in grouping. Bookcases or sliding walls now divide these large rooms into

---

1. In Phase I of the IGE evaluation of 156 schools (see Appendix B), Charles Evans fifth grade reading and math scores were the lowest. When academic aptitude was taken into account, the actual performance of Charles Evans School within the range of sample schools was at the 47th percentile in reading and at the 46th percentile in mathematics.

separate teaching areas. The walls are plain, and are decorated with student art works.

The teachers in Pierce school spoke proudly of their long history with Individually Guided Education. Some of the staff had worked on early projects of the Wisconsin Research and Development Center from which the current reform program had evolved. Pierce was used as one of several settings for films and other audiovisual materials about the IGE program, and various staff members have served as consultants in program development and implementation to the R and D Center and to school districts. The principal has commented that Pierce's long, highly visible involvement with IGE has produced a dynamic and creative program at the school.

Pierce is organized into four teaching units for kindergarten through sixth grade. Each unit is staffed by four or five teachers and an aide or student teacher, and serves approximately 100 students of several grade levels.

The typical classroom displays student artwork and worksheets and some student writing. Reading assignments and comprehension questions are listed on the chalkboard. Student progress charts hang on the walls. Desks are generally arranged in rows, with a long table indicating a teaching station. In many classrooms, a list of schoolwide objectives is displayed.

A typical day begins with a pledge of allegiance to the flag and a brief "sharing" time. In an effort to increase student contact with the teacher, reading is then scheduled with the homeroom teacher. At the beginning of the school year pupils are grouped by ability into three or four reading units within a homeroom; these remain fairly stable throughout the year. The assignments usually require reading a story from a basal reader, answering questions about it, completing exercises related to reading comprehension, or working with a phonics worksheet. While the pupils work, the teacher moves from group to group. Children in the primary unit who need special help go to the Instructional Materials Center to work with an aide on the Wisconsin Design for Reading Skill Development. Later in the morning children are given an arithmetic assignment, usually involving a few pages of exercises from their textbook.

After lunch, pupils are divided into different ability groups for math and move to different teachers for instruction. The rest of the afternoon is spent on social studies, science, art, music, or physical education, or in study period for completing unfinished assignments.

At the heart of the curriculum is the textbook, an accompanying workbook, and worksheets. Pupils are expected to complete a specific number of materials each year. Supplementary reading or special privileges in the Instructional Materials Center are available for those who finish their work early. Teachers reported that most of the pupils are members of slow groups and frequently do not finish the required grade level materials. Few children, though, are retained from one grade level to the next, even when their work indicates a lack of understanding and an inability to complete the materials designated for their grade level.

In talking about the school, Pierce teachers acknowledged their students' poor results on standardized tests of achievement.[2] They believed, however, that the school program provides the best educational experience possible, and that their pupils were working to the best of their abilities. The teachers added that the school provided an orderly day that was important for these children.

### Teacher Ideology: Pathology and Cultural Inadequacy

How did teachers in the Pierce and Charles Evans schools see the problem of teaching? What conceptions of knowledge and of learners did they bring to the practices of schooling? How did they define the mandate of schooling? In the technical schools the prevailing belief seemed to be that teaching involves uncovering student deficiencies in skills and implementing an instructional system to correct those deficiencies; the language of individualization, children's needs, and continuous progress expressed these beliefs. In the illusory schools, teachers were pessimistic, not sure they could overcome children's learning deficiencies; no technical or professional skill could make up for such "social defects" as uncaring homes and cultural indifference to academic values. The ideology of professional practice that emerges in the illusory schools is one of social pathology—a belief in the cultural inadequacy of the children who attend these schools. The knowledge and work transmitted in these schools is related to this view of social pathology.

Professionals in both Pierce and Charles Evans schools made frequent references to the unstable and unsupportive home lives of their pupils. Both schools are situated in communities regarded as "difficult" by their staffs: Pierce enrolls mainly pupils from white, low-income families, a number of whom receive welfare assistance; Charles Evans enrolls children of low-income black families whose economic position is even less secure. With few exceptions, teachers in the two schools generally believed that achievement at a "normal" rate was possible for only a few of their students. To teachers and principals alike, these communities were

2. In Phase I of the IGE evaluation of 156 schools, the Pierce fifth grade reading score was at the 41st percentile, and math scores were at the 30th percentile. When academic aptitude was taken into account, the actual performance of Pierce was at the 47th percentile in reading and the 46th percentile in mathematics.

characterized by poverty, broken homes, and a class culture that is indifferent or hostile to academic values and which creates social conditions that prevent pupils from learning. Whether or not these perceived conditions are realities, the professionals in the schools believe that they are.

At Pierce school, the awareness of a "poverty of culture" infused professional discussions and practices in a variety of situations. Discussions about grouping and achievement, for example, were framed not only around notions of ability or actual performance, but also around the social characteristics of the children. When talking about how Pierce school differs from other schools in the city, teachers mentioned home situations that left many children without supervision and without the kind of interaction with adults needed for success in school. One Pierce teacher continually returned to the need to adjust teaching to the students' lack of experience in "self-control" and in conforming to limits set by others:

Teacher: In this building children tend to be a little unstable. They don't come from the same type of an environment that the children do in some of our other schools in the school district. There are more stable buildings than this one . . .
Observer: What do you mean by stable?
Teacher: I mean this is an extremely active group of children. They have not been required in the home to sit down for periods of time with their parents for discussions . . . Now I'm not talking about all of our parents. Fortunately we do have a group of families [in which] there is a lot of interaction between the children and the parents, but there's no way of getting around the fact we have a lot of children in this building that are on their own a lot. They're used to being on the move, they're used to making their own decisions, and when they come to the school environment, which is a more structured situation, it's difficult for them. These kids need reassurance—"Yes, you are doing it right"— to try to keep them going and to [help them] develop a different kind of self-direction and independent skills. . . . [They have to learn] to follow a format a little more closely than they do when they're out on the street, for instance. They have to become more aware of time here. And we have to help children become more aware of doing things in specific times.

The perception of social pathology worked its way into the concrete interpretations of children's work at Pierce. As teachers interacted with children who looked and behaved alike, they perceived and treated some children differently than they did others. The teachers' actions were based on awareness of the social/cultural differences among the children rather than on differences in their academic skills and achievements.

Mrs. Q. explains that she really feels sorry for some of the students. They need so much love—"because of their background." "I used to work in a school with well-to-do kids before I came here." Pointing to two children, the teacher continued, "For example, you can tell the difference between those two kids." The children don't seem different to the observer, who asks "Why do you perceive them to be different?" "You can tell they're different by their backgrounds," the teacher replied. "That boy's mother is all mixed up. She's been married three times. He comes to school hungry. And he came to school yesterday on his birthday without a treat. The other girl, you can tell, comes from a good family. She's nicely dressed."

In another Pierce classroom, an observer was offered a similar social interpretation during a classroom lesson: "Diane . . . comes over to me and puts her arm around my shoulder. She says, 'I don't know how to do this.' [I] ask 'What do you usually do if you don't know what to do, Diane?' Diane answers, 'Nuttin'.' The teacher comes over to me and comments, 'Total lack of discipline in the home.' "

The perception of community pathology is also found in the school district in which Pierce is located. In an interview with a curriculum consultant, an observer was told that instability in the students' homes was one of the major problems facing the school district.

In Charles Evans school, where teachers are sensitive to black demands for better schools and more effective programming, they did not talk as much about the social conditions that limit academic performance. Nevertheless, physical characteristics at Evans reminded observers of the special situation at the school. The building was surrounded by barbed wire. Inside, all offices and unused classrooms were locked. The vice-principal fingered through a large mass of keys before he could find the right one to his office, and once inside, he offered an apology for the broken telephone, explaining that there had been a burglary the week before. The principal, when walking with observers to the front steps of the building, carried a key to regain entry. For security, only certain stairways could be used, and some exits were padlocked with chains running through the door handles. A notice on a bulletin board in the teachers' lounge told of the difficulty in educating high school students from the Charles Evans attendance area: "We [the observers] passed the bulletin board where they had an article about the school district setting up minimum competency for students. We asked one of the teachers what happens to the kids who don't meet the minimum standards. We were told they drop out. 'Yes, they drop,' she said; 'now we are giving career awareness for those who drop out.' Career awareness is to tell them what kind of jobs they can get when they drop out."

In discussions with teachers, the belief in social pathology entered into comments about students. Teachers were pessimistic about the prospects of obtaining good academic performances from the children. One teacher told an observer that many children may qualify for a clothing allowance under a federal program if they are from low-income families and also score below the eighteenth percentile on a standardized test of reading and math; the teacher suspected some parents of urging their children to do poorly on the tests so they would continue to get the clothing allowance. The idea that parents and pupils would be sophisticated enough to know when the test would be given and how to manipulate its results did not seem far-fetched to this teacher and several others.

Teachers at Charles Evans school were more sophisticated and sensitive in talking about the strains of poverty than their counterparts at Pierce. They publicly recognized that schools in low-income black communities had not provided a high quality of schooling and that teachers had to take some responsibility for the schooling that was provided. The principal, who is black, spoke of the problem of the school as the inability of the white teachers to relate. The assistant principal, who is also black, described the problem [in these terms]: "The white teacher comes in, isn't familiar with the background of a child, isn't familiar with the way they are handled, that they are aggressive, they curse and so on, and isn't able to deal with that." Understanding of the economic plight of parents was shown by a teacher who spoke about the lack of parent volunteers in the school programs: instead of defining the parents as the problem, this teacher referred to the lack of teacher initiative in involving parents and suggested that "maybe it's us."

While these views were sympathetic to the problems of students and of parents, the sympathy was for victims of the "sick" social conditions that produced unacceptable social behavior. In both schools, a chain of social (rather than pedagogical) explanations emerged to describe why children did not do well.

That outside conditions were perceived as limiting program development created a dilemma for teachers: their status and positions were dependent on their ability to project professional competence, but the everyday world beyond the school presented what were perceived as insurmountable obstacles over which teachers had no control.

In resolving the conflict between the social imperative of teaching the three Rs and the "reality" of insurmountable obstacles, an institutionalized response emerged in Pierce and Charles Evans: an image of professional expertise is projected to confront the view of community pathology. The confrontation serves to establish the idea that professional help can make a difference if the right conditions exist. The Pierce principal discussed the effectiveness of the school's program by comparing one boy's success to his brother's delinquency:

Well, there's a boy whose brother just got back from juvenile detention center. But because the boy knows that he has to master this program, it's a priority. . . . He wanted to prove that he could go even beyond what is expected. The teacher is comfortable, the kid's comfortable, and he'll succeed. But he knows what he's expected to do. It's clear. His mother knows. She loves him. And you know he may make it. I hope so, because he's got some cognitive power he's proud of.

The principal continued the conversation by emphasizing the "poor" situation of the child: "You wouldn't believe his home. . . . He has no father. But he's got some pride in himself because he can do some things. He knows what he can do. I know what he can do."

The principal's viewpoint indicates an ethos of individualism: students who are motivated can succeed because the correct conditions of schooling are already present. "We are going to make students responsible for their own lives, we're not going to blame a student's lack of progress on an alcoholic parent. Success is due to self-image, not home life. I believe the teacher can make the difference."

While accepting the idea that community conditions can influence schooling, teachers affirm the view that those outside conditions can hinder children's work in school. As a result, there is an emphasis on professional competence in the face of what seem to be overwhelming odds. The possibility of success exists only if children in school can overcome the debilitating elements of their home lives. On the other hand, when students fail to achieve their failure can be attributed to community pathology or a lack of individual motivation. Student failure is not seen as the result of the structural qualities and norms of schooling itself.

### Form and Illusion: IGE as Ceremony

A glance at the daily activities of Evans and Pierce schools reveals what one would expect to find in any American school: there are established times for teaching language arts, science, social studies, reading, and mathematics, and children go to the gymnasium for physical education, and have art and music classes. The curriculum at the two schools is given a particular nonconventional form through the technologies of Individually Guided Education. Units, small groups of children, and talk of instructional planning pervade the patterns of school conduct.

Looking more closely at the actions and behaviors in the schools, discrepancies and discontinuities emerge. Rather than engaging in any elaborate grouping or testing practices to determine instructional needs, instruction follows the sequences outlined in whatever teachers' manuals or textbooks are being used. As one probes further, this textbook instruction takes on a ceremonial quality. The nature of that ceremony, however, is different at Charles Evans than it is at Pierce. At Charles Evans, the forms of instruction are observed through the performance of passing out books, writing messages on the chalkboards, and talking about scientific or mathematical learning. At Pierce, a language of illusion permeates the interactions of the school, but the words about schooling have little to do with the actual instruction. In both schools, there is little actual follow-through in the teaching of subject matter. The overall impression of the schools is that of machinery visibly turning, but the movement and clatter of the gears and parts are not quite connected to the product that is claimed to be made.

The discrepancies and discontinuities between the form and the substance of schooling in Charles Evans and Pierce schools appear in the response of these schools to the IGE reform program. In both schools, reform is symbolized in a language that refers to "flexibility," "individualization," "grouping and regrouping," and "testing," and bulletin boards at their entrances announce that these are IGE schools. Yet when we tried to observe the regrouping of children, the implementation of a "systems" approach to curriculum, or the use of evaluation procedures, we were unable to find clear evidence that these schools were doing what they said they were doing.

Both schools reported that one of the central technologies of Individually Guided Education, the Instructional Programming Model (see p. 29), was instrumental to teaching in their institutions. The importance of this central IGE technology was recognized by the principal at Pierce: "Getting to . . . instruction, when you talk about the IPM you are really getting down to the nitty gritty . . . I feel very good about what we've done with the Instructional Programming Model as far as school-wide objectives, broad schoolwide objectives [go] . . . I think we've been pretty daring with the Instructional Programming Model and the skills of learning how to learn." Such public pronouncements, though, were inconsistent with the comments heard and the activities observed in the classroom. Teachers in Charles Evans had identified few objectives to guide teaching. One teacher at Pierce, while acknowledging the existence of objectives, asserted that there were no formal means of evaluation:

About eight years ago we were into a continuum-based curriculum and quite a few elements of IGE. Curriculum was based on continuums with many tests, criterion-referenced testing to key into these continuums. Then over a period of time we [went] back to the textbook-based curriculum, which children today have. . . . Whereas before we had many objectives for each continuum, now we have only four or five for each subject area. Also they are broader in scope. . . . There is no formal evaluation for objectives, and we may take tests from the books, and some teachers prepare materials.

These comments were consistent with the lack of testing observed in classrooms, and may explain why so little regrouping took place. In Pierce school, for example, most pupils moved each morning from a homeroom or home station to another room to join a reading group, usually one of three groups managed by a single teacher. Later in the day the pupils regrouped and moved to rooms or teaching areas within the unit for math instruction in homogeneous groups. Instruction tailored to each individual child was explicitly rejected by the Pierce principal, since, in his judgment, it was beyond the capabilities of the teachers and the resources of the school.

The "logic" of grouping would lead one to expect that the achievement level within each group would be strictly defined, that different assignments would be developed for each group, and that there would be more interaction between teachers and the homogeneous groups. Yet groups existed in which none of these conditions were met. A teacher at Pierce commented that "our groups are pretty stable this year. Regrouping is easiest when you have classes set up back to back. We can't do that much." And an observer at Pierce recorded that

after the teacher left, many students began to talk, so I decided to talk with them about their work. They seemed eager to talk to me. They told me about the spelling test, how hard it was, how many they had missed. Mrs. N. explained to me later that this spelling class was especially difficult to teach because there was such a great variation in the students' ability levels. I asked her if there was some reason why the students hadn't been regrouped, since there was such a wide variation in abilities. She said that she had requested a regrouping but was told to keep the group that she had. Also, her group had the least range of ability levels that could be arranged. She explained that, therefore, she had this spelling group for an entire year.

Groups in Pierce and Charles Evans usually remained stable once they were formed, rather than changing constantly in response to identified pupil needs. A common pattern of instruction emerged: students were assigned to groups, lined up, and moved from teacher to teacher. Each group might include students with a broad range of abilities; often groups that were formed on the basis of different abilities were assigned the same work. The implication that teaching would correspond closely to student abilities or levels of understanding was contradicted by what took place within the groups, as this observed incident at Pierce reveals:

12:15

The teacher takes roll. He says to the students, "I would like to give you two assignments. One: write a summary of what you learned last week about lumbering in the United States. Two: now if you don't want to go the creative route, there is a book here to use. You really have three options. One—review what you've learned. Two—read several chapters and summarize; do it like a book report. Three—read a chapter and answer the questions, especially for those of you who don't feel creative today. Okay, those people who want to use the book. Now I'm not going to let you out without doing anything." Students from the head of each row pass out the texts.

12:55

The period is over and the group leaves.

1:00

The teacher comes over to me, "Unless you want to sit through the same thing twice, you might want to go to another room. This is . . . what we do in social studies and science."

1:03

A new group of students enters and the teachers gives the assignment again. "Okay, you have three options," he begins. He continues with his description of the assignment.

A similar discrepancy occurs at Charles Evans. While one might expect that grouping is done to respond to different learning abilities of children and that groups of fewer students would be alike in ability or learning needs, this is not the case.

2:40

Science for 5th graders. Some students are looking at a science textbook chapter. It is about drug abuse—uppers, downers, and their bad effects. In talking to the students, it becomes clear that they do not know what the chapter is about since they cannot read the words in the text. Other students are busy copying a diagram of a human eye from the textbook. There are labels, but [on questioning] the students [the observer] discovers that they cannot (or will not) say why the labels are there, or how different parts of the eye function.

The principal and teachers at Charles Evans school rarely used the term "Instructional Programming Model" but their classroom practices were similar to those at Pierce. Neither school provided for constant and regular record keeping, an important element of IGE. One teacher at Evans told an observer

IGE begins with the overall school district objectives . . . The whole unit is pretested on the objective[s] and then grouped by ability. Every six weeks this happens again. A few pupils may be grouped differently when the sets of objectives come into play in reading and math, but most pupils tend to stay with the same teachers. "After six weeks of teaching, there is a posttest. Then we all go on to the next objective." The observer asks, "What happens to those who do badly on the posttest?" The teacher replies that these children are taught the same material in a different way. There do not seem to be any children who fit this description who can be observed during the time that the observer is present.

This form of grouping in both schools was related to the organization of instruction around sequences outlined in the textbook manuals used in the classrooms. Much of the formal schoolwork centered around the use of textbooks, textbook series, workbooks, and worksheets. Typically, a lesson began with the teacher asking a few "motivation" questions related to the lesson. A teacher might ask, for example, what a topic sentence is, or what a child would do if he or she were in a forest; then textbooks would be passed out in which students would read a story about a forest or locate topic sentences.

During a math lesson at Pierce, a teacher directed students "to draw three things you would like to buy, then add up how much it would cost you to buy them." The teacher then asked several children to use the workbooks that contained examples similar to the one just given orally. After completing the workbook assignments, some students came to the teacher's desk to have their worksheets corrected. Much time was taken up passing out and collecting books in this classroom. Once students got their books, the patterns of interaction in the class resembled recitation patterns found in the teacher's guide to the textbook.

Some teachers did not follow textbook manuals, but planned schoolwork to enable children to learn information and skills deemed necessary, and to relate what they learned to general ideas in science, social studies, and language arts. This differed from the general pattern of instructional organization and activities at Pierce and Evans schools, which can be briefly summarized. Early in the school year, groups are formed according to norm-referenced tests; these groups remain constant throughout the year. Instruction begins with teachers following the activities suggested in the teacher's manuals that accompany each textbook. The exercises in the teacher's manuals are reproduced in neat handwriting on the chalkboards. Children look at the books, write numerals or words on a sheet of paper or on a worksheet, or copy words or diagrams from textbooks or from the chalkboard. These actions appear to be productive. We will examine the distinguishing activities at each of the illusory schools more closely in the following sections.

### Curriculum without Content: Charles Evans

Looking at the form and context of textbook instruction in Charles Evans school, further discrepancies and contradictions between words and action emerge. While teachers and students went through patterns of behavior associated with reading, spelling, or mathematics lessons, little actual information and few skills seemed to be taught. We can classify the activities of teachers as "not teaching" or "illusory" teaching when the tasks that teachers set for students are independent of what the teachers know about student levels of understanding and ability (giving a child a book she or he cannot read); when teachers make decisions about instruction without taking into account feedback from students about ongoing achievement (the mistakes on tests are not corrected); or when teachers make no effort to explain ideas, to help students to acquire skills, or to guide them in self-instruction and the exploration of knowledge. In such "teaching," the categories of formal subject matter and the rituals of passing out the textbooks become devices to create the illusion that everyone is engaged in the tasks of schooling.

The teachers in Charles Evans school appeared to recognize that many of their students needed special assistance to enable them to achieve well. With the help of Federal Title I aid, the school had established a well-equipped multimedia room for teaching children in need of remedial help. During the two weeks that our observers were in the school, the room was only found in use once:

About 15 sixth grade students have been collected and brought to a room especially equipped for teaching remedial reading. There are cubicles fitted [with] viewers and earphones so that pupils can play tapes and watch cartoon illustrations of a story . . . Title I funds are used to pay for a computerized system in which pupils do exercises related to the cartoon and audio stories and reading tasks. The pupils' responses are mailed to a firm in Chicago, and the analyses of pupil responses are returned in the form of prescription cards, which direct pupils to the next lesson to follow.

As the children come into the room, they take their prescription cards from a folder attached to the wall. Others get manila envelopes stuffed with a workbook and worksheets. About a dozen pupils go to the cubicles where the audiovisual machines are. They listen to stories. Some look at lists of words as these appear on the viewer. . . . Two girls are filling out worksheets as they listen to tapes through earphones and watch cartoons appearing on the viewer.

As I come closer to these two girls it is obvious that the worksheet blanks they are filling in are unrelated to what is on the viewer. One girl asks me if I want to listen. I put on the earphones and hear a story that is different from the one that her worksheet questions are about.

At other times, the remedial room teacher may have kept closer control over use of the equipment. She had a plan for their use, and the pupils seemed knowledgeable and at ease with the materials and the machines. On the occasion observed, however, at least two students had decided by themselves which materials to use:

One of the girls said that she didn't like what her printout prescription card told her to do, so she simply chose a packet that she knew and liked and decided to do that one. Unfortunately, it had been mixed up with other packets, and this pupil seemed to be filling in the blanks at random. Her friend was also filling in worksheet blanks not related to what was being shown on the viewer. Her packet had apparently been mixed up as well.

Earlier, the remedial teacher had told an observer that the computer printouts were not much used in planning the reading program. While the printout identified children's deficiencies and gave prescriptions, the teacher said that she did not find the recommendations accurate for selecting materials.

Similar discrepancies were apparent in the schoolwork observed in other classrooms at Charles Evans. In one room, beautifully even hand-writing covered a portable chalkboard. Several students spent a whole period copying the assignment carefully onto a sheet of paper, while other children played quietly with each other or engaged in other activities. In another classroom, the teacher explained the multiplication of fractions and cancelling; as children tried to work the problems they had been assigned, it was evident that they did not understand the work because their papers were filled with errors. When one child asked for help, the teacher explained again carefully. Children still struggled, and it seemed likely that they were not at all ready for math at this level of difficulty. When one girl was asked, "How many thirds are in one?" she answered, "One?" In another teaching area, children were reading from a textbook written for their grade level about economics in India. The children seemed unable to say what the essay was about and unable to react to any of the concepts in it. It was difficult, if not impossible, for them to read this text. Still, they sat quietly, and by the end of their work time, one child had made a beginning at answering the questions at the end of the chapter by copying the chapter title on a piece of paper.

These observations illustrate how the order, procedures, and mechanics of the classroom tasks had become the paramount values of the formal curriculum at Charles Evans. Instruction was intended to make children look busy and productive. Students were continuously scolded for talking, moving from their seats, or looking up from their books or papers. For the most part, pupils tried to follow the directions of their teachers, but some could not do the work; if they could not do the work, they remained quiet and appeared to be busy. A few children sailed ahead, but most appeared to flounder.

There were teachers and pupils in the school for whom a day meant more than activity without significance. The two teachers who were responsible for kindergarten children at Charles Evans expected their pupils to learn to manage themselves when the teachers were working with other groups. They also expected very young children to learn beginning word recognition skills—skills which were not usually taught until the first grade in this district. In an awards assembly observed at Charles Evans, 23 kindergarten children were given awards because they had made such good progress in beginning reading. This feat was all the more noteworthy because these children were not a special group of high achievers, and because in the same year fourth, fifth, and sixth graders in the school were reading at from four to twelve months below grade level on norm-referenced tests.

In a fifth grade class, there was evidence of teaching that pushed children beyond a routine acquaintance with subject matter:

"What was the main idea of the paragraph?" [the teacher asks.] A child answers. "What was the slogan? Complete sentences please." The teacher helps the child answer by giving her a start: "The man's slogan was . . ." The girl repeats and finishes the sentence. The teacher asks the children to infer from the story, "Why did he say anything? Wouldn't they notice him if he just walked along?" The children answer eagerly. The teacher asks them to relate events in the story to their own experience with the question, "Have you ever heard anyone call out what he is selling?" One child tells about peddlers near her house calling out, "Red wine and watermelons." The teacher laughs but accepts the answer as appropriate.

In this incident, the teacher encouraged children to get the meaning behind the words of a story by interpreting them through their everyday experiences. Such instruction, however, did not represent the general classroom experience at Charles Evans school.

The conventional routines of schooling are apparent in Charles Evans. Attendance is taken; children move to different rooms or work areas; assignments are given and children sit at desks or tables writing away busily. The form of conventional school subject matter also appears. Children study reading, mathematics, social studies, science, and language arts. It *looks* like learning is going on. Work areas are reasonably quiet even when children move in or out. Children don't shout or wrestle on the floor or throw spitballs. If the work that pupils do is not comprehensible to them (copying words that can't be read, writing numerals instead of computing), at least there is the illusion that assignments are being completed and of classroom "productivity." But a link seems to have slipped out of the chain that binds teaching to learning.

### The Language of Illusions: Pierce School

The illusory nature of the school curriculum at Pierce was dramatized by the language used to discuss school curriculum objectives. The principal thought of instructional objectives as a key factor in instructional planning. The work of teachers was to identify and reach a consensus about broad school goals and to translate these goals into more precise lesson objectives. Statements of objectives were prominently displayed in Pierce school. An observer described the display in one room:

The room is a large open space divided into two classrooms, with some bookcases separating the two classes and teachers. In the front of the room there are large cutout letters on the wall saying, "Who's on the right track for spelling?" Underneath that is a sign saying, "Challengers: Who knows nouns and verbs?" Then [the letters spell out] the objectives for each month: September, following directions; October, getting the main idea; November, using supportive detail; January, sequencing ideas and events; and so on.

Upon looking more closely at the curriculum objectives in the school, however, they seem abstract and almost noncommittal about what children would learn. At a staff meeting, the principal distributed a ditto sheet listing schoolwide objectives; the staff was to edit them before incorporating them into a curriculum statement. The unedited objectives included the following main points:

1. Each Pierce learner will demonstrate at least 80% mastery of the attached priority objectives in language arts, math, and media skills.
2. Each Pierce learner will be able to state the following monthly schoolwide comprehension objectives: September, following directions; October, getting the main idea; November, using supportive detail; January, sequencing ideas and events; February, using context clues; March, drawing conclusions; April, inferring and predicting outcomes; May, separating fact and fiction.
3. Each Pierce learner will take part in at least one of the following three programs in order to develop positive skills in getting along with people: (A) hi-ho; (B) tutoring; (C) foreign language tutoring.
4. Each Pierce learner will take part in at least one of the following creative enrichment programs per quarter, to apply skills to life situations: (A) environment; (B) school newspaper, (C) career education; (D) special interest units; (E) schoolwide reading; (F) special resource people; (G) creative art productions; (H) media center enrichment . . .
5. Positive community communication and involvement with Pierce children will be brought about by using special resource people, having children do something for the community, and having special school programs like celebrating Pierce School's 50th anniversary.

Scrutinized closely, these objectives give little information about what a child is actually to learn in school. Most of the objectives are procedural in emphasis: students will take part in this or that, or will achieve 50 percent mastery of something called priority objectives. A priority objective refers to some general category of instruction (following directions or comprehension) and to the ability of the child *to state* the objective: "Each Pierce learner will be able to state the following schoolwide comprehensive objectives. . . ."

The language of objectives at Pierce school possesses a peculiarly opaque quality, as though one is not expected to see through the language to some referent, but rather to find the referent in the language itself. Its

imagery projects harmony and order, but the actual syntax is discon-
nected and vague. These language characteristics emerged in an administrator's explanation of the school program: "Without a doubt it structures
things for the teacher, yet allows . . . flexiblity for the teachers to enrich,
to do certain creative projects even within the realm of the objectives. It
is sort of a self-pacing thing. It doesn't let you get bogged down by one
concept or another. Instead you center your planning around four to five
. . . concepts."

The concepts of flexibility, creativity, and objectives reappeared in
another conversation: "The whole concept [of objectives] is a paradox of
flexibility . . . the objectives are so broad that nobody really understands
the attributes within the objectives and, you know, you've got a problem
if [the objectives] so sterilize education in terms of behavioral concepts
that they don't allow for individual creativity for learning or curiosity—
expanding things within your child."

On examining these passages, it is not at all clear how teachers used
objectives to organize the daily work of the school. How did the flexibility
of objectives affect schooling practices? Were teachers to aim at the
schoolwide objectives, or to follow their own interests? Several comments
suggested that the objectives had been stated so broadly that a teacher
with imagination could justify almost anything as an attempt to achieve
the schoolwide goals.

We can think of the language of objectives, instructional programming,
units, flexibility, and self-pacing as a ceremonial language. It creates an
image of schooling: a vision of efficiency and competent professionals.
After all, if the September objective is "following directions," if schooling
involves a "paradox of flexibility," if signs exist around the school to
proclaim these visions, and if children can repeat the objective of the
month, then schooling may seem to be doing what it is thought to do.

At Pierce, language allowed professionals to substitute the correct
words for actions. A child reciting the correct objective of the month to
the principal was believed to be an example of good education. The
principal saw it this way:

You see, I ask, "How can I support you [the teachers] to bring about better
education?" They'll say, "Would you make sure that you check out the math
objectives?" So, upstairs [when] they have math from 12:15 to 1:15, I make it a
point to get in all 10 rooms and ask five kids their objectives in that hour. They
know I'm coming and they want me to come. . . . I found that three out of five
kids didn't know their objectives, the first time. After that every kid knew the
objective every time.

To a teacher it was "awfully nice to have the principal come in . . . I
simply [gave him] the feedback. Out of 50 kids, 46 kids knew their

objectives. The first time I think there were 38. We were in pretty good shape already. Next go around it went up to 47. And the next time it was 50 out of 50. And I asked some kids that you wouldn't expect to know . . ." The illusory language, the language aimed at creating an image, was aimed at students as well as adults. The language was not just a facade; it had implications for what and how students were taught. In one classroom neatness and orderliness continually emerged as paramount values in the actions of a teacher who washed the chalkboard after each use rather than erasing it; the chalkboard and the ledge for chalk rarely showed a speck of chalkdust. As the children in the class were given their report cards, the conversation focused on the penmanship grades of the group. The teacher commented to the class: "It is very important that what you do appears good and has good penmanship. It has to look good."

Schools are public institutions, and because they must meet demands for public accountability, people in schools create talk that projects images of the importance of their work. The verbal images, however, are almost always ambiguous. Whether one approves of a school's teaching "the basics" should depend upon what the school elects to call "basic." Knowing that a classroom's average achievement in reading is at the sixtieth percentile compared to some national norm does not say whether the test measures what one wants to call achievement. Whether pupils who are engaged in the act of writing are acquiring academic knowledge as they do so depends upon what they are thinking about and why they are writing.

While all institutions generate talk to justify their social arrangements, a particular type of talk occurred in Pierce school to give meaning to the practice of schooling. The professionals engaged in energetic but circular semantic ballets in which language became its own referent. In our analyses of technical and constructive schooling, we found that the language of instruction did refer to the subject matter, skills, and knowledge being taught. This is not often the case in the illusory schools, where the symbols of schooling create illusions about the meaning of activities and events that have little or no actual substance.

The lack of substance in the teaching at Pierce and Charles Evans creates a double edge to the meaning of the illusion in these schools. The first and most obvious is that children participate in what seems to be traditional schooling but most are not being taught its content and skills. Second is that the rituals of classroom life establish a particular relationship between the children of the school and the categories of schooling. By participating in the routines of classes labeled reading, science, mathematics and so on, children are being taught that these categories are central for judging the competence of the individual pupil. Yet most children may be taught that they are personally incompetent, while the organizational forms make the content seem available. The content and skills are actually inaccessible to most children. What seemed, initially, a lack of substance, may simply be a different kind of substance.

## Form as Substance:
## The Social Messages of Illusory Schooling

The ceremonies, rituals, and language of Pierce and Charles Evans schools created the illusion that what was expected to happen in schooling actually was happening. That illusion, however, was repeatedly contradicted by patterns of conduct in the schools. But we must recognize that no school practice, however illusory, is without meaning and value; that no form is without substance. In part we argued at the conclusion of the previous section that there was a substantive meaning to the lack of follow-through in the teaching of the formal subject-matter: children were being taught the importance of the formal categories of schooling and their own incompetency in relation to mastery of its content and skills. But the social message of illusory schooling had another quality related to the belief in community pathology.

As we have seen, the objectives that children recited and the focus of classroom discourse in Pierce and Charles Evans schools were only tangentially related to the formal teaching of subject matter. What the processes of instruction reflected was a belief in community pathology— and the need for the schools to enforce morality. In the illusory schools, certain values and behaviors were valued which the children who came to the school did not have. The manners, behaviors, and knowledge that the children brought to school were not valued.

Although optimism about the school mandate pervaded technical and constructive schooling, the staffs in the illusory schools were pessimistic about conventional goals of instruction. The day-to-day activities in the illusory schools gave priority to teaching what were considered the necessary behaviors, self-control, and attitudes, rather than formal schoolwork. It was the social messages in the instructional processes which gave definition to the concept of knowledge and work.

Obedience to school authority was a compelling norm that guided classroom teaching in these schools. Teachers were quick to construe students talking or moving about without permission as the beginnings of disobedience. Typically, according to an observer at Pierce, a sharply worded directive kept pupils in line: "As a group of students enter the room and sit down many begin talking to each other. The teacher turns to them. 'This group is much too noisy,' she says somewhat harshly. She turns back to some of the things on her desk. Several seconds later she turns again to the children and says, 'I have a feeling I was talking to myself.' Then she walks to the front of the room to give direction to [classroom activities]."

Physical coercion or its threat was a means for enforcing control and obedience. In at least one situation a teacher at Pierce was observed shaking a student roughly, and at Charles Evans a paddle was available for children who misbehaved. As children entered in the morning a teacher commented, "If you're not quiet, you'll get three." Another teacher, who had been nagging, scolding, threatening punishment all morning, threatened to use the paddle, saying, "If you go on talking, you can talk to this." The sound of the paddle smacking a child was heard.

Technology was also used to maintain control and order. On one occasion the television at Charles Evans was employed as an "electronic sedator" for children in an upper-grade class who had completed their work and others who were returning to or leaving the area as lunch time approached. When a child asked if he could turn on the television, the teacher responded that it was a good idea but that

12:02

"no one is to be talking. Everyone turn around." The lights are dimmed in this area as the TV comes on. The screen shows Guatemalans cutting bananas and loading them on a boat. A narrator says, "The provision of medical services tends to undermine the Indians' faith in magical meanings," and continues with similar opaque abstractions. The narrator introduces a professor of anthropology who lectures for several minutes about the culture of poverty. The teacher says, "Just let your mind rest," to those children who are talking to one another in the room.

12:14

The program ends with the reading of a poem about "negritude" by an African poet, "For love is black, joy is black, the air is black." Several children stare at the TV, but they do not seem to be participating in any noticeable way.

12:15

A new program, "Electric Company," comes onto the TV. Very lively performers, loud and funny. Pupils continue to watch solemnly without sound or smile. "Adventures of Letterman" tells about a person who changes his name from Wetterman, when he gets into a wet rage, [to] . . . Betterman. As the performers on TV go from word to word (e.g., web, wed) the pupils say the words after the TV. Many seem now to be involved and participating with the program.

12:30

As children respond by laughing at a particularly funny incident, the teacher glances at the clock and announces, "Time to line up for lunch." The TV is turned off and children line up and leave, breaking abruptly their focused attention.

While the children exhibited a number of different reactions to the television programs, their responses seemed unrelated to any formal instructional purpose. The pedagogical intent was perhaps summarized by the teacher's comment, "Just let your mind rest."

The emphasis on obedience to conventional rules and acquiescence gave structure to the lessons in the classroom. A reading lesson at Pierce, for example, by stressing the mechanics of the task, required consistent behavior on the part of all those involved. To stray from the procedures was to receive an immediate demand for conformity:

The teacher calls on Jerry to read. "Jerry, would you stand up and read, please." Jerry gets up from his seat. The teacher asks Jerry's partner for his book so that she can follow along. Jerry stands and reads from a list of words at the end of the book, somewhat hesitatingly. "Thank you Jerry," she says, "please sit down." "Della, would you read," she says. As Della begins to read another list of words, Jerry whispers a bit with his partner. Without looking [at] Jerry, the teacher says, "Jerry, you may go to the quiet room, please." He gets up and goes to the closet in the corner. Another child whispers. The teacher says, "John, go outside, please." And then, "Della, please continue." The boy immediately goes outside. Della reads her list of words. This format continues for about 15 minutes.

The work pattern during an art lesson at Evans also stressed conformity. Children were to cut out pieces of paper that had been predesigned to give the shape of pilgrims.

The teacher introduces a two-part art project, making male and female pilgrim figures. "The first part of the lesson," she says, "is not art, it's just following directions. What we end up with is all the same so we can't consider that art. The second part, however, is art because everyone in the class will draw their own face." The teacher demonstrates cutting the pilgrim figure from a large piece of paper, speaking as she cuts and describing each part of the process. The teacher tapes the project on the board for display and asks the students to rearrange the tables with several [students] sitting at a desk. All the students then fold the paper, and the teacher begins the demonstration again, explaining how to hold the paper if you are left-handed or right-handed. . . . About a half-hour later . . . the students have completed their cutting and they start coloring the faces.

Faced with perceived difficulties of community life and cultural pathologies, teachers at Charles Evans thought that Individually Guided Education provided technologies that could give greater organizational control over children from the inner city. One teacher told an observer that the IGE program was "good for inner-city children. They are not stable—they move around a lot, and it allows you to test them and know where they are." The principal recounted how he had come to the school at a time when there had been a good deal of student misbehavior and teacher mobility. The introduction of the unitized structure had helped, he believed, to create a more secure and orderly place.

The emphasis in the illusory schools on rules to be obeyed should be considered more closely. To establish a rule is also to express a tacit message about what values should underlie the structure of control. The rules of illusory schooling are not what we might associate with the conventional "management skills" or discipline children should learn in order to master formal schoolwork. In the technical and constructive schools, teachers expected everyone to know how to act to accomplish their work, even though they might need reminders. In the illusory schools, teachers believed that children did not know how to act, and that the first task of schooling was to establish the behavior necessary for schooling. The social process of instruction in the illusory schools emphasized values related to the children's character formation, such as cooperation, hard work, respect for property, and the delay of gratification. Teachers perceive these behavioral and attitudinal characteristics as lacking in the children's home environment. At Pierce school teachers and a guidance counselor developed a motivation program to help children learn to get along with each other.

Both social values to be accepted and those to be rejected were dealt with. In a primary class sharing period at Pierce, when the teacher asked "What don't we tell in sharing time?" a student responded, "About people getting drunk or breaking windows and things like that."

Some of the value teaching at the illusory schools entailed more positive symbols. At Charles Evans, the entire school assembled for an awards ceremony to celebrate the obedience and willing assistance of children from all grades. The distribution of certificates of good performance was punctuated by singing, dancing, and dramatics.

A child goes to the microphone and calls the assembly to order. He asks for the children to sing "America the Beautiful." The children sing and then say the Pledge of Allegiance. A teacher comes to the microphone to lead "silent" prayer (which consists of words, "Lord, help us follow thy way," etc.). A group of children sing and act out the song "Happy Feeling."

Awards are given for perfect attendance; five children get them. Awards are given for good conduct; two children get them. Helper awards are given; five children get them. These are all in the pre-kindergarten unit 1. All applaud when the awards are given. Two boys near me, one in third grade and the other in second grade, tell me they are not getting awards this time. They did at the last assembly. They liked getting the awards. They say awards are for being at school, being good, and helping. The most important thing about school, they say, is learning. They want to learn to read and write.

Twenty-three children in unit I kindergarten receive awards for "Achievement in Reading." All have started vocabulary for first grade reading. In addition, three get awards for letter recognition. Awards are also given for perfect attendance to 16 of the pupils.

Four pupils in unit II are given helper awards for "teacher cleanup helper." The teacher says, "Two students have improved their behavior. They are really trying." These students get citizenship awards.

A child recites, "A good citizen is quiet, doesn't bother others, doesn't run in the halls, uses good table manners, eats all the food, and is not a litter bug." There is applause.

The principal congratulates the winners of awards for attendance, citizenship, and scholarship. He asks those who did not get awards to raise their hands. He gives them "an award" for being a good audience. He asks the award winners to applaud them.

The character traits publicly rewarded in the school assembly reflected a deep-seated belief among the professionals that schooling is an "objective" institution in which success or failure is determined by an individual's motivation and ability. As the principal of Pierce school commented, all his teachers were good and the individual who was motivated would overcome the debilitating effects of the community. This same ideology is expressed in a lesson at Charles Evans which, at least outwardly, seems concerned with writing outlines. The initiation sequence of the lesson, however, lasts longer than the period for writing and, as it unfolds, a completely different purpose emerged—to establish certain values toward schooling.

Teacher: What bores you in school?
Pupil: Tests.
Teacher: Now wait. Don't say something fictitious. (Teacher talks about how this is poor response. Need to like test so others can evaluate you. Not enough to say don't like tests.)
Kids try to say some teachers are not fair. Teacher won't accept. Points out that teacher may be justified by poor classroom behavior and the poor behavior was really the cause of the teacher's "unfairness." He writes "Poor Classroom Behavior" on board as part of outline of students' pet peeves.

The teacher's comments seek to impose three types of values upon the children: (a) school practices are appropriate and should be accepted (valued) by the children ("children need the tests"); (b) children should use the evaluative criteria of schooling as a way of evaluating themselves; (c) problems which children define as the school's ("teachers are not fair") should instead be considered as the problem of the children themselves ("poor classroom behaviors"). The children's interpretations are disregarded and the teacher imposes definitions which establish the benevolence of institutional arrangements and inadequacies of the children's actions.

The processes that emphasized obedience and social values affected children differently. Some children acquiesced, as did the child who responded to a question about the school-wide objective for the month:

I asked four children if they can tell me their objectives for the day. None of them were able. Finally one girl said, "Hand my work in on time." I challenged her that this is probably her objective for every day. She agrees.

In another class, children respond to a teacher's question about their work with a similar internalization of expectation and value:

Teacher: I'm going to give you some problems to work on paper. What will you do when you get the paper?
Students: Work quietly. (They answered almost in chorus.)

Approximately 10 percent of the students at Charles Evans school were usually rewarded for being high academic achievers. Some also received rewards for internalizing the norms of behavior that others had failed to accept. Award winners were living reminders to others in the school and to people outside the school that learning was taking place. At Charles Evans, students whose work was at or above grade level were selected by teachers to join the "Listeners and Learners." The rewards of membership in this group included trips to plays and concerts, visits to interesting places, and recognition by classmates and parents as high achievers.

A curious anomaly was created when one child, who was chosen by her teacher to be a Listener and Learner, found out that she could not join because she was also eligible for the school remedial program. An observer reported the painful consequence:

One of the first graders has squeezed herself against the wall and looks away from her teacher. She is crying and angrily refuses to go to one of the remedial teachers when her classroom teacher asks her to do so. The teacher explains to [the observer] that she was a very good worker, very independent, that is, she was able to follow directions well and complete her assigned work easily. She was selected to be in Listeners and Learners. Her standardized test scores were low enough, however, to qualify her for special help in reading and math. The principal insisted that she could not participate both in the school's program for academically capable children and the federal remedial program. Her teacher decided the remedial help was more crucial. The teacher seems to sympathize with the child's distress, and she (the teacher) is upset that what she felt was best for the child has turned her from an acquiescent and productive student into a sullen, resistant one.

The principal at Charles Evans school explicitly identified Listeners and Learners as a way of recognizing academic achievers, and insisted that conforming classroom behavior was not a criterion for selection. It is very likely, however, that conforming behavior did enter into a teacher's judgment of "above grade level" achievement. As a result, members of the club were likely to represent students who internalized approved norms of behavior (hard work, cooperation) as well as academic achievement.

To summarize, a distinction exists between curriculum as the formal subject matter of schooling and the "curriculum" of social processes at Pierce and Charles Evans schools. The formal curriculum at these schools is a ritual involving little follow-through or substantive work, although, as we argued in the previous section, the rituals of teaching the formal subject-matter may have significance in what children are taught about the relationship of school knowledge and themselves. The social processes of instruction, however, do yield other social values and meaning: the acquiescence to external authority, respect for property, delayed gratification, and hard work required of a moral person are emphasized. Often the image of the school as an institution conveying moral values is juxtaposed to the community and children's homes to indicate the benevolence of institutional arrangements and the inadequacies of the home environment.

### School District, Community, and the Ceremonies of Schooling

The relations of the illusory schools to their students' parents and to the school districts were subtle and contradictory. While our data collection procedures focused upon the schools and limited our researchers' involvement with external agencies, certain district and state policies and practices emerged and were identified as factors that influenced and legitimated the illusory quality of schooling. Many activities undertaken by the school staffs were viewed as public relations efforts in response to pressures for change and increased efficiency; their purpose was to convince parents that the schooling was efficient and benevolent.

The "school-community relations" component of the IGE model is intended to increase parent participation in and understanding of the reform program. In the illusory schools, however, school-community activities had a more specific meaning: parents' interactions with professionals functioned both to legitimate school practices and to separate professionals in the school from parents in the community.

The consequences of school-parent relations were more apparent at Pierce school than at Charles Evans, possibly because the staff at Pierce was more practiced in using the special language of Individually Guided Education, which has its own code words for professional authority and legitimacy. It may also be possible that the social dynamics of an inner city community create a gulf between residents and the professional members of any official institution, so that any separation of the two groups is evident even if the professionals use relatively direct and transparent language.

Parents were invited to Pierce Elementary School on special days to enlist their support in carrying out the school objectives. While comments and opinions were invited, parents were expected to respond to the professionals' agenda. That many, if not most, parents accepted this as reasonable was evidenced by occasional statements, such as one parent's comment that "teacher-parent communication at Pierce is excellent," and by the high level of participation by parents in teacher-parent discussions sponsored by the school.

In one such discussion, parents were asked to give their ideas about values and values education at home and at school. An observer reported the exchange:

Teacher: I think that respect is an important value for children to acquire.
Parent 1: Yes, respect. I would say in addition something that I heard the other day. I thought it really captured a lot of the values that are important to me. It went like this: "Don't hurt yourself, don't hurt others, and don't hurt things."
Teacher: Yes, but that's very general. [Observer: said in very much of a "teacher" tone; the parent seems somewhat taken aback.]
Parent 2: Well, maybe, don't hurt yourself by being lazy.
Parent 5: Or don't hurt yourself by being dishonest.
Parent 4: In reference to things, I would say, don't hurt yourself by breaking your toys.
Teacher: I think we're really answering question two, and we haven't answered question one yet. I'd like to go back to question one: What values do you feel are important for your children to acquire?
Parent 1: Well, one big thing is to respect older people.
Teacher: It seems we're bogged down by the word "values."
Parent 1: Well, honesty, truthfulness. Those are values. [Observer: seems to be getting a little uneasy.]
Teacher: OK. Now, question two, how do you do it? What methods are used in your home to impart the values you feel are important?

It is only after the parents agreed to the school priorities that their contributions were accepted. Parent comments seemed to be "heard" only when they filled in a picture outlined in advance. A few teachers encouraged parents to contribute directly to the curriculum planned for their pupils. In most interactions between professionals and nonprofessionals, the professionals apparently found it necessary to seem to share decisions with parents while attempting to maintain control.

Closer scrutiny of the dialogue between teachers and parents at Pierce reveals that the emphasis continually shifted to behavioral norms and attitudes that the teachers wanted parents to accept as morally appropriate and, if possible, to enforce in their homes. In one teacher-parent discussion group, the teacher defined the issue to be discussed as permissiveness. The discussion began with a question about what signs parents interpreted as permissiveness in our society. The discussion ended with parents defining permissiveness as "lack of discipline" and deciding that "the source of permissiveness is in the home and [that permissiveness is] transferred to the school." Another group, referring to responsibility in the home, stated that "responsibility begins when children are very young and put their toys in the box." In still another group, parents talked about what disciplinary measure should be used at home and in school:

One of the parents in this group suggested, and others nodded agreement, that discipline should be not just standing the child in a corner, but standing the two children who were fighting together in the corner with their hands around each other. A disciplinary measure which most parents didn't agree with was that of taking away meals, but taking away treats was [seen as] a good idea. There was consensus among parents that they wanted to be informed about any disciplinary problems at school. They also felt that the whole class should not be disciplined when only a few were causing the problem. The group wanted a program for self-awareness; [there was] a suggestion that this would be helpful so that people [wouldn't] take out their frustrations on others.

The teacher brought the meeting to a close, thanking all the parents for coming and encouraging their feedback and further communication.

While thanking the parents for their "feedback" and "communication," the teachers were in fact directing specific messages to the parents about what norms of behavior and etiquette they expected both from the parents and their children. The discourse might be viewed as a mechanism by which the school projected the ideology of pathology onto parents, and through which the parents seemingly internalized the ideology. The mechanism is subtle: questions are framed that allude to the debilitating qualities of the home and the need for parents to change their ways if schooling is to be successful.

It was clear in later interactions at Pierce that not all parents accepted the problems as they were defined by the school. The principal recognized that "there are some parents who are very unhappy with where their students are in reading and math." However, he was optimistic that with proper "communications" these parents would come to understand the school program better. The principal justified his efforts to have parents accept the school's objectives by saying that "society is forcing us by pushing us to be accountable."

The use of the illusory language to separate teachers from the community also legitimated the actions of professionals. Language became a referent for teachers who needed to believe that they were competently fulfilling the mandate of schooling. A teacher at Pierce school was explicit about ways objectives establish the reasonableness of what occurs in his school, for the parents as well as for pupils:

Parent: Do you find writing the objectives captured all the important things you wanted to capture?

Teacher: No, that doesn't mean that's all you'll teach. That just makes you aware of the things that you really should hit. . . . It just means that we have focused on some things. Parents are aware of them. Kids are aware of them. And kids are saying, "I have to learn how to add. I have to learn how to subtract." It's making kids more conscious of what they're working on. It's just a way of getting people—parents, kids, and teachers—to agree on what we're trying to get across.

The relationship of professionals to parents at Charles Evans Elementary School was different in quality from that at Pierce. An official effort was made to bring parents into the school on a regular basis, rather than on special days under carefully controlled conditions. An attractive room, furnished with comfortable chairs and tables that could accommodate small discussion groups, was set aside for the use of parents. However, the room stood empty most of the time, except when teachers used it. Professionals said they were disappointed by the lack of parental response to school invitations, but there may have been some feeling of relief mixed with the disappointment. Most of the black teachers and some of the white teachers seemed to understand how difficult it was for parents to come to school during the day, and little blame was placed on parents for their lack of participation. The symbols of welcome and reaching out appeared to be contradicted, however, by the barbed wire and locked doors.

In considering the variety of policies and practice that affected Charles Evans and Pierce schools, we find both active and passive forms of legitimation. These involve school and district emphases upon "public relations" to gain community acceptance of school programs, and district and state policies and practices that emphasize the "surface" aspects of schooling. All forms of legitimation, however, shifted attention from what was actually occurring to the illusions—to what people believed should be occurring. At Charles Evans and Pierce schools, the focus of school accountability was deflected by public relations from what was done to what was said.

The role of public relations in school legitimacy was illustrated by the ceremonial uses of IGE at Charles Evans and Pierce. Professionals viewed the technologies of IGE as part of the way the schools expressed their relations to their communities. District administrators and school principals talked about the pressures placed on the school by the public— pressure to improve reading and mathematics achievement scores, and to create rational, efficient organizations. In response to these demands, IGE technologies provided parents with information such as objectives and test scores that enabled them to feel that they knew what was going on in the schools. A district elementary school coordinator commented:

I am a great one for PR. I think parents are very important in education and I think we have to keep them informed as to what we are doing with their children. I think as long as they know, they are going to be happy. But I think once we start trying to get sneaky with them, this is when we get the uproars.
Observer: Are you thinking of something in particular when you say that?
Coordinator: Well, I just think they want to know what is going on as a taxpayer, myself having two children in public school system. I feel I want to know what is going on as a parent. . . . We say we go for 80 percent mastery, say of five objectives at third grade. You have five raw objectives, knowing multiplication facts; recognize a half, a third, a quarter, and [other] fractions; and tell time to the five-minute interval.

Teachers and principals at Pierce school used the IGE program to relieve pressure from different groups within and outside education. This political use of the program was succinctly described by the Pierce principal: "The central office bends from political influence more than it used to. An example of this is special education. They like IGE because the kids can mainstream, yet get extra help. Another example is the high achievers. People like it [IGE] because kids can go as fast as they want." At other times, the principal talked about how the board of education had passed a resolution supporting the IGE philosophy because its objective-based curriculum helped to respond to the parental push for the "back-to-basics" and minimum competency standards.

Other educational practices also helped to create acquiescence to the illusory quality of schooling. These emphasized the surface aspects of schooling, projecting rationality and consistency in the formal structure while ignoring underlying rules and implications. The rituals of record keeping and precise curriculum organization were maintained, but the school districts did not allocate the money to hire personnel for implementing the IGE instructional program. The form became a substitute for the practice. An observer in a math class at Charles Evans reported that "the teacher went to each kid to help and check answers. When I began helping, it was apparent that even two of us could not help each child on all of the problems during a class period. I talked with the teacher about aides for the classroom. There were no paid aides available for assisting teachers in record keeping or classroom work."

The principal of Charles Evans commented that he felt depressed by contradictory districtwide policies regarding goals of instruction and staffing ratios, and by district central office expectations for pupil achievement that were not appropriate for particular pupils. Some pupils could not read the science textbook that the central office had purchased in quantity for their grade level. Such contradictions, the principal reflected, were of little interest to school district bureaucrats accounting for costs, seeking organizational consistency, and attempting an "equal" assignment of resources throughout a district.

The practices of state departments of public instruction may also focus attention on ceremonial aspects of schooling. In Pierce school, for example, teachers talked about a state-administered survey intended to "probe the depth of knowledge the staffs had about IGE." The principal considered how the survey directed attention to the appearance rather than the substance of the program: "It calls for more homeroom accountability; I prefer productivity, but the school board isn't interested in that."

School district policies and practices in providing special remedial programs may also help to maintain the illusory quality of schooling by treating remediation as ritual and ceremony. Both the Charles Evans and Pierce school districts employed special teachers to work with low-achieving children, but this help took particular forms. At Pierce, a reading teacher came to the school for an hour and a half a day, and then went to another school. At Charles Evans, students were brought into a special reading room once or twice a week to work on a program created and evaluated a thousand miles away in Chicago. In these schools, remediation meant taking students out of classrooms for special activities. Remedial work was not systematically derived from or integrated into the ongoing life and work in the classroom; remediation was a limited and fragmented effort that failed to consider the total program or milieu of the pupils. Such special help can be viewed as a gesture—necessary, but symbolic all the same.

To summarize, the policies and practices of the schools, school districts, and states appear to accept criteria of program development and evaluation that legitimate the conditions of schooling found in Pierce and Charles Evans. Procedural questions and surface characteristics are used to project institutional competence and benevolence. Public relations efforts serve to establish the superiority of school morality and behavior. While the evidence suggests that practices and policies external to the schools act to legitimate illusory schooling, we realize that these relationships need to be treated more systematically than our data permit.

## Conclusion:
## The Social Predicament and Illusory Schooling

The illusory schools are confronted with a social predicament which the staffs do not perceive to be of their own making. The conventional mental learning of skills and knowledge is thought to be unattainable for most students. Children are seen as deficient because of the debilitating effects of home life and community. Teachers view the children who come to the schools as poorly equipped with the sensibilities, manners, and awarenesses appropriate for learning. Patterns of schoolwork are concerned with learning how to act; the operative conceptions of schoolwork and knowledge emphasize the development of obedience and acquiescence to institutionalized social authority, and acceptance of certain aspects of middleclass culture.

The nature of illusory schooling is illuminated through its discrepancies and contradictions. The organization of instruction and the routines of schoolwork and teaching are often without content. The language of "meeting childrens' needs," of individualization, and of grouping is circular, and becomes questionable when referred to concrete actions. The routines and language forms at Pierce and Charles Evans schools, however, help to project an image of schooling as rational, productive, and competent.

In all schools there are discrepancies between what the schools hope to do, what they think they are doing, and what they actually do. The type and extent of these discrepancies at Pierce and Charles Evans lead us to distinguish between technical and constructive schooling, on the one hand, and illusory schooling on the other. In technical and constructive schooling, the formal categories of the subject matter play a significant role in the organization of schoolwork and knowledge. The integration of content and personalization of knowledge give a particular meaning to constructive schooling. The fragmentary and hierarchical organization of knowledge, together with precisely specified forms and types of work, provide meaning for technical schooling. In illusory schooling, in contrast, the subject matter objectives that children recite, the emphasis in teachers' conversations, and the norms of classroom discourse create a definition of knowledge and work only tangentially related to any formal curriculum. The messages of the instructional processes in illusory schooling concern community pathology and docile student behavior. The formal curriculum content in these schools is secondary to the institutional purpose of developing a controlled and morally correct student population.

That subject matter is secondary does not mean that illusory school teachers do not value the formal curriculum of elementary schooling.

They do. They state explicitly that it is important for children to learn how to read, to do mathematics, and to be creative and imaginative. The teachers are discouraged by their pupils' poor results on standardized tests of achievement. But they find consolation in the belief that they do the best that they can, that their pupils are working at the upper levels of their abilities, and that school provides a valuable respite from the socially disorganized home lives from which the teachers believe their pupils come. The one goal that the teachers believe they can achieve is to make each school into an orderly, busy place where children are safe, and where they can learn the "right" attitudes and behaviors that will help them as they get older.

The conditions of illusory schooling provide an implicit explanation of why children do not do well. The logic of such schooling might be described in the following way: children in these schools come from broken homes, do not have adequate discipline or the correct attitudes for schoolwork, and have few or no educational materials available to them in the home; these conditions make it difficult or impossible for them to learn properly. To the professionals at the illusory schools, it is irrelevant that most of these conditions are also found in suburban middleclass communities, and that some studies of low-income black children indicate that their environments can be stimulating and intellectually challenging and that their language forms are rich in expression and meaning.[3]

The social predicament that teachers perceive results in something of a siege mentality at Pierce and Charles Evans schools. In response to pressures from school district and community, much professional thought and energy goes into creating an image of schooling that will satisfy critics or deflect adverse criticism of poor achievement in reading, math, and other academic areas. That image is projected by certain symbols that respond to the question, "What do we want parents (or school district administrators) to think about our school?" The symbols generated to answer that question are not the same as those involved in answering questions such as: "What are we doing? How can we tell people what we do?"

At Pierce and Charles Evans, the haze of words and practices symbolic of productivity create an illusion that pre-empts the attention of outsiders. The appearance of schooling responds to the outsiders' expectations: children writing words on paper are learning to spell or are practicing composition; children looking at books are reading; a quiet, orderly school is one in which pupils are acquiring information, pursuing ideas, and improving their academic skills.

The symbols of productivity and success acquire greater potency and are more easily accepted in the communities because they are legitimated

---

3. See, for example, Labov (1972) and Brice-Heath (in progress).

by professionals in the schools. Edelman (1977) has commented on the use of language to reassure people that government is accomplishing what its supporters expect: "Everyone is susceptible to that symbolization and socialization; popular talk, recurring political rhetoric, and sophisticated political theorizing all reflect it" (p. 143). Edelman points out that most people are unable to free themselves from background assumptions about capacities and motives. These taken-for-granted assumptions color observations and make it difficult to see "the worlds people inhabit in their everyday lives. . . . With such suspension of background assumptions, an observer begins to recognize that it is *language* about political events rather than the events themselves that every one experiences; that the unintended consequences of actions and language are often more important than the intended ones and the conventional observation . . . chiefly tell(s) us which symbols are currently powerful, not what 'reality' is" (p. 142).

In schooling, as in government and other institutions, symbolic practices have consequences for professionals: people who talk about individualization, meeting children's needs, curriculum objectives, and school-community relations become convinced that they are talking about reality. They divert their own attention from what actually goes on, or persuade themselves that they are providing the best possible schooling by (for example) repeating the words which describe the technologies of Individually Guided Education. Such technical terms as unitized schooling, criterion-referenced and standardized measures, diagnosis and prescription, and instructional methods create a symbolic system that provides an illusion of productivity, and which relieves pressure on teachers and administrators by producing an appearance of work.

Illusory language also helps to create a distance between professionals and their clients and, in effect, reduces the professionals' responsibilities to their clients. At Pierce and Charles Evans schools, public language serves as a protective screen for both teachers and parents. To some extent, "Kennedy Is a Kid's Place" and the language of "systems of instruction," discussed in previous chapters, serve the same function, but at Pierce and Charles Evans the protective nature of the language is its dominant function.

The illusory schools are not merely inventions of teachers and principals. School district administrators and parents, as well, want to believe that the schools are meeting their responsibilities and that all is educationally well. All surface signs at Charles Evans and Pierce schools point to productive school programs; all participants in the schools, including the pupils, collaborate in the illusion of productivity, appearing to justify the idea that self-discipline and hard work lead to substantial achievement.

While arguing that the daily practices of illusory schooling are characterized by certain assumptions, implications, and consequences, we need to clarify two points. First, examples of technical and constructive teaching methods are found in both illusory schools. But this is not to say that these are the distinguishing institutional conditions of illusory schooling. The sustaining norms, beliefs, and patterns of the illusory schools concern the ideology of pathology, the importance of ritual as a means of creating social cohesion, and the missionary quality of social interactions.

Second, to some extent the ideologies and practices of all six schools that were studied overlap. For example, the classroom activities at Clayburn school contain some illusory qualities: there are occasions on which children in this school engage in the rituals of reading and mathematics without being taught the content of the lessons. Achievement scores are low as well. In contrast to the illusory schools, however, the Clayburn staff is optimistic about the students' abilities to learn from their teachers. The configuration of instructional procedures, patterns of interactions, and norms of discourse at Clayburn add up to technical rather than illusory schooling.

At this point, we can raise a question that we've asked about each form of schooling: What are the principles of authority, legitimacy, and social control of illusory schooling? In earlier chapters we have argued that institutional life maintains forms of social control, and we have challenged the popular belief in a common or standard school by our descriptions of different forms of social control and power that are maintained under the guise of schooling. The significance of illusory schooling lies in its peculiar form of order and control, and how this relates to the schools' social predicaments.

To clarify the nature of control and authority in illusory schooling, we must first consider the ways in which ritual and ceremony create meanings and provide interpretations of social life. Ritual and ceremony are cultural enactments; they induce both moods and metaphysical conceptions that are important in shaping consciousness.[4] The conventions and proprieties that emerge in social intercourse help to define reality and to fuse that world with the products of the imagination. The conventions of schooling, therefore, can be viewed both as ways to help individuals to enact roles and to help them relate to the social order.

Ritual and ceremony are important to all of the schools in this study. Passing out textbooks, taking tests, and playing roles help to maintain the myth of continuity, formal equity, and opportunity within the school setting. They also help to maintain formal authority and respect. The

---

4. See Geertz (1973) and Bernstein (1977:54-66) for discussions of ritual and ceremonies as forms for creating social cohesion and consensus.

children's criticism of lessons in the constructive school, for example, bolstered the authority of the teachers, who could permit or deny such criticism. The rituals of grouping, teaching, and setting precise evaluation criteria in the technical schools provide an image of an efficient community worthy of support by parents, children, and professionals.

The implications of such ritual for the social order beyond the school involve the particular school practices that establish homogeneity and its opposite, differentiation. Standard rituals, accepted by consensus, create an illusion of a unified, nationwide moral system: in all schools, universal patterns of behavior are practiced that enable staff and students to assume that certain universal meanings underlie their experiences. It is believed that in all parts of the country, and in different social and economic communities, teachers and students in schools can talk about recess, English class, or test-taking with common understanding. All schooled people can empathize with each other about these experiences. Even nonschooled people and dropouts understand the potency of the school experience.

This consensus, however, is deceiving. Not everyone has the same experiences or the same degree of success. Within schools there are differentiating rituals and ceremonies that define groups and that award status; where rewards must be limited, schools arrange fair competition for the scarce prizes. The differentiating rituals are tests and grades. The grouping patterns and textbook assignments given in the classroom announce assigned levels of competence. The assumptions underlying such rituals are never verbalized or made explicit, and the rituals themselves obscure the values they transmit and inhibit analysis.

On a broader scale, rituals differentiate schools in different communities according to their potential to compete in the meritocratic system. Differentiating rituals often take the form of compensatory educational programs, discussions about student diversity and individualization, and different learning and teaching styles, although at the same time the myth of schooling as a homogenizing institution is maintained. The rituals of differentiation relieve the pressure for equality of results.

It is through their rituals of differentiation that the significance of illusory schooling and the nature of its social control may be understood. The rituals of the illusory schools may convey three social messages related to consensus and differentiation.

One message concerns the categories of the subject matter of schooling: like children in all schools, students in the illusory schools are taught that there are important and unquestioned categories of knowledge and skills, each with its rules and particular content that must be mastered in order to participate successfully in the social world. The categories that shape school instruction are only some of the possible ways of organizing the knowledge that is available in society. The selection of particular forms of knowledge for schools must be considered as representing interests of particular social groups that have power and status. All children learn that science, social studies, and math are the categorical imperatives of life, and with a few rare exceptions, all children in our culture are expected to appreciate and acknowledge them. The sacred character of certain culturally agreed upon categories of knowledge, and the legitimacy of the experts who generate that knowledge, are among the celebrations of illusory schooling.

A second message conveyed by the differentiating rituals of the illusory schools proclaims that most children in the schools will not succeed in mastering the formal curriculum and in dealing with the categorical imperatives of the larger social world. Inherent in this message is one of the contradictions of illusory schooling: while all are to acknowledge the importance of the sacred categories and their rituals only certain people have access to their rules and systems of meaning, and the children in the illusory schools, on the whole, are not those people. The ideology of community pathology underlying instruction posits that the commonsense world and norms of these children are inadequate and often dysfunctional. Thus the perspective of the illusory school views the institution as competent and the person as incompetent. Student failure is personal, a result of inadequacies of personality or community. The sacred categories of schooling remain sacred and unchallenged—and they remain inaccessible.

The third social message of illusory schooling is conveyed by the emphasis on social control and therapy. This behavioral or "expressive" form of schooling involves obedience to social and moral rules, and awareness of a code of conduct that lies outside the children's cultural experience. That the "other" rules are to be considered superior suggests that the social conditions of the community produce difficult, if not insurmountable, obstacles to success.

The rituals and ceremonies of illusory schooling imply a meritocratic competition in which the few winners deserve to win and the losers deserve to lose. Through these rituals, the schools preserve the vestiges of the social order, and in doing so justify their place in the larger society, even though they provide neither the tangible activities found in technical schooling nor the substance found in constructive schooling.

Illusory schooling represents a form of social consciousness. At one level, the official rhetoric that justifies schoolwork provides an acceptable version of what the school is accomplishing, while it relieves professionals of the burden of continuously reexamining and changing their practices to accomplish the purposes they have agreed upon. At a different level, the emptiness implicit in working hard when there is little to work at, in succeeding only in ritual activities, has a potentially more powerful consequence in the low-income communities such as those that surround Charles Evans and Pierce schools: except for a fortunate few whose abilities will lead them to genuine accomplishment, children will take little from the illusory schools. This schooling offers little to illuminate and improve their daily lives as they become mature people in their communities, to prepare them for further and more demanding schools, or to help them achieve occupational successes that create new life options for them. As the children from these schools grow up and develop their abilities to provide for themselves, they may learn that for them self-discipline means acquiescence to control by others, and that hard work makes them tired. While such knowledge can be the beginning of an awakened social consciousness, it can also lead to self-destructive despair and defeat in the face of harsh social realities.

We can look at the social conditions of illusory schooling from two possibly contradictory perspectives. One emerges from the view of pathology: the two schools provide children with a secure haven from a world that is sometimes dangerous and, it is believed, often unstable; while schools cannot overcome the debilitating aspects of the outside social, economic, and political world, schooling can compensate for it. From a different perspective, illusory schooling serves a mediating function between the rulers and the ruled: through persuasion and consent—not through coercion or force—and through patterns of work and communication, illusory schooling legitimates the moral conduct and direction of will of certain dominant elements in society. While legitimating a particular moral conduct in society, it also reinforces the failure of those in the schools who do not have the social and cultural resources necessary to adopt that conduct.

# 7

## The Social and Political Complexity
## of School Reform

The aim of Individually Guided Education is to create a single organizational and curricular form that is effective in any community or social context. IGE assumes psychological differences among students; the central technologies of the reform program circumscribe the variety of responses that these psychological differences require of teachers. Implicit in the IGE implementation literature are the beliefs that (1) school knowledge should consist of information and skills which can be precisely specified in advance of teaching; (2) information and skills are cumulative and can be arranged in a hierarchy that translates into a temporal series, with the simpler preceding the more complex; and (3) teachers should respond to different learning styles by varying the pace of teaching, the size of student groups, and the material and equipment used to instruct students.

Underlying the reform technologies and the emphasis on individual variation are the assumptions that the reform will make schooling meritocratic, and that each student will progress according to his or her ability regardless of the social conditions from which the child comes. The belief that schooling can be a rational, efficient, and objective response to individual differences is not unique to IGE; it is drawn from broader educational thought about school accountability, curriculum as management, and systems perspectives on school organization (Kliebard 1979). The

161

unique quality of the IGE reform program is that it offers a comprehensive organizational, political, and curricular system that appears to respond to demands for a true meritocracy.

We find, however, that Individually Guided Education neither creates a common or universal condition of schooling nor frees schooling from the constraints of different social conditions. Our data uncover configurations of schooling that respond as much to community and professional interests as they do to students' differing capabilities. In each of the three kinds of schooling we have identified, the use of IGE technologies is shaped by distinct assumptions about teaching, learning, and schooling, and does not provide a consistent and universal mechanism for distinguishing among pupils' psychological traits.

The ways in which a school reform effort responds to different social contexts and predicaments is the focus of this chapter. We ask two questions: What are the salient institutional strains, tensions, and contradictions that create particular conditions of schooling? How does an effort at school reform relate to a school's predicament? In our search for answers, we will reconsider the conceptions of professionalism, work, and knowledge that were maintained in the schools investigated, and re-examine the interplay of occupational imperatives and community interests that shaped the conditions of schooling in which Individually Guided Education was implemented. Initially, we will consider the relationship of professional ideologies and social/cultural patterns in order to illuminate the way pedagogical practices are formed and legitimated. We will go on to clarify the social function of the reform program, examining IGE as part of the ceremony and ritual of schooling. The educational research and development model and its emphasis on individualization as a psychological and procedural element devoid of cultural and social location is then analyzed. Finally we will consider how research and evaluation, as configurations of assumptions, procedures, and concepts, not only fashion findings about schooling, but also articulate judgments about what the social and school worlds should be. Conventional investigative approaches, we will argue, hide conservative implications under the guise of descriptive inquiry. Suggestions are made for developing a more comprehensive perspective on the social and political complexity of schooling and its reform.

## Institutional Variations, Professional Ideologies, and Social/Cultural Factors

Our investigation of six schools that use Individually Guided Education has revealed three institutional configurations, which we have labeled technical, constructive, and illusory.[1] In each of these institutional configurations a different style of work and conception of knowledge were maintained; each required different behaviors and competencies of its students. The observable teaching practices in all of these schools were similar (teachers planned units of instruction for large and small groups, children read textbooks, and tests were used for evaluation), yet these practices were carried on within particular systems of meaning that created different definitions of learning, individualization, teacher accountability, and pupil responsibility. In each kind of institution the content of schooling (such as reading, writing, and mathematics) was related to different purposes, and was developed within different patterns of social relations and authority. And it was also within these social contexts that IGE was implemented and given purpose and meaning. Our use of the three categories of schooling, the reader should be reminded, are meant to suggest family resemblances in which the schools are grouped around complex patterns that point to similarities, overlapping and logically direct and indirect links, yet are not logically similar by having identically determined characteristics.

Conventional descriptions of school programs, school climate, and change tell us that all of the schools investigated were to some degree successful. Each of the schools had similar pupil-staff ratios and instructional expenditures and staffs of similar levels of education and experience. Morale in each of the schools was reported to be high. Principals took active roles in developing and maintaining support for the IGE program at their schools. People in leadership roles outside the six schools thought that the schools had developed successful models of the IGE program and were, by implication, exemplary elementary schools.

This conventional wisdom ignores, however, several important dimensions of schooling: social relations in the schools, the schools' particular definitions of the individual and of learning, and the corresponding principles of authority, legitimacy, and control established for both teachers and students. To explain the variations in the conceptions of knowledge and work found in the schools, we must analyze further the professional ideology that dominated each school, the surrounding community, and the perceptions of the school mandate that guided professionals as they worked to define the school programs. Our data do not permit us to formulate precisely the interaction of elements external to schooling that produce a particular institutional condition. What we can provide is a

1. It is important to distinguish between studies about the initial implementation process of an innovation, such as those of Miles (1980) and Smith and Keith (1971), and this study, which focuses on schools that have gone through the initial processes and are considered models of the reform effort.

description of professional ideologies and of how professionals perceive
the demands of communities, together with some of the contradictions
that develop as a result of these interactions.

The influence of professional ideology on the meaning of the daily activities of schooling is apparent when we compare technical, constructive,
and illusory schooling. Despite the fact that IGE implementation literature includes extensive descriptions of the program's goals and technologies, teachers and principals in the six schools translated the slogan
"individualization" in a way that responded to certain beliefs they already
held about children and learning. In the technical schools, children were
considered deficient with respect to a body of predefined knowledge
and skills. The underlying psychology of learning was behavioristic, and
knowledge was held to exist outside the minds of individuals. Individualization, in technical schooling, was a matter of pacing children
through specific levels of information and skills. In the constructive
school, knowledge was considered to be personal; individualization involved the child in a communicative process that would enable him or her
to exercise control in interpersonal situations. In the illusory schools,
since the children's backgrounds were seen as pathological, the individualized instruction was therapeutic: appropriate social values and behaviors could be sought and acquired, together with those minimal
academic skills that students were able to acquire, given the social constraints under which they were thought to live.

These different professional ideologies defined the appropriate means
by which children were to engage in social relations, comprehend the
world, and improve their social and cultural conditions. The technical
schools' emphasis on procedures and efficiency, for example, standardized knowledge and separated the conception of work from its execution;
this in turn produced fragmented and oversimplified tasks that removed
from the activities of schooling the possibility of creating a self-organized,
self-motivated, and self-renewing community. In contrast, the emphasis
in the constructive school on developing facility with language and responsiveness to the subtle variations of social situations offered practice in
controlling interpersonal relations. This emphasis in communication
skills, however, devalued knowledge related to certain kinds of physical
labor. And finally, the ideology of pathology which permeated illusory
schooling promoted the establishment of a moral basis for the socialization
of children, in which schooling assumed a missionary quality.

These professional ideologies were both sustained by and subjected to
pressures from school districts and state departments of education, and
from the community. One form of pressure has been exerted by the recent movement for public accountability in education. As a result, several
states have imposed criterion-referenced measures to test the range of

skills and information a child has acquired at certain grade levels. The purpose of such tests is to provide professionals with a mechanism to demonstrate publicly their efficiency in meeting certain goals of public education.

The test results of one of the technical schools, in which criterion-referenced measures adopted by the state were given, were printed in the county newspaper along with the results from other schools. The principal continually stressed how important these test scores were to the local school superintendent. Observations of the day-to-day interactions in this school revealed instructional procedures similar in form and content to those of the state tests. In the case of illusory schooling, specific school district and state practices emphasized the surface qualities of school programs and, in doing so, may have legitimated the established school value and authority structures. District administrators supported existing school programs in all but the constructive school, and often identified the schools we studied as models for other schools.

While we can point to different professional ideologies in the schools studied, there appears to have been little open conflict over or discussion of the assumptions, implications, and consequences of the ideologies. Conflict over ideology was found only at Kennedy school, between professionals in the central office (who wanted to standardize curriculum and learning objectives to provide consistency and greater accountability within the district) and the teachers (who believed in a constructivist ideology and wanted to maintain autonomy in curriculum planning and implementation). External pressures for consistency affected the definitions of pedagogy maintained at Kennedy, as teachers had to respond to and in some cases challenge and modify district policies. Among school districts and the other schools of the study a consensus on pedagogical practice seemed to exist; there was only occasional evidence that some teachers were not committed to the existing pedagogical definitions.

As significant as the differences between professional ideologies might be, a second important factor in the definition of schooling was the relationship between ideology and the professionals' perception of the immediate community served by the school. In each of the schools studied, professional ideology was related, in part, to a definition of the kind of student being taught, and each of the three forms of schooling offered different perceptions of students. The sense of what professionals could (and should) accomplish was shaped both by abstract beliefs about schooling and children and by a set of obligations and limitations arising from the professionals' perceptions of their clientele. Professional definitions and descriptions of student populations entailed claims about the children's "needs," and meeting these "needs" was said to be the overall obligation of the school. However, the social characteristics of the children's community were treated by teachers as psychological traits inherent in the individual that constrained the possibilities of schooling. Clear examples of such constraints were found in two quite different schools, Pierce and Kennedy.

At Pierce parents (and consequently their children) were seen by the staff as irresponsible, careless, and socially pathological. This viewpoint placed a great burden on the school. Professionals responded by using disciplinary and therapeutic measures to compensate for what they believed were the unhealthy conditions of family life. At Kennedy, on the other hand, the definition of schooling was constrained by the perception that the children were from homes where parents provided the sensibilities, awarenesses, and skills necessary to achieve in school. Interactions among teachers, parents, and children revealed that, while the teaching of basic skills was valued, the children were perceived as able to learn these skills easily; thus schooling could be devoted to intellectual and social development, which had a different epistemological basis.

The parents in each school studied were seen as having lifestyles, values, and social orientations which called for specific school responses. Staff perceptions of students and parents merged with staff ideology to form patterned responses that shaped the daily life of the school. Their perceptions of students also enabled teachers to classify certain attributes as "good" and others as less desirable.

That professionals perceive pupils as carrying different personal and social characteristics is probably inevitable and not necessarily undesirable. Differences do exist among students, and certainly some differences are a result of the fact that children spend a substantial part of their time among people and in settings outside of school. Relations with families and friends and activities in the neighborhood can be thought of as sources of educational experiences; however, these experiences may or may not enhance the characteristics of the "good pupil" envisioned by the professionals. The problem with the vision, however, is that a school staff defines its mandate in relation to that ideal, often ignoring the actual linguistic competencies, cognition, and reasoning patterns of the children who come to the school. Studies of minority and poor communities, for example, reveal the complexity and richness of the language patterns found among the cultural and social groups within them; but because the expectations engendered by social myth and social manner deny these competencies, schooling may ignore or define as incompetent the experience and thought of children from such communities.[2]

2. For a provocative discussion of class language and ideology, see Bisseret (1979) and Bernstein (1975).

While this discussion might suggest a correspondence between peda-gogical practices and broader social/cultural conditions, such a simple for-mulation would not capture the dynamics of the relationships found in the schools and their communities.[3] These schools are not mirrors which reflect general social conditions in society. The different technical school communities, for example, represent a wide range of social and economic conditions. Clayburn is located in a rural community where most people work in agricultural or low-status service occupations; achievement scores were below the national mean. Maplewood can be characterized as a com-munity of skilled blue-collar workers located in a suburb of a large metro-politan area; achievement scores were above the national mean. In both schools, the technical, functional emphasis of the instructional program appears to be related to the occupations of the children's parents. Yet Belair, the third technical school, which is located in an affluent, busi-ness-oriented community and in which achievement was substantially above national norms, presents a different picture. The style of work and knowledge in this community seems to be related to certain social/cultural beliefs, including community religious beliefs, rather than to the occupations.

A correspondence between pedagogical practices and community so-cial/cultural characteristics is also challenged by the economic similarities between one of the illusory schools (Pierce) and one of the technical schools (Clayburn). The differences in their programs, we can hypothe-size, may be related to geography and to community norms. In Clayburn's rural southern community interactions in the school take place against a background of extended family relations that often go back for generations; in this school, there was a sense of optimism about children's learning. Pierce teachers, in contrast, perceived a community with a tran-sient population that had few neighborhood ties; this perception was reflected in the ideology of pathology that dominated school discourse. In these schools and communities, social class is important, but it is not independent of other dimensions of social/cultural life.

Those who would introduce educational reform measures must recog-nize that their intentions, goals, and technologies are profoundly subject to the specific dynamics affecting a particular institution. Reformers should expect that their programs will be interpreted, modified, and used in accordance with the professional ideologies which are asserted through institutions, as well as in response to conditions outside of institutions. The relationships between professional ideologies, communities, and

3. For discussion of this issue, see Giroux (1981), Wexler (n.d.), and Meyer et al. (1979).

classrooms are neither simple nor direct. They are mediated by signals and pressures exerted by parents, communities, and occupational groups outside the school, as well as by the interactions within the school.

The identification of different institutional configurations of schooling does not suggest that technical, constructive, and illusory schooling are points on a continuum. They are not IGE from most to least, nor are they schooling from best to poorest. They should be considered as configurations that refer to particular conditions of work, knowledge, and professional ideology. At a surface level, each of the schools revealed facets of technical, illusory, and constructive practices. But while specific practices in each of the schools may be isolated and identified, they should not be confused with the interrelated and dynamic elements and social values that are the essence of each of the three institutional configurations. There are crucial differences among these configurations that are found in the interweaving of work, knowledge, and professional ideologies into social patterns that inform teachers and pupils. Finally, it must be recognized that some teachers and children did not fully commit themselves to the patterns of school conduct, but instead were detached from the ongoing flow of events and meanings. These atypical situations, in the course of analysis, proved not to influence the meanings of schooling under consideration. This does not mean, though, that the atypical teacher or child could not be studied in order to understand the points of vulnerability in institutional arrangements.

In considering the different pressures that interact to produce particular kinds of schooling, we need to recognize that schooling gives form to certain social and community interests, and that it is not at all a neutral endeavor. The six schools in this study are distinguished by different styles of thought and action that are passed on to the children as ways of maintaining relationships with the world. In the previous chapters, we have argued that each institutional condition offered different visions of society, rules for individuals establishing relationships with the social world, and principles of legitimacy by which to judge the adequacy of these social relations.

### Reform as a Mechanism of Occupational Legitimation

Having described the reform effort and its effects in the six schools, one might ask, why were professionals willing to accept a reform program which would reorder the ways teachers interact and would pose a threat to the existing social organization? One way of answering is to recognize two altruistic motives: many teachers thought the program would produce better educational experiences for children and more productive professional tasks for themselves. Our analysis, however, also indicates that the reform program responded to the institutional imperatives of stability and legitimacy. To focus solely on teachers' and planners' intentions—on sincerity and the desire to make schools better—would be to gloss over the social functions of reform and obscure the complexities of the schooling.

Another approach to understanding the acceptance of the reform effort is to consider reform as a label with social significance. All reform programs feature rituals, ceremonies, and particular language styles which create a feeling, for both the public and professionals, that things are getting better. The dramaturgy reinforces belief in institutional processes and professional competence; it makes social organizations seem progressive, responsive, and above all, consumer oriented. The ability to generate new symbols of affiliation is important to institutional stability and credibility (see Meyer and Rowan 1977). The regeneration of social commitment is imperative in institutions, like those in our study, in which different outcomes are produced.

To view reform as a legitimating mechanism compels us to consider the function of IGE apart from its impact upon the instructional processes in schooling. The ceremonies of the reform program, such as team teaching or computerized record keeping, can be used to justify and to legitimate a variety of institutional practices, and to provide symbols of credibility by suggesting that the institution is meeting its social mandate.

The legitimating function of reform programs is apparent when we consider the tensions that exist between the school and its outside constituencies. Although schools have a social mandate to "educate," the specific outcomes of schooling cannot be evaluated like the products of a car manufacturer. What the public demands of schooling is generally ambiguous, ambitious, and sometimes heroic: schooling should enable individuals "to compete successfully in the adult world of work," "to be more active and productive citizens," or "to understand the changing and complex world we live in." These expectations provide schools with their social and moral mandate; yet, upon scrutiny, meeting these goals has been more than they have been able to accomplish even with the support of religion, family, and government. The ambiguity of school goals, therefore, creates a need for a general feeling of trust among those outside the institution toward those who must carry out the schools' social mandate.

The tensions between schooling and its outside constituencies are compounded by the belief that schools and other institutions should be efficient—a belief that permeates the fabric of American life and its patterns of conduct (Mumford 1966; Noble 1977). Schools are popularly believed to have specific technologies that can contribute to the efficient fulfillment of their social and moral commitments. In fact, the technologies necessary to create an efficient and rational institution to fulfill such mandates do not exist. Even the technologies of Individually Guided Education, however comprehensively used, can respond to only a limited requirement of the school mandate: the teaching of skills and information. As variations in achievement scores of the six IGE schools indicate, the reform technologies were not always successful or efficient. Belief in the efficiency and rationality of schooling is further complicated by the tension between two schooling functions: schooling's role as a normative, political enterprise, and its role as an industry whose products are clearly defined and physically available.

In addition, what is meant by schooling is not universally agreed upon. Throughout its history, schooling has responded differently to different groups in society. The emergence of social studies as a curriculum field, for example, was meant to provide new immigrants, blacks, and American Indians with the norms, attitudes, and habits that would make them productive workers in American industrial society (Lybarger 1981). Such instances exemplify the belief that schooling requires a differentiated response to the varying social, cultural, and economic circumstances of its clientele. At the same time, the ideal continues to be that of a common school, the same for all classes and groups of people.

One solution to these dilemmas of schooling is to create rituals and ceremonies that produce an image of a rational enterprise. The IGE system of instruction, with its consistent procedures and testing practices, yields an image of schooling in which all participants are treated equally and objectively. The precision of the language used in IGE instruction and evaluation enables teachers and principals to talk about their work in a way that conveys accuracy, rationality, and organization. To be able to demonstrate that 75 percent of the fifth grade has completed Level 25 in mathematics, point to a graph that illustrates this feat, and pull out a folder which contains a child's test scores creates a sense of control and projects an image of competence.

In the schools investigated, IGE's language of precision was used by staff members to convince district administrations and the communities that they were offering better, more progressive ways to educate children. The display of IGE symbols in these schools generated status for the institutions. In the technical schools, professionals considered it significant that the district superintendents viewed their schools as models for others in their districts. The superintendents also saw IGE as one of many districtwide innovations which conveyed to the public a sense of district progressiveness and of the efficient use of tax dollars. The constructive and illusory schools were similarly pointed out as examples of district responses to the professional mandate.

Public and professional support might be considered a well-deserved by-product of school efficiency and accountability. Our data show that the language and ceremonial practices of reform schooling are, in part, political in nature.[4] The imagery they create responds to general social myths about institutional rationality and efficiency; they do not directly refer to the actual knowledge, work, and social values found in the daily life of schooling.

In the schools in this study, the language forms and ceremonies associated with IGE created not only symbolic forms to attract community affiliation, but also a belief among professionals in the coherence and purposefulness of their work. The committee meetings, the curriculum systems, and the record keeping helped to reinforce a sense of accomplishment and esprit de corps among staff members. A survey among professionals in the schools indicated a high correlation between the perceived level of IGE implementation and job satisfaction. The feeling of satisfaction and commitment, however, did not necessarily reflect uniform meanings for the social organization of the schools. In the various schools IGE was used differently to respond to different definitions of the school mandate. The language and ceremonies of the reform that produced such satisfaction can be viewed as having provided psychologically compelling activities which strengthened affiliation among those who participated.

The importance of reform in developing the occupational commitment of teachers should not be underestimated. Activities in schools tend to be fairly routine for both students and teachers. Teachers have regular hours, assigned periods for breaks, standard materials and books, and, typically, limited interactions with children and other adults. Differentiating roles, career ladders, and sabbaticals are among the traditional mechanisms used to overcome the ennui produced in school environments. Reform programs can offer new mechanisms for total staff involvement. A continual search among school district personnel for something new and innovative helps to draw attention away from the routine and the mundane. In consequence, morale is often raised and commitment to the stability of the organization developed. Staff morale, job satisfaction, and personal efficiency, therefore, should not be viewed solely as psychological factors; each needs to be considered in reference to the institutional patterns that sustain commitment and affiliation.

## Research and Development:
## The Professionalization of Reform

The importance of research and development efforts can be seen within the context of legitimation. The prestige of the IGE schools in our study

4. The nature of the political in schooling discussed here differs from the nature of the politics of interest groups and decision-making found in political science. By the term "political" we refer to the symbolic manipulations and social practices that produce affiliation

was enhanced by their affiliation with the Wisconsin R and D Center that developed the Individually Guided Education program. Teachers saw themselves as participants in a significant effort that went beyond their specific schools and districts. The organization of staff members, administrators, school consultants, and academicians into a national movement also gave credibility to teachers and their schools. The sense of importance felt by staff members was enhanced by involvement in the IGE network and participation in leadership institutes.

The legitimacy of IGE in the studied schools was further reinforced by our own research efforts. We approached the selection of schools by asking leaders in the field to identify those schools that they thought provided model IGE programs. Our selection process tended to reaffirm the staffs' faith in what they were doing. It was proudly announced in one state's educational newsletter that one of the schools was a "finalist" in the IGE evaluation study of exemplary schools.

To think of reform as part of the life that sustains an occupational group enables us to explore further the legitimating function of the IGE program through its educational research and development model. Our intent is to consider educational research and development as a social endeavor rather than as a scientific project detached from social meaning, and to locate that social endeavor within the context of schooling. Thus our concern is not with what knowledge or curricula have been produced through research efforts; rather, it is to identify the general model of change underlying the research and development efforts that produced IGE and other school reforms, and to consider the implications of these reforms for the status, privilege, and power arrangements found in schools.

The model of change formulated by the national research and development centers had a center-to-periphery orientation; that is, centralized groups would develop the knowledge and programs necessary for school reform, and then disseminate the programs to the nation's schools. The belief that a universal method of reform could be devised for all schooling is expressed in the Individually Guided Education program. According to IGE, reform is rooted in the psychology of individual differences—children are seen to have different learning styles and rates. The task of reform is to increase learning efficiency by identifying technologies that make more effective implementation of school goals possible. IGE does this by integrating differential psychology with systems analysis to create a clearly defined and universal set of procedures for the differentiated

---

to and legitimation of institutional conditions. See Edelman (1970); Young and Whitty (1977).

pacing of all students, and an administrative scheme to operate the procedures.[5] Individualized instruction is intended to discover how students differ, especially when they lack skills or information, and then to commit student time to learning the skills and information that is lacking. The integration of differential psychology with systems analysis led to the IGE unit organization and Instructional Programming Model, central technologies in the reform program's effort to make instruction respond efficiently to diversity among students.

The flaw in this model of change is apparent when the logic of individual differences and individualization is examined. Individual variation is a psychological abstraction which isolates human traits, aptitudes, and attitudes from the school setting, cultural environment, and social circumstances in which children function. It assumes that "individual differences" exist apart from the social setting of schooling and that they can be "treated" in a logical and administrative fashion.

One consequence of psychologizing school change is failure to consider, except in a limited sense, the impact of social structure upon individual development. In our study of IGE schools, the emphasis on individualization blinded program users to both the significance of social structure for schooling and the dynamics of that structure.

The irony of the Research and Development Center approach is that it had the unintended consequence of conserving existing pedagogical relations rather than changing them. In none of the schools in our study were the technologies of IGE used as the Research and Development planners had envisioned them. The focus upon administrative efficiency in the technical schools transformed technique into a moral domain; the planners, in contrast, valued IGE technologies as means to develop the more general goals of schooling. The selective use of the IGE technologies in the constructive schools also had consequences that were different from the planners' intent. Rather than starting with a hierarchical program of skill development that would lead to more abstract conceptual thought, skill activities were integrated with problematic and aesthetic activities in ways that limited the utility of mastery teaching. The unit structure and grouping procedures were used to focus on priorities other than instructional programming. In illusory schooling, the technologies of IGE legitimated the very school values and practices that the program was meant to overcome. In none of the six schools were the existing conditions of schooling changed; instead, the old conditions were given a new source of credibility and reasonableness through the symbolic form and practices of the reform itself.

---

5. See Chapter 2 for a discussion of the purposes, assumptions, and technologies of the Wisconsin R and D program, Individually Guided Education.

Because of the social factors that influence definitions of ability, competence, and achievement, individualization cannot be viewed solely as a
psychological problem when applied to schools. The concepts of individual differences and individual development are related to liberal
theories which view the political order as the product of individual signa-
tures to a social contract (DeLone 1979). Belief in the social contract and
the role of the individual has shaped social and educational reform: deep-
seated tensions and contradictions in adult society are to be resolved
through a genuine effort in schooling to help children help themselves.
Early educational reforms such as those proposed by Horace Mann, as
well as the recent accountability and back-to-basics movements, stress
the need to increase the efficiency with which schools provide equal
opportunities for children of different aptitudes and talents. The interest
of educational reformers in children's psychological traits also has roots in
more widespread social transformations, in which increasing differentiation and specialization in the occupational structures of economic and
intellectual life have produced the need for different talents and activities. The irony of liberal reform, as DeLone argues, is that by focusing
almost exclusively upon the individual apart from his or her social context, reform efforts have brought about different, but not equal treatment, and have sustained intergenerational inequalities.

These considerations compel us to look again at the implications of the
Individually Guided Education program. Putting the reform program in
neutral (apolitical) and universal language obscures the contradictions and
dilemmas embedded in the conduct of schooling. The liturgy and technologies of the program are a ceremonial mask concealing the reification
of existing school values and practices. Emphasis on a universal method to
improve children's abilities and skills draws attention away from the differential conditions of schooling and the biases of those conditions. Efforts
to define the problem of schooling as the management of individual development, however, enhance the legitimacy of those who manage and
those whose standards define development.

### Educational Research and the Mystification of Reform

We must consider research as a configuration of assumptions, procedures, and concepts that not only shape our findings but also articulate
values that direct us in challenging social situations (Popkewitz 1978,
1980; Popkewitz, Tabachnick, and Zeichner 1979). Inherent in research
are deeply held convictions about institutional possibilities and the role of
the individual as one who intervenes in social life. To engage in research
about schooling is to organize and categorize conceptions of the patterns

of schooling. Research also involves submitting language to rules which establish a style or form of thought. The act of definition is an act of affirming what is important in social and educational life, what should be given credence in school affairs, and, implicitly, what can be reasonably and appropriately changed. From the perspective of this investigation, the practices of educational research must be viewed in relation to the reform effort itself.

We can begin to clarify the nature of bias in educational research and evaluation by considering certain assumptions that underlie conventional research practices. Schooling is commonly viewed as a rational system, the elements of which yield specified outcomes (such as academic achievement or acculturation) and interact to produce a consensus on how school goals should be met. School research and reform is expected to identify more precisely the school system's properties, and to improve the efficiency of its interactions by developing appropriate technologies (see Easton [1971] and Simon [1969] for discussions of the world view underlying much of contemporary educational research).

The researcher treats the organization of schooling and the behavior of teachers as having distinct and analytically separable parts or elements. For example, teaching can be studied independently of learning; praise by teachers can be studied in relationship to student achievement. The trouble with these assumptions is that they take for granted the goals and purposes of schooling. The tendency among researchers is to accept the program developers' statements of intent and their categories and technologies of change, and to test the extent to which a reform program has been implemented within the schools. The effect of such separation, isolation, and fragmentation is to obscure and mystify the very social relations, meanings, and assumptions of schooling that need to be made problematic.

We can examine how the biases created by these assumptions are incorporated into research by considering two prevailing approaches to understanding the effects of reform. One is called the "fidelity" approach; the other can be labeled the "process of implementation" approach. In each instance, under the guise of descriptive and neutral inquiry, the research effort assumes the constancy and normative appropriateness of existing school arrangements or reform programs.

An example of the fidelity approach and its normative implications can be found in the measurement Level of Use (Loucks et al. n.d.) developed at the University of Texas R and D Center. Level of Use attempts to determine the faithfulness of a school's use of a reform program to the developers' program description. Criteria associated with six different levels of implementation (from non-use to integration and renewal) guide the researcher in determining the fidelity of implementation. The assumption behind these criteria is that the important question to ask about reform concerns the degree of correspondence between the planners' descriptions and actual school use.

Our data suggest that the problem of reform implementation is not adequately explained by measuring levels of use, and that the adoption or adaptation of reform involves a range of social meanings, interpretations, and implications that must be related to the institutional configurations of schooling. In each of the Individually Guided Education schools we studied, participants developed definitions, imposed beliefs, and established priorities as they implemented and used the IGE technologies. In the illusory schools, for example, patterns of conduct pointed to specifically defined meanings of teacher and student competence, learning, and individualization. According to conventional logic, one of the illusory schools might have been labeled a non-user or a mechanical user and eliminated from consideration;[6] the other might have been labeled a creative user because of staff talk about how the school had modified the program. From our perspective, the labels "non-use" and "creative use" obscure the substantive meanings of the reform in its institutional setting. In the illusory schools, the reform ceremonies functioned as political acts which protected the substantive practices of the schools from external scrutiny; the ceremonies also taught docility, but little was expected and elicited in the way of academic achievement from students. The image of reform was significant because the illusory schools were located in communities in which school programs had traditionally failed their clientele, the poor and minorites. The Levels of Use labels would have obscured the significance of the illusory schools' uses of the reform program.

Some researchers have argued that the fidelity approach is inappropriate, and that research needs to focus upon the actual process of implementation, to examine the unanticipated as well as the anticipated outcomes of reform, and to utilize more open-ended research techniques such as field methods and intensive interviewing (see, e.g., Fullan and Pomfret 1977). Recasting the problem to include "qualitative" measures of the implementation process, however, has not been accompanied by a reexamination of the basic assumptions that guide fidelity research. Studies of implementation processes have, for example, narrowly defined "unintended consequences" as those elements which foster or impede the incorporation of behaviors identified by the reform into a school organization. It is assumed that the social processes of schooling are functionally related to the ongoing system, and that these processes are devoid of

6. "Mechanical" use is a classification found in the Levels of Use schema. It is *not similar* in meaning to our term "technical schooling."

social values, assumptions, and implications other than those related to efficient management. The study of implementation processes, while expanding inquiry to consider what actually occurs as a reform program is used, still tends to legitimate existing meanings, values, and assumptions.

Gross, Giaquinta, and Bernstein's (1971) case study of a school district's reform effort contains just such a conservative bias. The study sought to discover whether the behavior patterns and role changes described by the program planners actually developed. Observations revealed that the reform, a problem-solving approach to curriculum, was not implemented because the necessary knowledge and skills were not made available to teachers during the program's implementation phase. The study provides insight into the factors that influence the actual uses of a reform; it does not, however, make problematic the social values and knowledge underlying the social relations of schooling.

The normative quality of implementation research is further illustrated by the widely publicized Rand study of educational reform. This four-year, federally funded study used a combination of questionnaire, interview, and observational techniques to investigate whether "existing forms of federal intervention would be likely to produce real improvements" (Berman and McLaughlin 1978:4). The researchers assumed that reforms were being incorporated into common schools in which there were no issues, strains, or contradictions other than those brought about by the reform technologies. A major criterion for judging the success or failure of a reform was "institutionalization," that is, whether the program continued after the federal "seed" money had disappeared.

The Rand study assumed that the reform planners' definitions and categories for measuring change should be accepted for research purposes. This assumption, however, should not be made without analysis; such analytical criticism is not present in the Rand study and, as a result, the research is self-validating and conservative. This is particularly evident in its conclusions. Having accepted the program designers' proposals as a valid definition of reform, Berman and McLaughlin make policy recommendations concerned with increasing the efficiency of program implementation. They argue that the government should provide technical assistance to help schools adapt reform programs in order to produce more consistent outcomes; that federal assistance should be given to help local districts adapt programs to the needs of the community; and that implementation assistance should be process-oriented to help districts identify problems and carry out solutions.

The Rand study illustrates a number of assumptions and implications of the study of reform. In reading its recommendations, one is struck with the view that change and reform are technical in nature; tied to a planner's or school district's identification of "needs." From the perspective of the IGE study, this technical orientation is open to criticism. One of the major findings of the IGE study is how different schools give meaning to the slogan "needs." Need was defined by the staffs in the constructive, illusory, and technical schools in relation to priorities and beliefs within each school's social context; inherent in each definition were different assumptions about and values concerning schooling, social relations, and authority.

To posit levels of use, renewal, or local adaptation as the criteria of reform is to obscure the fundamental characteristics of schooling as a social, moral, and political enterprise. If the power arrangements, interests, and inequities in schooling remain unscrutinized, it makes no difference whether change is oriented by a center-to-periphery model like IGE or a decentralized, local "needs" model like that suggested by the Rand study. To isolate the use of reform technologies from the differentiated institutional relations and social rules that operate in schooling is to reduce the problem of change to a technical and superficial level. When that happens, the biases of social organization rest unexamined, and reform may in fact give new credibility to those institutional rules and priorities that brought about the initial intent to change.

Under the assumption that schooling should be a rational, efficient system, variations in the implementation of reform programs have been discussed in the literature (Fullan and Pomfret 1977). These discussions also assume that the constraining conditions of social context can be held constant, and that the problem of reform is to identify the vulnerable points in a school's organization which permit or hinder a program's acceptance and use. Changes in schooling are commonly thought of as being most productive when reform follows a sequence that begins with research and goes through development and diffusion to adoption and adaptation. Implementation, evaluation, and research all focus upon the adequacy of information and motivation, the availability of financial and administrative support, the level of use of the program, and the effects of the innovations. The central assumption is that the more that is known about an innovation and the more commitment there is to it, the more often adoption or adaptation will occur. The operative conception of change is quantitative, and the process of change is defined as a linear movement from research to development, diffusion, and adoption/adaptation.

Adoption and adaptation involve incorporating reform technologies into a variety of social contexts.[7] In each of the schools in our study,

7. For comprehensive discussions of the issues involved in implementing change drawn from case studies, see Stenhouse (1979); Tamir, Blum, Hostein, and Sabar (1979); Firestone and Corbett (1979); and Lundgren and Pettersson (1979).

participants developed definitions, imposed beliefs, and established priorities that reflected particular institutional conditions. In part, these conditions were related to professional interests; in part, they were related to the social and community elements in American life. The meaning of reform is found by tracing the relationships among the technologies of reform and the professional and community interests that are worked out in day-to-day activities in the schools.

### What Might Be Done: Some Suggestions for Research

The attempt to understand the relationship of reform to institutional patterns is not new. Waller's *Sociology of Teaching* (1932) discusses how appearances and the seemingly pleasing exterior of school life often conceal institutional interests and their consequences. Sarason's much-cited book, *The Culture of the School and the Problem of Change* (1971), provides data from a variety of reform projects to illustrate the importance of classroom patterns and behaviors as determinants of the use of educational innovation. More recently, Wolcott's (1977) study of the clash of professional beliefs concerning implementation of an accountability program in a school district uses the constructs of culture and subculture to explore how an apparently technical innovation expresses or challenges subcultural ideologies.

These studies enable us to understand some of the important occupational and social dimensions of schooling. What the IGE study has illustrated, however, is that competing professional interests have implications not only for people who are processed in school, but also for the knowledge distributed through school pedagogical practices. The study further illustrates that school practices are influenced by social and cultural orientations, and by the wider transformations that take place in society at large.

The relationships that we have found among social, cultural, occupational, and pedagogical practices suggest that the problem of reform in institutional life needs to be recast. To do so will require extending the concept of school as an institution to articulate more clearly the social and cultural meanings that impinge upon school life. These relationships can be formulated as questions:[8]

1. What conceptions of knowledge and work exist in pedagogical contexts?
2. How do occupational ideologies and practice influence the pedagogical context?

8. For a more extended discussion of this problem, see Popkewitz (1981).

3. What are the relationships among teaching/learning, occupational structures, and the social/cultural orientations of the communities in which the schools are located?

The IGE study has pointed to the importance of understanding how these sets of relationships affect institutional life, and what meaning they give to reform. Their specific content and dynamics contain unresolved questions and issues. For example, how do specific social/cultural characteristics filter into the school to influence instructional practices, and what are the implications of teachers' different and potentially conflicting perceptions of their occupational role? Professionals do have relative autonomy in establishing pedagogical practices, but how is this autonomy exercised to create, sustain, and renew occupational ideologies? What are the roles played by state and local education agencies, teachers associations and unions, and teacher-preparation institutes in establishing and legitimating school practices?

The interplay of these sets of relationships requires methods of inquiry that respond to the complexities of the problem. The issue, however, is not one of qualitative versus quantitative measures, or process versus output measures. Questionnaire and field study techniques need to be incorporated into research designs to provide descriptions of ongoing activities, the meaning that such actions have for those involved, the interpretations people give to their own actions and the actions of others, and the regularities and correlations exhibited in school practice.[9]

The history of social and political reforms efforts suggests that their effects cannot be uncritically accepted, and that—no matter how benevolent the intent of the reformers—unforeseen, unplanned, and unwilled consequences must be considered in ways that permit the researcher to go beyond the assumptions and priorities of those who administratively define the "system." Our research suggests that the distinction between intent and effect is important in studying schooling and reform efforts. While the intent of reform may be noble and sincere, planned social intervention is fraught with unanticipated and sometimes undesired consequences. The curriculum reform movement upon which IGE is based was built upon certain assumptions about educational change and reform, and our research has raised questions about both the reform and its underlying assumptions. The study of six elementary schools identified as exemplary of IGE illustrates the complexity of making schools better. Schools are social and political enterprises characterized by interests that cannot be taken for granted.

9. Bellack (1978) provides an excellent analysis of different research traditions in teaching, and offers a synthesis for the problem discussed here.

*Appendices*

*References*

*Index*

# Appendices

## Introduction

This study of IGE was part of a larger evaluation project organized within the Wisconsin Center for Individualized Schooling. The evaluation project had two interrelated purposes: first, it was to test the assumptions that underlie IGE; second, the concrete study of IGE was to serve a more general theoretical interest in the problem of school change and reform (see chapter 1). The interplay of the two interests of evaluation and research made the project different from conventional approaches to program evaluation, and was what made the project appealing to the authors, who before the evaluation were faculty members in the Department of Curriculum and Instruction but were not involved in the Wisconsin Research and Development Center.

The entire evaluation project was administered separately from the other projects within the R and D Center. Two of the principal investigators had no involvement with the program and could approach it as "strangers." The third investigator had worked with the early development of the IGE program, but had not been involved with the project for a number of years (his past experience, however, proved valuable as the authors sought to understand the historical development of IGE and its original purposes).

The evaluation project was divided into five phases : (1) self-report questionnaires and achievement measures collected in 156 schools, discussed in Appendix B; (2) a "verification" study involving observations in a sample of the 156 schools, intended to check the validity of the self-report data; (3) the study of institutional factors developed in this research report, the methodology of which is reported in Appendix A; (4) an evaluation of curricula produced by the R and D Center; and (5) an analysis and synthesis of the previous four phases.

## Appendix A:
## Design and Procedures of the Study

The problem of understanding the "effects" of Individually Guided Education required that we develop a research design and procedure that situated the reform in the social context of schooling. It was essential that the research be directed at illuminating the patterns of institutional behavior and the meaning participants gave to their actions in school settings. We sought to understand how the IGE technologies were used in school settings, and what forms of schoolwork were associated with phrases like "meeting children's needs" and "individual differences." However, we never conceived of our task as merely reporting in unanalyzed form the life in these schools from the participants' point of view. From the very beginning of the research, we were concerned to develop a critical/ analytic stance toward what was seen and heard. That critical stance was built, in part, upon the assumption that all reform programs, such as Individually Guided Education, ought to be problematic. By that, we mean that we "bracketed" or put aside the intentions and definitions of the program designers in exploring the program's use in schools.

The task of exploring the institutional effects of IGE language and technologies was performed through direct observation in the schools. We wanted to understand, through conversations and interviews, the meaning the actors gave to the various actions required by the reform programs.

By observing the use of IGE and understanding its meaning for the teachers and administrators who implemented the technologies, an institutional portrait could be created. The design of the study (presented as a "given" in the original proposal for the evaluation project) called for intensive case studies of six IGE schools. To create a pool of IGE schools from which to select specific institutions for observation, survey data gathered in Phase I of the evaluation project (see Appendix B) was used to identify those schools that reported implementation of various IGE components. The self-report data helped to distinguish between schools in which staff members believed IGE had been implemented and schools that were only nominally affiliated with IGE. These data were supplemented by a survey of people reputed to be knowledgeable about IGE to determine which of the schools reporting high implementation could be recommended as exemplary IGE schools. Among these people were members of the Wisconsin R and D Center staff who had worked with various schools to implement the program, individuals in state departments of public instruction who had first-hand knowledge of IGE in their states, and individuals who had worked at implementing IGE at a variety of sites.

After a list of exemplary IGE schools was established, seven members of the evaluation project, including the three authors of this report, visited 17 schools to assess the possibility of using them as sites for studying the reform in depth. Two observers visited each school for two days to verify the implementation of IGE technologies. Typically, a school unit meeting or an instructional improvement committee meeting and several classrooms were observed and detailed notes were made. Teachers were interviewed to obtain an initial judgment about the extent to which IGE was understood and practiced. The principal was always interviewed to get an overall impression of the school, and to ascertain the willingness of the school to be studied on an intensive basis.

Following the site visit, the observing team wrote a report for other research team members based on the observations and interview data gathered. Subsequently, a team member presented an oral commentary on the data in the written report; this became an important methodological technique throughout the research. The presentation initially took the form of an argument as to whether or not the school should be selected as a research site. During the presentation other team members cross-examined the individual's interpretation of the data and application of criteria for final selection.

The initial criteria, of course, addressed the degree and quality of IGE implementation. This was done to ensure a sample of exemplary IGE schools before in-depth studies began. Criteria also dealt with the distribution of schools across a range of social classes, and racial and geographic categories. From those schools identified as exemplary of IGE, we intended to select six which also provided demographic diversity. The research team was confident at first that the process of selection would quickly yield examples of both diversity and the reform measures in operation. However, selection was more difficult than expected because some of the highly recommended schools were, in fact, not exemplary in that they had not implemented one or more features of IGE. Out of the 17 schools visited, 4 were selected for a first round of intensive study. We decided to postpone selection of two additional schools until we obtained more information about other sites and gained some perspective through the study.

After the research team concluded its field work in the four schools, the process of selecting two additional sites was continued. Again, information provided by persons who knew the field was important in identifying exemplary IGE schools. A final selection was made after team members visited three additional sites, and reconsidered those sites previously rejected. The final two selections were significant in that they contrasted in outward characteristics, yet both seemed to be strong IGE schools. One was an inner city school serving a low-income black population, while the other was in a small city with a middleclass white population. As it turned out, these schools both added dimensions to the evaluation study which the previous selections could not provide.

Approximately 30 weeks of fieldwork were done during a year and half period. Eight weeks in the spring of 1977 were spent visiting the schools selected in the reputational sample to acquaint us with the settings of IGE; another 20 weeks were used to collect data in the six schools selected. Three to four week-long visits to the schools were made over the 1977–78 school year, with the exception of one school which was visited for only two weeks.

The procedures of research followed the patterns found in most field study methods. Data were gathered through observations in classrooms and interviews with teachers, principals, parents, and district administrators. In all cases the people at the sites were informed that the purpose of the research was to describe and evaluate IGE in operation. Assurances were given that our purpose did not include the evaluation of individual teachers or schools. Team members were given cordial and cooperative treatment in every school, and with only one or two exceptions, teachers seemed unconcerned about the prolonged presence of observers in the classroom. In many situations the researchers taped interviews to preserve the exact language and thoughts of teachers and administrators. Despite the rather frank statements that sometimes came out in these interviews, at no time did teachers show a reluctance to have their views recorded.

In addition to the formal interview data, copious notes were taken describing the classroom activities of both teachers and students, and in many instances observers recorded their comments verbatim. Observers also provided commentaries or interpretive statements to put the data into perspective. This material, typed up and transcribed from tapes, was distributed to the other members of the research team, and a meeting of the team was held to discuss the data and the interpretations offered by the observers. In the debate that followed the data were examined for completeness, consistency, and the extent to which they sustained data gathered at other sites.

At each of the sites the pattern of visits was essentially the same. Each of the research team members took primary responsibility for data gathering at one site; this meant that the individual was to make at least three one-week visits to that site. The visits were spaced to allow events to progress at the school, and to allow the researcher a chance to digest the data and to receive advice and criticism from the other team members. In addition, each of the three principal investigators made a two-day visit to those sites for which he did not have primary responsibility; this procedure gave each team member an opportunity to have first-hand knowledge of all six schools, and provided a basis for informed discussion when data and interpretations were presented. These brief site visits were also used by the primary observer to obtain comparative views that might confirm or challenge his perceptions of the school for which he was responsible. The fact that each of the observers had visited all of the schools gave a perspective to the data which would not have existed otherwise. In all, the team spent about 130 days over an 8 month period observing and interviewing at the six sites.

The analysis and interpretation of the data began with the first visitations and continued through the writing of the research report. In general, the methodology of analysis and interpretation can be described as a version of the constant comparative method. There was an explicit attempt from the beginning to make comparisons both within and between sites. The focus of discussion was on the meaning, use, and interpretation of IGE which characterized each of the schools. Through discussion and debate within the team there gradually emerged the most appropriate and useful categories for describing and interpreting the ongoing life within the institutions, and for conceptualizing the similarities and differences observed.

After discussions of a visitation, the primary observer returned to the school with new questions regarding patterns of institutional life. At first it appeared that schools adopting IGE looked and acted very much alike, but eventually we discerned different institutional patterns among the several schools. It was not until after the data collection period that three general categories of schooling emerged: the technical, the illusory, and the constructive. These categories reflected significantly different configurations of work, knowledge, and professionalism in the implementation of IGE.

A constant comparative method was also used to compare the data gathered by observers with the perspectives of the IGE developers, the users of IGE in the schools, and, of course, the perspective that the research team was developing. In other words, we were constantly asking how the viewpoint of the developers differed from that of the IGE users, and in what ways each of these constituents might see school reform differently than the researchers. The research team was consciously in the process of making explicit the differences between their own frame of reference and that of the developers and users.

Another way in which the procedures were comparative was internal to the development of the research team's interpretation of the data. While the research team members were in general agreement on many important issues, each brought a unique set of background experiences to the task, which acted as a filter in processing the data. Each was able to argue for particular interpretations of the data and add to the cumulative understanding that eventually emerged. There was constant intellectual challenge to the ideas put forth; no one came away from the discussions unscathed. There was pressure to defend interpretations of data, to ask different questions on the next visit, and to interview people who held a different set of assumptions.

The observational data of this study were supplemented by aggregate data collected in Phase I of the evaluation effort. These data included: self-report surveys for 156 schools, which assessed implementation of IGE technologies; reading and mathematics achievement scores for the second and fifth graders in those schools; and a survey of teachers' and administrators' perceptions of teaching and learning. These data helped us to compare the specific schools of our study with a larger sample of IGE schools.

## Appendix B:
## A Brief Overview of the Phase I Study

This appendix describes the procedures used to gather self-report staff data, and pupil achievement, aptitude, personality development, and cognitive ability data in a sample frame of 156 IGE schools, of which the six schools discussed in this research report were a part. The sample survey data were collected as part of the first phase of the IGE Evaluation Project conducted by the Wisconsin Research and Development Center for Individualized Schooling. Professor Price, Professor Romberg, D. Stewart, P. Klopp, A. Buchanan, and T. Janicki were responsible for the collection and analysis of the data. Because the authors of this report have used the Phase I data throughout the text to illustrate aspects of the interpretation, it is appropriate to offer a discussion of the design and procedures of the Phase I study.

### Information from the Sampling Frame

To select the six schools studied in this investigation, the research team used information that had been collected before the start of the evaluation to create a sampling frame for the Phase I study; the team also used a reputational survey. The sampling frame information came from the IGE Schools Questionnaire of March 1976, which had been sent by the Wisconsin R and D Center to schools that had identified themselves as having an IGE program. The schools were asked about the implementation of various IGE features and practices that the Center had recommended. Each questionnaire was filled out by one respondent, typically the principal of the school, and was thus a "self-report" based on the individual's perceptions. The questionnaire was not intended to evaluate a school's "IGE-ness." The information obtained from the questionnaires was used to construct seven variables that served as the basis for creating a sampling framework. The seven variables were:

1. A rating of the staff organization in terms of its congruence with recommendations in IGE literature

2. Age of the program as an IGE program
3. Extent (across curriculum area) to which the Instructional Programming Model was reportedly being used
4. Rating for "facilitative environment," a component of the IGE model
5. Rating of the organization of children in the school in terms of its congruence with recommendations in IGE literature
6. Reported use of Wisconsin R and D Center curriculum products (products intended to be compatible with the Instructional Programming Model)
7. Demographic information about the community served by the school

To form a sampling frame for the Phase I study, seven orthogonal dimensions were formed from the seven variables by using principal components analysis (see Price 1977). The first of the seven principal components reflected the tendency for some schools to rate themselves high on the first six variables, and for others to rate themselves low. The first principal component was therefore used in Phase III as a general index of the extent to which a school reported itself as having implemented the various features and practices befitting of an exemplary (orthodox) IGE school.

Data collected as part of the Phase I study included self-report questionnaires given to each school staff, the results of standardized tests of academic aptitude, achievement, and personality development given to second and fifth grade students, and of a battery of cognitive ability tests given to fifth grade students.

### Staff Instruments

Questionnaires for the school staffs were based primarily on several existing instruments, modified in content or format to meet the requirements of IGE terminology and certain technical constraints, such as machine-readable response forms. A detailed discussion of the content and original source of each instrument, as well as its relationship to the variables of interest in Phase I, appears in Stewart (1980).

These instruments were printed in three questionnaire booklets for distribution according to respondent group: the Instructional Improvement Committee and principal, the Grade 2 and Grade 5 test units, and all members of the professional staff. One instrument, the verification copy of the Spring 1977 IGE Schools Questionnaire, was provided separately for the principal. Machine-readable response forms were developed to accompany each questionnaire booklet. A booklet, response form(s), and pencil were packed in an individual envelope, preprinted with identification numbers and directions for distribution, completion, and return by the respondents.

The time required for an individual staff member to complete the questionnaires varied according to the number of respondent groups to which he or she belonged. Since the unit leaders of the Grade 2 and Grade 5 test units were usually members of all three respondent groups, they invested the greatest amount of time—245 minutes. The estimated working time for each booklet was:

Instructional Improvement Committee
Questionnaire                                                                        25 minutes

General Staff Questionnaire                      100 minutes
Unit Questionnaire                               120 minutes

General Staff Questionnaires      Every professional staff member assigned to an investigated school at least one-third time during the 1976–77 and 1977–78 school years was asked to complete the general questionnaires. By setting this requirement it was expected that all support personnel, such as guidance counselors and remedial teachers, would participate in the evaluation, but that staff not yet familiar with IGE or not an integral part of school operations would not do so. Aides were not included because of the problems associated with involving instructional aides but not clerical aides.

The estimated working times of the five general questionnaires (combined in the single staff booklet) were:

| | |
|---|---|
| Staff Background Information | 20 minutes |
| IGE Implementation Survey | 30 minutes |
| Job Satisfaction Survey | 20 minutes |
| Assumptions About Conditions of Effective Schooling | 15 minutes |
| Assumptions About Learning and Knowledge | 15 minutes |
| | 100 minutes total |

On the Staff Background Information form, each staff member provided data on his or her assignment and position in the school, professional and IGE-related training and experience, and professional activities, as well as personal information.

The IGE Implementation Survey was designed to indicate each respondent's judgment of local implementation of seven IGE components on a five-point scale that ranged from *no implementation* to *ideal implementation*. There were 77 statements or concepts in the survey, each related to one of the following components: Multiunit Organizational Administrative Arrangements (MUS), Instructional Programming for the Individual Student (IPM), Curricular Programs (CURR), Evaluation for Decision-Making (EVAL), Home-School-Community Relations (HSC), Facilitative Environments (ENV), and Continuing Research and Development ( R & D).

The Job Satisfaction Survey measured eight aspects of job satisfaction on a five-point scale ranging from *not satisfied* to *very satisfied*. The eight aspects, surveyed in 50 items, were: co-workers, career function, school identifiction, financial considerations, working conditions, pupil relations, community relations, and administration.

Staff members were asked to indicate the relative need for each condition listed in a set of 28 statements called Assumptions About Conditions of Effective Schooling. The statements had been derived from IGE literature which defined desirable conditions for teaching and learning. Responses were on a five-point scale ranging from *strongly disagree* to *strongly agree*.

In the last general staff questionnaire, Assumptions about Learning and Knowledge, school personnel reported their feelings about a set of 28 statements related to open education. Response choices again ranged from *strongly disagree* to *strongly agree,* on a five-point scale.

Unit Staff Questionnaires     Staff evaluation materials for both test units, grades 2 and 5, were identical. However, to insure that the two test units responded separately, the covers of the unit questionnaire booklets were printed in different colors, and both the covers and envelopes indicated the appropriate grade.

All members of each test unit, except aides, were requested to respond to the questionnaires if they met the following criteria: (A) assignment to the unit at least one-third time in both the 1976–77 and 1977–78 school years, and (B) direct involvement in planning instruction for unit students in reading, mathematics, and/or language arts. These criteria were meant to allow and encourage part-time unit members such as reading specialists or learning disability teachers to respond, and yet avoid participation by personnel unfamiliar with unit operations.

The three questionnaires in the unit booklet, and their estimated working times, were:

| | |
|---|---|
| Role of the Staff Teacher | 10 minutes |
| Instructional Practices in Reading, Mathematics, and Language Arts | 60 minutes |
| Instruction and Research Unit Structure and Function | 50 minutes |
| | 120 minutes total |

Each unit staff member responded independently to the first two questionnaires, while the unit staff as a group was asked to complete the third.

Role of the Staff Teacher surveyed the number and kind of instructional and advisor contacts teachers and special teachers had with students. Instructional Practices in Reading, Mathematics, and Language Arts assessed separately four aspects of individualized instruction—rate, media, grouping, and learner assessment—for each of the three content areas. The Instruction and Research Unit Structure and Function questionnaire surveyed unit membership, meeting schedules and reports, utilization of meeting time, and the role of instructional and clerical aides. Also incorporated into this questionnaire were topics of special concern in the evaluation: record-keeping and grouping/regrouping practices, time allocationed to different curricular areas, and number of instructional objectives.

Instructional Improvement Committee Questionnaires     If an Instructional Improvement Committee (IIC) was operating in the school, members were asked to complete by consensus the Instructional (Program) Improvement Committee Structure and Function Questionnaire. Topics surveyed in this questionnaire included membership, meeting schedule and reports of meetings, time allocation to various tasks, and development of schoolwide instructional objectives in the various curricular areas. If no IIC was operative in the school, the principal was asked to describe in brief narrative form on the response sheet the governing body or leadership group or person, and to complete the section on schoolwide objectives. The IIC booklet also included a question regarding the demography of the school attendance area. Demographic categories were based on the community types developed by the National Assessment of Educational Progress project.

The verification copy of the Spring 1977 IGE Schools Questionnaire was distributed with the ICC materials. Principals were asked to verify or update the information previously provided. Of particular importance were changes in the school's organization, and in the extent of application of the Instructional Programming Model (the addition of another subject areas in which the IPM was applied, for example). The estimated time required for completing the IIC and principal questionnaires was 25 minutes.

### Student Instruments

Across the 156 Phase I schools from which student data were received, approximately 5,500 students at Grade 2 were tested, and 5,800 students at Grade 5. Most schools tested between 24 and 50 students at each grade. These students were preassigned by the Wisconsin R and D Center to one of four test groups at each grade. Also preassigned were the tests to be administered to each group. The Short Form Test of Academic Aptitude (SFTAA) was the only test administered to students in all groups. Since the total time requirement was approximately 90 minutes for Grade 2 students and approximately 120 minutes for Grade 5 students, the tests were scheduled to be administered in three separate sessions.

Table 1. Phase I Student Tests

| Test | Grade(s) |
|------|----------|
| Short Form Test of Academic Aptitude (SFTAA)[a] | 2,5 |
| Comprehensive Tests of Basic Skills (CTBS), Form S[b]: | |
|     Reading Vocabulary | 2,5 |
|     Reading Comprehension: Sentences | 2 |
|     Reading Comprehension: Passages | 2 |
|     Reading Comprehension | 5 |
|     Mathematics Computation | 2,5 |
|     Mathematics Concepts & Applications | 2,5 |
|     Spelling[c] | 5 |
| Self-Observation Scales (SOS), Form C[d] | 2,5 |
| Locus of Control[e] | 2,5 |
| Concept Attainment Abilities (CAA): | |
|     Number Series | 5 |
|     Number Relations | 5 |

Table 1. Phase I Student Tests (Continued)

| Test | Grade(s) |
|------|----------|
| Picture Class Memory | 5 |
| Remembering Classes: Members | 5 |
| Omelet | 5 |

a  Grade 2: level 1; Grade 5: level 3.
b  Grade 2: level C; Grade 5: level 2.
c  Administered as a CAA word fluency substitute.
d  Grade 2: primary level; Grade 5: intermediate level.
e  Not used because of low reliability.

Listed in Table 1 are the tests administered to both grades. Test copies of the SFTAA, CTBS, and SOS were purchased from the commercial publisher; machine-scorable SFTAA and CTBS test books were used for Grade 2, and reusable test books for these two measures were used with a SFTAA-CTBS combination answer sheet for Grade 5. Since each CTBS Reading and Mathematics test was assigned to a specific group, students used only a portion of a test book or answer sheet.

The SOS is a group-administered, self-report instrument with empirically determined scales that measure the way children perceive themselves and their relationships to peers, teachers, and school. The primary level measures four dimensions of a child's self-concept: self-acceptance, social maturity, school affiliation, and self-security. Seven dimensions are measured at the intermediate level: self-acceptance, self-security, social maturity, social confidence, school affiliation, teacher affiliation, and peer affiliation.

The five Concept Attainment Abilities (CAA) tests (Harris and Harris 1973) are from a battery of tests that was developed as part of a previously completed R and D Center project. Only students in Grade 5 participated in that study. In our Phase I study, the CAA tests were administered to assess student cognitive skills in three categories: numerical ability, memory, and word fluency. The correspondence between these categories and the tests was:

| Cognitive Ability | Test |
|-------------------|------|
| numerical | Number Series |
| | Number Relations |
| memory | Picture Class Memory |
| | Remembering Classes: Members |
| word fluency | Omelet (an anagrams test) |
| | Spelling (CTBS) |

Since comparable tests are not available for Grade 2, the CAS tests were given only at Grade 5 for the Phase I evaluation.

## Other Documents

Readers interested in more detail about the Phase I study should refer to reports from that study. Details about the instruments used can be found in a working paper by Klopp, Buchanan, Stewart, and Romberg (1979). An overview of the variables derived from those instruments can be found in Technical Report 475 by Price, Janicki, Howard, Stewart, Buchanan, and Romberg (1978). A summary of the study's findings can be found in the paper by Price, Janicki, Romberg, and Stewart (1980).

# References

## Chapter 1:
## School Reform and Institutional Life

Anyon, J. 1976. Ideology and U. S. history tests: a study of bias. Paper presented at the annual meeting of the National Council of Teachers of Social Studies, April 1976, Washington, D.C.

Apple, M. W., and King, N. 1978. What do schools teach? In G. Willis, ed., *Qualitative evaluation: concepts and cases in curriculum criticism*. Berkeley: McCutchan.

Becker, C. 1932. *The heavenly city of the eighteenth-century philosophers*. New Haven: Yale University Press.

Becker, H. 1952. The career of the Chicago public school teacher. *American Journal of Sociology* 57: 470–477.

Berger, P. L. and Luckmann, T. 1967. *The social construction of reality: a treatise in the sociology of knowledge*. Garden City: Anchor Books.

Bledstein, B. J. 1976. *The culture of professionalism*. New York: W. W. Norton.

Braverman, H. 1974. *Labor and monopoly capital: the degredation of work in the twentieth century*. New York: Monthly Review Press.

Cusick, P. A. 1973. *Inside high school: the student's world*. New York: Holt, Rinehart, and Winston.

Durkheim, E. 1977. *The evolution of educational thought; lectures on the formation and development of secondary education in France*. P. Collins, trans. originally published 1938. London: Routledge and Kegan Paul.

Edelman, M. J. 1977. *Political language: words that succeed and policies that fail*. New York: Academic Press.

Esland, G. 1971. Teaching and learning on the organization of knowledge. In M. F. D. Young, *Knowledge and control: new directions for the sociology of education*, pp. 70-116. London: Collier-MacMillan.

Feyerabend, P. 1978. *Science in a free society*. London: New Left Books.

Goodlad, J. I., and Klein, M. F., and Associates 1970. *Behind the classroom door*. Worthington, Ohio: S. A. Jones.

Hamilton, D. 1975. Handling innovation in the classroom: two Scottish examples. In W. A. Reid and D. F. Walker, eds., *Case studies in curriculum change: Great Britain and the United States*, pp. 179-207. London: Routledge and Kegan Paul.

Hughes, E. 1958. *Men and their work*. Glencoe, Ill.: The Free Press.

Ilyenkov, E. V. 1977. *Dialectic logic: essays on its history and theory*. Moscow: Progress Publishers.

Jackson, P. W. 1968. *Life in the classroom.* New York: Holt, Rinehart, and Winston.

Kallós, D., and Lundgren, U. 1976. *Lessons from a comprehensive school system for theory and research on curriculum.* Research Report. Stockholm, Sweden: Department of Educational Research, School of Education.

Keddie, N. 1971. Classroom knowledge. In M. Young, ed., *Knowledge and control: new directions for the sociology of education,* pp. 133–160. London: Collier, MacMillan.

Lasch, C. 1977. The siege of the family. *New York Review of Books* 24, no. 19 (November 1977): 15–18.

Popkewitz, T. 1975. Reform as political discourse: a case study. *School Review* 84: 311–336.

Popkewitz, T. S. 1977. The latent values of the discipline-centered curriculum. *Theory and Research in Social Education* 4: 41–60.

Popkewitz, T. S. 1979. Educational life and institutional reform. *Educational Researcher* 8: 3–8.

Popkewitz, T. S. 1981. Antagonistic meanings and institutional life. In B. R. Tabachnick, T. S. Popkewitz, and B. B. Szekely, eds., *Study of teaching and learning: trends in Soviet and American research,* pp. 114–126. New York: Praeger Publishers.

Popkewitz, T. S., and Wehlage, G. G. 1977. Schooling as work: an approach to research and evaluation. *The Teachers College Record* 79: 69–86.

Rose, S. 1972. *The betrayal of the poor: the transformation of community action.* Cambridge, Mass: Schenkman.

Sarason, S. 1971. *The culture of the school and the problem of change.* Boston: Allyn and Bacon.

Silberman, C. E. 1970. *Crisis in the classroom: the remaking of American education.* New York: Vintage.

Stake, R. E. et al., eds., 1978. *Case studies in science education.* Vols. 1 and 2. Washington, D.C.: U. S. Government Printing Office.

Stevens, W. K. 1972. Review of the Carnegie commission report. In B. N. Schwartz, ed., *Affirmative education,* pp. 5–7. Englewood Cliffs, N. J.: Prentice Hall.

Taylor, C. 1977. Interpretation and the sciences of man. In F. R. Dallmayr and T. A. McCarthy, eds., *Understanding and social inquiry.* Notre Dame, Ind.: University of Notre Dame Press.

Willis, P. E. 1977. *Learning to labor.* England: Saxon House.

Young, M. F. D. ed., 1971. *Knowledge and control: new directions for the sociology of education.* London: Collier-MacMillan.

# Chapter 2:
# Individually Guided Education As Social Invention

Askov, E., and Otto, W. 1972. *Teacher's planning guide: word attack.* Minnesota: National Computer Systems.

Begle, E. G., 1968. Curriculum research in mathematics. In H. J. Klausmeier and G. T. O'Hearn, eds., *Research and development toward the improvement of education*, pp. 44–48. Madison: Dembar Educational Research Services.

Frayer, D. A., and Klausmeier, H. J. 1971. *Variables in concept learning: task variables*. Theoretical paper no. 28. Madison: Research Center for Cognitive Learning.

Gideonese, H. D. 1968. An output-oriented model of research and development and its relationship to educational improvement. In H. J. Klausmeier and G. T. O'Hearn, eds., *Research and development toward the improvement of education*, pp. 157–163. Madison: Dembar Educational Research Services.

Katzenmeyer, C. G. 1977. Measurement in individually guided education. In H. J. Klausmeier, R. A. Rossmiller, and M. Saily, eds., *Individually guided elementary education*, pp. 151–182. New York: Academic Press.

Klausmeier, H. J. n.d. The Wisconsin Research and Development Center for Cognitive Learning. Mimeographed. Madison.

Klausmeier, H. J. 1977. Instructional programming for the individual student. In H. J. Klausmeier, R. A. Rossmiller, and M. Saily, eds., *Individually guided elementary education*, pp. 55–76. New York: Academic Press.

Klausmeier, H. J. 1968. The Wisconsin Research and Development Center for Cognitive Learning. In H. J. Klausmeier and G. T. O'Hearn, eds., *Research and development toward the improvement of education*. Madison: Dembar Educational Service.

Klausmeier, H. J., and O'Hearn, G. T., eds., 1968. *Research and development toward the improvement of education*. Madison: Dembar Educational Service.

Klausmeier, H. J., Rossmiller, R. A., and Saily, M., eds., 1977. *Individually guided elementary education*. New York: Academic Press.

Klausmeier, H. J., Goodwin, W., Prasch, J., and Goodson, M. 1966. *Project models: maximizing opportunities for development and experimentation in learning in the schools*. Occasional paper. Madison: Research and Development Center for Learning and Re-Education.

Liphan, J. M.., and Fruth, M. J. 1976. *The principal and individually guided education*. Reading, Mass.: Addison-Wesley.

Liphan, J. M., and Klausmeier, H. J. 1976. IGE as a self-renewing system. In J. M. Liphan and M. Fruth, eds., *The principal and individually guided education*, pp. 1–26. Reading, Mass.: Addison-Wesley.

Otto, W. R., and Askov, E. N. 1973. *Wisconsin design for reading skill development: rationale and guidelines*. Minneapolis: National Computer Systems.

Otto, W. R., Saeman, R., Houston, C., McMahan, B., and Wojtal, P. 1967. *Prototypic guide to reading skill development in the elementary school*. Working paper no. 7. Madison: Wisconsin Research and Development Center for Cognitive Learning.

Quilling, M. R. 1968. Controlled experimentation in research and instruction units. In H. J. Klausmeier, J. L. Wardrop, M. R. Quilling, T. A. Romberg, and R. E. Schutz, *Research and development strategies in theory refinement and educational improvement*. Theoretical paper no. 15, pp. 10–13. Madison: Research and Development Center for Cognitive Learning.

Quilling, M. R., Cook, D. M., Wardrop, J. L., and Klausmeier, H. J. 1966. *Research and development activities in R & I units of two elementary schools of Milwaukee, Wisconsin 1966–1967.* Technical report no. 46. Madison: Research and Development Center for Learning and Re-Education.

Romberg, T. A. 1968. The development and refinement of prototypic instructional systems. In H. J. Klausmeier, J. L. Wardrop, M. R. Quilling, T. A. Romberg, and R. E. Schutz, *Research and development strategies in theory refinement and educational improvement.* Theoretical paper no. 15, pp. 14–18. Madison: Research and Development Center for Cognitive Learning.

Romberg, T. A. 1977. Developing mathematical processes: the elementary mathematics program for individually guided education. In H. J. Klausmeier, R. A. Rossmiller, and M. Saily, eds., *Individually guided elementary education.* New York: Academic Press.

Wiersma, W. 1977. Evaluation for instructional decision making. In H. J. Klausmeier, R. A. Rossmiller, and M. Saily, eds., *Individually guided elementary education,* pp. 183–236. New York: Academic Press.

# Chapter 3:
## Daily Life and Public Language: Three IGE Schools

Popkewitz, T. 1980. Global education as a slogan system. *Curriculum Inquiry* 10(3):303–316.

# Chapter 4:
## Making Schools Efficient: Technical Schooling

Braverman, H. 1974. *Labor and monopoly capital: the degradation of work in the twentieth century.* New York: Monthly Review Press.

Collins, R. 1979. *The credential society: an historical sociology of education and stratification.* New York: Academic Press.

Edelman, M. J. 1977. *Political language: words that succeed and policies that fail.* New York: Academic Press.

Meyer, J. W., and Rowan, B. 1977. Institutional organizations: formal structure as myth and ceremony. *American Journal of Sociology* 83(2):340–363.

Noble, D.F., 1977. *America by design: science, technology and the rise of corporate capitalism.* New York: Alfred A. Knopf.

# Chapter 5:
## Exploring Ways of Knowing: Constructive Schooling

Bernstein, B. 1977. *Class, codes and control: towards a theory of educational transmissions.* 2d ed., vol. 3. London: Routledge and Kegan Paul.

Gouldner, A. W. 1979. *The future of the intellectuals and the rise of the new class.* New York: Seabury.

Nisbet, R. A. 1976. *Sociology as an art form.* New York: Oxford University Press.

Popkewitz, T. S., Tabachnick, B. R., and Zeichner, K. 1979. Dulling the senses: research in teacher education. *Journal of Teacher Education* 30, no. 5: 52–60.

## Chapter 6:
## The Image of Substance: Illusory Schooling

Bernstein, B. 1977. *Class, codes and control: toward a theory of educational transmissions.* 2d ed., vol. 3. London: Routledge and Kegan Paul.

Brice-Heath, S. (in progress). Questioning at home and at school: a comparative study. In G. D. Spindler, ed., *The ethnography of schooling: educational anthropology in action.*

Edelman, M. J. 1977. *Political language: words that succeed and policies that fail.* New York: Academic Press.

Geertz, C. 1973. *The interpretation of cultures.* New York: Basic Books.

Labov, W. 1972. The logic of nonstandard English. In A. Cashdon and E. Grugeoled, eds., *Language in education.* London: Routledge and Kegan Paul.

## Chapter 7:
## The Social and Political Complexity of School Reform

Bellack, A. 1978. *Competing ideologies in research on teaching.* University Reports on Education, 1. Uppsala, Sweden: Department of Education. University of Uppsala.

Berman, R., and McLaughlin, M. 1978. *Federal programs supporting educational changes. Vol. 8. Implementing and sustaining innovation.* Santa Monica, Calif.: Rand.

Bernstein, B. 1975. *Class, codes and control: theoretical studies toward a sociology of language.* New York: Schocken Books.

Bisseret N. 1979. *Education, class language and ideology.* London: Routledge and Kegan Paul.

DeLone, R. A. 1979. *Small futures: children, inequality and the limits of liberal reforms.* New York: Harcourt, Brace and Jovanovich.

Easton, D. 1971. *The political system: an inquiry into the state of political science.* New York: Alfred A. Knopf.

Edelman, M. J. 1970. *The symbolic uses of politics.* Urbana, Ill.: University of Illinois Press.

Firestone W., and Corbett, H., III. 1979. *Rationality and cooperation in external assistance for school improvement.* Philadelphia: Research for Better Schools.

Fullan, M., and Pomfret, A. 1977. Research on Curriculum and Instruction Implementation. *Review of Educational Research* 47: 335–397.

Giroux, H. A. 1981. *Ideology, culture and the process of schooling.* Philadelphia: Temple University.

Gross, N., Giaquinta, J., and Bernstein, M. 1971. *Implementing organizational innovations.* New York: Basic Books.

Kliebard, H. M. 1979. The drive for curriculum change: the United States, 1890–

1958. I—the ideological roots of curriculum as a field of specialization. *Journal of Curriculum Studies* 11(3): 191–202.

Loucks, F., Newlove, B. N., and Hall, G. E. n.d. *Measuring levels of use of the innovation: a manual for trainers, interviewers and raters.* Austin, Tex.: Research and Development Center for Teacher Education, University of Texas.

Lundgren, U. P., and Pettersson, S., eds. 1979. *Code, context and curriculum processes.* Stockholm: Stockholm Institute of Education.

Lybarger, M. 1981. *The origins and rationale of the social studies curriculum: 1900–1916.* Ph.D. diss., University of Wisconsin-Madison.

Meyer, J. W., and Rowan, B. 1977. Institutionalized organizations: formal structure as myth and ceremony. *American Journal of Sociology* 83:340–363.

Meyer, J., Tyack, D., Nagel, J., and Gordon, A. 1979. Public education as nation-building in America: enrollments and bureaucratization in the American states, 1870–1930. *American Journal of Sociology* 85(3): 591–613.

Miles, M., 1980. School innovation from the ground up: some dilemmas. *New York University Education Quarterly* 11(2): 2–9.

Mumford, L. 1966. *Technics and civilization, the myth of the machine.* New York: Harcourt, Brace, Jovanovich.

Noble, D.F. 1977. *America by design: science, technology and the use of corporate capitalism.* New York: Alfred A. Knopf.

Popkewitz, T. S. 1978. Educational research: values and visions of social order. *Theory and Research in Social Education* 6(4):20–49.

Popkewitz, T. S. 1980. Paradigms in educational science: different meanings and purpose to theory. *Journal of Education* 162(1):28–46.

Popkewitz, T. S. 1981. The social contexts of schooling, change and educational research. *Journal of Curriculum Studies.* 13(3):189–206.

Popkewitz, T. A., Tabachnick, B. R., and Zeichner, K. M. 1979. Dulling the senses: research in teacher education. *Journal of Teacher Education* 30(5):52–60.

Sarason, S. 1971. *The culture of the school and the problem of change.* Boston: Allyn and Bacon.

Simon, H. 1969. *The sciences of the artificial.* Cambridge, Mass.: M.I.T. Press.

Smith, L., and Keith, P. 1971. *The anatomy of educational innovation: an organizational analysis of an elementary school.* New York: Wiley.

Stenhouse, L. 1979. *Curriculum research and development in action.* London: Heinemann Educational Books.

Tamir, P., Blum, A., Hostein, A., and Sabar, N. 1979. *Curriculum implementation and its relationship to curriculum development in science.* Jerusalem: Israel Science Teaching Center.

Waller, W. W.. 1932. *Sociology of teaching.* New York: Wiley.

Wexler, P. n.d. Structure, text, and subject: a critical sociology of school knowledge. Mimeographed.

Wolcott, H.F. 1977. *Teachers as technocrats: an educational innovation in anthropological perspective.* Eugene, Oreg.: Center for Educational Policy and Management, University of Oregon.

Young, M., and Whitty, G., eds. 1977. *Society, state and schooling: reading on the possibilities for radical education.* Delves Close, England: Palmer Press.

## Appendix B:
## A Brief Overview of the Phase I Study

Harris, M. L., and Harris, A. W. 1973. *A structure of concept attainment abilities.* Madison: Wisconsin Research and Development Center for Cognitive Learning.

Klopp, P., Buchanan, A., Stewart D. M., and Romberg, T.A. 1979. *Conduct of the study: Phase I of the IGE evaluation.* Working paper no. 258. Madison.: Wisconsin Research and Development Center for Individualized Schooling.

Price, G. G. 1977. *Sampling for Phase I of the IGE evaluation.* Working paper no. 223. Madison: Wisconsin Research and Development Center for Cognitive Learning.

Price, G. G., Janicki, T. C., Romberg, T. A., and Stewart, D. M. 1980. *Summary of the causal model analysis based on a large-scale survey of IGE schools.* Madison: Wisconsin Research and Development Center for Individualized Schooling.

Price, G. G., Janicki, T. C., Howard, J. A., Stewart, D. M., Buchanan, A. E., and Romberg, T. A. 1978. *Overview of school and unit variables and their structural relations in Phase I of the IGE evaluation.* Technical report 475. Madison: Wisconsin Research and Development Center for Individualized Schooling.

Stewart, D. M. (adaptor) 1980. *Results of the IGE evaluation Phase I: scores and results of the in-depth analysis.* Working paper no. 291. Madison: Wisconsin Research and Development Center for Individualized Schooling.

# Index

JACKET DESIGNED BY CAROLINE BECKETT
COMPOSED BY NASHVILLE COMPOSITION CO., INC., NASHVILLE, TENNESSEE
MANUFACTURED BY MALLOY LITHOGRAPHING, INC., ANN ARBOR, MICHIGAN
TEXT AND DISPLAY LINES ARE SET IN CALEDONIA

Library of Congress Cataloging in Publication Data
Popkewitz, Thomas S.
The myth of educational reform
Bibliography: pp. 195–201
Includes index.
1.  Curriculum change—United States—Case studies.
2.  Individualized instruction—Case studies.
I. Tabachnick, B. Robert.     II. Wehlage, Gary.
III.  Title.
LB1570.P6     372.19'0973     81–70011
ISBN 0–299–08840-5     AACR2